To my son Alex.

May you be as enthusiastic about life as I am now, learn from my mistakes and be inspired by some of my successes. More importantly, give everything a go with your eyes wide open. Whether it's playing sport, strumming a guitar or selling stamps, your mama and I will be there cheering you on.

Acknowledgements

I've had great fun writing this book but I could not have done it alone. My good friend Alex Spink, rugby correspondent for the *Daily Mirror*, travelled alongside me through most of my career and I would like to acknowledge his enormous help in piecing these tales together. Together we have trawled my mind for those moments that brought a smile or, for that matter, a tinge of embarrassment.

Well, I've never claimed to be perfect.

Matt Dawson
August 2013

CONTENTS

PROLOGUE

Olympic Stadium, Sydney
6 July 2013

It was lunchtime across Britain and Ireland, closing in on midnight in Australia, when finally it happened. Sixteen years searching for a series win in the southern hemisphere was brought to a glorious conclusion by Warren Gatland's Lions.

As the final whistle blew in Sydney to spark scenes of celebration not seen in this Olympic Stadium since England won the World Cup there in 2003, my mind raced back to 1997. To Durban in South Africa, where I was lucky enough to play for the last Lions team to come out on top.

As Gatland's Lions partied like it was 1997 I thought back to that night at Kings Park, where we clinched the series and shortly after I sat on the loo as the phone rang in my pocket. It was Harvey

1

Thorneycroft, my team mate from Northampton, calling to congratulate us and wondering if I was free for a word.

'Sure pal,' I said as he switched his mobile to speakerphone and, unbeknown to me, the sound of my post-match ablutions were broadcast to a packed clubhouse back home where Lions fans had gathered to watch us finish off the world champions!

That seems a long time ago now: the carefree scrum-half with the full head of hair, albeit shaved tight to my skull, is no more. I am married to the beautiful Carolin, we have a son, Alex, who is the joy of both our lives, and rather than play rugby any more I talk and write about it in the media.

The history books show a sixteen-year gap between parties. They highlight my try in Cape Town and Jeremy Guscott's dropped goal in Durban, then fast forward to this summer and the try-scoring brilliance of George North and the near flawless goalkicking of Leigh Halfpenny. But that only scratches at the surface of what the Lions have been about since the game of rugby union became a professional sport.

This book, my personal voyage through that period, attempts to delve far deeper. To chart the peaks and troughs, the laughs and fallouts, the pleasure and the pain. I have experienced the best and worst of these times, I have known acclaim and criticism, been showered both with bouquets and brickbats. Above all, though, it is the fun and camaraderie that springs to mind when I think of my time in the red shirt.

I hope I reflect that in this book. The stories I recount are told with affection for the characters involved and, I hope, a fair degree of accuracy. If there is the odd exaggeration, please forgive me for that.

Finally, it would be remiss of me not to thank all those who made it possible for me to fulfil my lifelong dream of becoming a

PROLOGUE

Lion. There are too many to name here, team mates and coaches at every stage of my career at school, club and international level. But three I must mention are Sir Ian McGeechan, Sir Clive Woodward and Warren Gatland.

Geech coached me at Northampton and capped me as a Lion. He has also done more than any other individual to steer the Lions through the choppy waters of professionalism. Clive enabled me to become a World Cup winner and gave me the chance at least to partially redeem myself with the Lions in 2005 after the offence my newspaper diary caused four years earlier.

Last, but not least, Gats reignited my career when he signed me to play for Wasps. And this summer it was his coaching skill and courage as a selector that put the Lions back on the pedestal where they belong. It was fantastic to see.

CHAPTER I

LIVING ON MY NERVES

It's May 1997 and I'm bricking it.

The squad has been announced, I've received the letter inviting me to become a British and Irish Lion, driven to a hotel in Surrey and been handed a room key. Oh, and by the way, you're rooming with Scott Gibbs.

'What?'

Yep, Scott Gibbs, the great Wales centre. Sharing a room with me. He's been to a World Cup and played on a Test-winning Lions side in New Zealand. He has twenty-nine Wales appearances and three years of rugby league under his belt. I've got five England caps, none of them in this year's Five Nations Championship.

'Are you sure about that?' I ask the guy on reception.

'Quite sure.'

'Holy shit.'

I drag my kitbag over to the elevator and push the call button. I look around, wondering what I have let myself in for. I am out of my depth. I've never met Scott, know nothing about him as a person, only his reputation as a fantastic player, the guy who, at the age of twenty-two, kept three-time Grand Slam-winning England captain Will Carling out of the 1993 Lions' Test midfield and then crossed over to rugby league and played in a World Cup.

As I put the keycard in the door a big part of me hopes he's out.

'All right Matt?' says this friendly Welsh voice as the door swings open to reveal a half-dressed Scott, his Lions gear strewn all over the floor. 'You want me to steam your shirt?'

'You what?' I gasp.

'You'll need a shirt for tonight. Don't worry about it, I'll do it.'

Before I know what's happening I'm handing this legend, whom I have only just met, a white shirt out of my bag. He disappears into the bathroom, hangs it on a rail in the shower cubicle, turns the water on hot and closes the door as the steam starts to rise.

'How good's that?' he laughs, a few minutes later, reappearing with my pristine crease-less shirt. 'You'll never have to iron another shirt again.'

You know what? I haven't.

Contrary to what some may think, none of us are born know-alls. Take Jason Leonard, England's most-capped player, a man who achieved everything in rugby union – and still had time for a good drink!

Jason was capped by England when he was just twenty-one. That might not sound remarkable these days as half the current England team seem to have broken through at around that age. But for a front-row forward in the early nineties it certainly was. Jeff Probyn, for a while England's most-capped prop, didn't play his first Test until he was thirty-one.

LIVING ON MY NERVES

Jason always appeared to me to be pretty much on top of things so imagine my surprise to learn of a conversation he once had with Paul Rendall, another great England prop of yesteryear. Rendall was universally known as Judge, a nickname given by Bill Beaumont when Paul was nominated to dispense justice in a players' court on a tour of Australia, when he was still uncapped. It stuck, particularly after he had passed sentence on team manager Geoff Cooke, ordering him to eat a daffodil sandwich.

'Judge,' Jason asked, quite seriously one day. 'Why don't you have a nickname?'

Jason takes up the story. 'I'd just got so used to calling him Judge that I never considered it a nickname. The abuse I got for the question was unbelievable. Judge took me to one side and said: 'Look, no one minds you making a complete prick of yourself every now and again, but for God's sake don't let the backs hear you say things like that. You're a forward and have a reputation to uphold. Stupid comments are for backs only.'

Jason appeared in five Test matches for the Lions on three separate tours between 1993 and 2001. His rugby talent was absolutely phenomenal and it's no surprise to me that he's currently working his way up the Rugby Football Union towards the presidency. But rugby being rugby, reputation is no protector against banter. Not when you put your foot in it.

'I'll probably be best remembered for the washing-machine story,' he admits, and recalls how a journalist interviewed him a few days before he played his first home game for England and wanted to know how proud he was to represent his country.

'Really proud,' Jason recounts in his autobiography *Full Time*. But that isn't proud enough for this reporter who asks the question again. 'Look, very,' says Jason, who is then asked what the shirt means to him. 'Oh God, I don't know. It just makes me proud.' You can guess what the reporter comes back at him with. Yep. 'How proud?' Jason by now has had enough, so to try to bring the interview to an end he flippantly replies: 'So proud that when I put my England kit in the washing machine I watch it going round and round because I'm that proud of it.'

That seems to do the trick and the reporter puts the lid on his pen, shakes Jason's hand and says his goodbyes. England are staying in the Petersham Hotel and when the paper arrives the next morning Jason's joke comment has been taken seriously and is the banner headline. He walks into breakfast where many of his team mates are already tucking in. No one says a word, they just move their heads round and round in unison.

'I was being sarcastic! I was joking!' He's wasting his breath.

Imagine making a fool of yourself like that? I don't have to, I've been there. I was playing for England B at the time, that's the team that became England A before being re-branded, for some reason that I still can't quite fathom, as England Saxons.

I'm in camp with the B boys and as per normal on the Wednesday before matches we make our way down Richmond Hill from England's swanky team hotel perched high over one of the most picturesque stretches of the Thames to visit the Park Avenue nightclub.

Adedayo Adebayo, who played on the wing for Bath and won six full England caps, has organised our evening and I have only one question for him. 'How the hell are we going to get back in without the management wising up?' Ade smiles. 'Daws, don't worry about that.'

It transpires he knows the pretty girl in reception – I'll say no more than that – and she assures him she will let us in through the conservatory round the back. Ade was quite a ladies' man and on this occasion he is accompanied by a girlfriend who has brought some pals over for a few drinks. We party in Park Avenue until finally the girls' lift home arrives.

I have been getting on well with one of our companions and it seems only right and proper that I should offer to take her to lunch the following day. I make a note of her address on the back of my hand, a street in Fulham just around the corner from Craven Cottage, and agree to meet at 2pm.

Morning comes and we have training at the Bank of England sports ground in Roehampton. It is a mucky day and by the time the session ends my kit reflects it. I am dripping with mud. Training has run over and I'm late for my date.

Suddenly I am reminded of that scene from *Top Gun* where Tom Cruise is late for dinner with Kelly McGillis after playing a game of beach volleyball with his pal Goose. Maverick, that's Cruise, jumps on his motorbike and turns up all sweaty and horrible at her house. Charlie (McGillis) opens the door and, bold as brass, he asks if he can come in for a shower. That's such a great line, I think to myself. I've got to try it.

So there I am in a taxi, inching its way through heavy traffic on the Fulham Palace Road, sitting on a towel to keep the seat clean and the driver sweet. This is going to be great, I tell myself as I pay the cabbie and tell him, grandly, to keep the change, all 20 pence of it.

I check the door number, press the bell and look up and down the street while I wait for my lunch date to let me in and laugh with me at the joke while showing me up to her shower room and handing me a sumptuous Egyptian cotton bath sheet. The road is quiet but for an old dear making a dog's dinner of reversing into a parking space that would comfortably house the Space Shuttle. I'm still watching this painful process when the door opens. I look round and smile, winningly I think, only to be met with a blank stare.

'And you are . . . ?'

Looking at me is a well-dressed woman in her late forties whom I have never seen before. Unbeknown to me the girl I have agreed to meet is a live-in nanny. Too late to change the game-plan now.

'Can I come in for a shower?' I ask the lady of the house rather too boldly as her nanny stands behind her, half way up the staircase, doubled over in silent laughter. The reply I receive from the woman standing there, looking at me askance it has to be said, is short and sweet. 'Er, no actually you can't.'

I'm rooted to the spot, mud trickling down my legs into socks rolled round my ankles thinking, 'What the hell do I do now?' After what seems an eternity, she breaks the silence. 'Right, well you'd better come in. 'To the kitchen. You can have a coffee.'

To be fair, I think she actually gets the joke. As I sit there trying to make polite conversation, her expression says 'Nice try son, fair play for giving it a go'. At least that's what I tell myself as I drain the cup and get up to leave, apologising as I go for the mud on her Tuscan-tiled kitchen floor.

If re-enacting Hollywood movies wasn't my strong suit back then, what was, I hear you ask? Think of some of the stuff I've done on TV since and you may conclude that I was a nause when it came to quizzes, that I could perhaps cook a bit and maybe, just maybe, put one foot in front of the other on a dance floor. Er, not exactly. I did watch every episode of *A Question of Sport*, lying on my front in our living room at home with my dad getting more and more annoyed as I beat him to almost every answer. And for as long as I can remember I have been a decent cook – as long as you like tuna sweet corn pasta, corned-beef hash and mushroom risotto. But *Strictly Come Dancing* . . . I was deluding myself.

Nothing in my life will ever compare to the horror of dancing on live television. I'll come back to my *Strictly* experience in more detail later, but for those who see me as a cocksure sportsman, let me offer you a glimpse of the other me and confess right away that without doubt, appearing on *Strictly Come Dancing* was the most nerve-racking experience of my life. Just thinking about it now makes me want to throw up.

It is 2006, I've not long hung up my rugby boots when my agent phones to ask whether I fancy *Strictly*. I don't hesitate. How hard can it be?

It would be an exaggeration to say dancing had been a central theme running through my life. That said, my grandma would go for a spin in Liverpool every week with dance partner Brian, and during my childhood in Birkenhead I would be instructed to sit with her in front of the box every week and watch *Come Dancing*.

I also went through a breakdancing phase after we moved to Marlow, me in a red shiny tracksuit – over my Kevin Keegan Southampton football kit – my mate Spencer Tuckerman in blue. We'd practise on the lino in my kitchen and perform at the Holy Trinity C of E disco. I'd then hook up with Donny and Marlon from the nearby estate and we'd body pop at Donny's house, providing one of us had a 50 pence piece for the electricity meter.

Backspinning to Ollie and Jerry's *There's No Stoppin' Us* soundtrack to that classic movie *Breakin'*, was my party piece. I'd finish the routine by balancing on my hands. I once even took part in a dance-off at Liston Hall in Marlow.

But my 'career' hit the skids when Donny, Marlon and I were in town one weekend and I thought it would be cool to go into a shop and steal a party streamer spray. No sooner was it in my jeans pocket than I felt a tap on my shoulder. The store called the police, the police called Mum and the daughter of Chief Inspector Thompson went ballistic. The upshot was that I received a police warning, Dad grounded me and Mum said I couldn't hang out with Donny and Marlon any more.

So call it unfinished business or simply arrogance but when the call comes from my agent offering me *Strictly*, I jump at the chance. It will it be good for my media profile away from rugby, methinks, and let's face it, if Darren Gough is reigning champion, it can't be that hard.

Oh, how wrong you can be.

As the start of the series gets nearer I'm loving the training and the dancing and think I am doing all right. There is an unofficial eve-of-series golf day at which all the competitors turn up and muck about. Everyone is there, from actors I have barely heard of to sporting legends Mark Ramprakash and Peter Schmeichel. We spend the day laughing and joking, sort of weighing each other up. Aside from Ramps and Peter there is Spice Girl Emma Bunton, Radio One's DJ Spoony, BBC newsreader Nicholas Owen, comedian Jimmy Tarbuck, singer Mica Paris, TV presenter Carol Smillie and actors Ray Fearon, Claire King, Louisa Lytton, Jan Ravens and Georgina Bouzova.

I come away from the golf in high spirits, convinced I'm going to be okay. Then comes the eve-of-show dress rehearsal. We're down to do the cha-cha-cha, a modern ballroom dance originating from Latin America. It is all about small steps and swaying hips. Watching one or two of the others go through their routine the reality of my situation slaps me square in the face. I am not even near to where I need to be.

I go into a bit of a panic. More than a bit in fact. Full-blown. There is a lot of glitz, glamour, acting and razzmatazz on display, but none from me. Not in my routine.

My partner, Lilia Kopylova, won the show the previous year with Goughie and she picks up on my alarm. 'Matt, you'll be fine. You'll be fine,' she says over and over again. I know I won't.

We do our rehearsal, I completely balls it up. My footwork is all wrong, I forget all the steps. I know it is crap. I feel myself freefalling into a gaping void with nothing to grab on to, because I know the next day we are going to have to perform in front of the nation, live on BBC1 with however many millions of people tuning in to watch me make a complete fool of myself.

I might never recover from this.

I start to feel giddy, like I am going to faint. I need fresh air. I rush out of the studio and try to calm myself. I take a couple of slow deep breaths then flag down a black cab, which takes me straight home.

'No chat tonight Drives, if you don't mind. Cheers.'

The taxi pulls up outside my house. The place is in darkness, there is nobody in. I draw the curtains, turn off my phone and start to count.

'One . . . two . . . three . . . step . . . two . . . three . . .'

I go through the routine, imagining Lilia dancing with me, then sit down and panic. I get up and do it again, get it wrong and panic again.

This goes on all night.

What I've failed to grasp is that on this show you have to throw every part of yourself into it, you've got to embrace wearing dodgy clothes and be able to laugh at yourself.

I haven't got that at all. When invited, I thought, 'Great, learn how to dance, meet Bruce Forsyth.' That was it, as much thought as I gave it. I didn't realise the commitment, I didn't do my homework.

I try to approach it as a rugby player would learning team moves. 'Right, let's crack this, one and two and three . . .' But my head is spinning with all the numbers to count, moves to execute, positions to put my body in. There's no flow to it. It absolutely freaks me out.

Little do I know that Lilia has left half a dozen messages on my voicemail urging me to call her back. She needs to know I am all right. I'm not. I'm shitting myself. But there is no way out.

We all get anxious when we step outside our comfort zone. And in rugby terms, for a kid who was still in effect an international rookie, the British and Irish Lions in 1997 was a place well outside of mine. So when a few of the Northampton boys sit down round a table in the old Trinity Pavilion at Franklin's Gardens the night before the squad is announced, there are a lot of nerves.

It is the place at Saints where we have all our team meetings and meals and on this occasion there is only one topic of conversation for Gregor Townsend, Paul Grayson, Jonny Bell and myself. Into the room walks Ian McGeechan, our director of rugby and, far more relevantly at that precise moment in time, head coach of the '97 Lions.

'Come on Geech, this is ridiculous,' I say. 'Give us half an idea whether we're in or not.'

McGeechan is big on words of reassurance. His management style is to encourage and bolster confidence, rather than rant and shatter it.

But he laughs, and walks out. Unbeknown to us, one of us has missed out. Jonny will be left at home. Embarrassing folk isn't Geech's style either. I know that now. At that time I assume I'm not in, to the point that I agree to team-mate Allen Clarke cutting off all my hair in the unlikely event I am picked.

The following morning we are out on the training field, and I'm doing extras with the kickers at the end of the session. No one's heard a word from the Lions and it's reached a point where nobody wants to ask. Out the corner of my eye I spot Allen jogging towards us. He's got this ever so slightly mad look in his eyes and something in his hands. What is that? Looks like a pair of scissors . . .

'Oh f**k, I'm in!'

Sitting in the pub with Paul Grayson, England's first-choice fly-half and my great mate, I run my fingers through the bristle on my head where once was a rather trendy 'curtain' hair style. In front of me on the table is a pint of beer, my fifth or sixth of an increasingly emotional evening.

'We're only British Lions, Grays,' I slur. 'Happy days.'

We leave the pub and weave our way back to his house in Chapel Brampton, a village on the outskirts of Northampton, where we pick up where we left off while flicking through his collection of video tapes in search of *The Greatest Lions Moments*.

What I know about the Lions at this point could almost be written on the back of a postage stamp. I'm aware there were some great Lions tours in the far-off days before sport enjoyed the wall-to-wall live coverage it does today. I guess, like most people, the tours of 1971 and 1974 stand out in my mind because the Lions won those series in New Zealand and South Africa with the great names from my childhood: Gareth Edwards, Barry John, JPR, Gerald Davies and Phil Bennett.

And not to forget Willie John McBride, widely regarded as the greatest Lion of them all. Not only did Willie John break every Lions appearance record and become a ridiculously successful player and captain, he also came up with the most famous call in rugby history: '99'.

Unless you sell ice creams for a living the mere mention of '99' will evoke images of brawling rugby players on far-flung pitches. Willie John invented it. He had grown so sick on previous tours of seeing key Lions players targeted with violence in provincial games shortly before Test matches that he decided the 1974 Lions in South Africa would take matters into their own hands.

His concern was not only that he could lose players to injury, but that matches could also be lost as his players were distracted by a thirst for revenge. Far better, he thought, that the first time the opposition start something, the Lions finish it 'on our terms' – and in such an emphatic way that there's no repeat.

He suspected Eastern Province might be the team to try it on so, even though he wasn't playing in the match, he went to the team meeting the night before. 'Tomorrow, if anything happens,' he recalled in his autobiography, *The Story of My Life*, 'we are all in it together – and I mean all. You belt the guy that is nearest to you as hard as you can. Whether he has been the one guilty of the illegal act has nothing to do with it. If that doesn't stop it, you haven't hit him hard enough. Then, once you've done that, it's all over and we are back playing rugby.'

His attitude was 'hurt one of us and you hurt us all'. He insisted his players would not start any trouble but if the opposition chose to, they would learn a painful lesson. The call, he said, would be '999'. Too much of a mouthful was the consensus. Okay, then '99'.

Next day the game kicks off and sure enough, as Willie John had predicted, Eastern Province target Edwards, one of my scrum-half heroes and surely the greatest No. 9 ever to play the game. As he passes the ball he is hit with a rabbit punch on the back of his head.

'Down went Gareth,' Willie John said. 'And, within seconds, down went half the Eastern Province team. Almost before I could blink there were five or six of the local team laid out on the pitch. It looked like some terrifying tornado had just swept across the ground, flattening almost everyone in its path. Players who were standing around suddenly found themselves on the ground, their jaws aching or bleeding. Others were hit so hard that they didn't feel anything for some time. It looked like carnage and it was – which was exactly the desired effect.'

The Lions won the series 3–0.

Willie John, Gareth, JPR, Benny . . . my mind is overwhelmed by the legends in whose footsteps I am about to follow as I arrive at Lions HQ with Grays and our Saints club mates Nick Beal and Tim Rodber. I am petrified. I don't know where to go, how to behave. Other than my three mates I don't really know anyone as I haven't played against a lot of them in internationals and I haven't figured at all in the Five Nations due to first a medial knee ligament injury then England coach Jack Rowell picking Andy Gomarsall instead.

Gomars had done okay but thank God I had Ian McGeechan as my coach at Northampton. He told me not to worry about the Five Nations, that he would monitor my fitness and form and that I would have 'probably seven club games' before the Lions select the tour party. He said it might count for something, it might not.

Austin Healey says it definitely did. Austin, like me, is a scrum-half. He was born in Wirral, four miles down the road from my birthplace in Birkenhead, and he also won a few caps for England. He never tires of telling me that I was selected for the 1997 Lions only because Geech was my club coach. His running joke, even to this day, is that whenever he knocked on a coach's door he'd see me coming out of the shower. Hilarious, eh? Yes, of course, there was an element of luck involved. I went despite being probably third-choice England scrum-half and Geech did take me based on my club form alone. But I had played well for Saints and was putting in the performances.

Geech knew me and the way I prepared for games and felt I was a 'Test match animal'. He had a fatherly presence about him and felt protective towards his players. I think because I was interested in how we ran the game at Saints I caught his attention. Geech and I talked a lot together about strategy and tactics. We seemed to be on the same wavelength. We knew exactly what the other wanted to get out of the game and out of the players in the Saints team. He used me very much as his voice and his mind on the field.

'As a barometer for the whole team,' was how Geech put it in his autobiography *Lion Man*. 'Matt and I never had a problem with each other. We talked a lot about his game.' His day-to-day knowledge of me swayed the balance in my favour ahead of

Gomars, Kyran Bracken, Ireland's Niall Hogan and Scottish duo Gary Armstrong and Bryan Redpath.

There was no 'them and us' when it came to management and players at Northampton. A lot of the boys were living in villages on the outskirts of town and we often ended up at a pub in Pitsford, where Geech was living. He'd come down and we'd all have a drink together. That was a different planet from the one rugby inhabits now, where you rarely see management and players out together.

The nineties were different from the professional rugby world in which we now reside. Union was amateur until 1995, something we played in our spare time when work commitments allowed. Although it went pro almost overnight, some of the amateur habits, happily, took a little longer to shake off.

At Northampton our concession to the brave new world was that rather than go to Auntie Ruth's bar in town for a beer and an eve-of-match chill-out on a Friday night, we'd do it on the Wednesday.

One occasion sticks in my mind. Tim Rodber, Paul Grayson and I were working on a new drop-goal routine. Rather than pore over video footage, we each poured another beer, then got down to business. Rodders stood at one end of the room, holding above his head two bar stools as posts, while Grays and I took turns 'converting' plastic pint glasses full of ale through the uprights.

We were good mates with the owners and the doors were long since locked and the curtains lowered. Soon after we passed out, only to be woken at 5am by what we thought was a bomb going off. In fact, it was two bottles of champagne simultaneously exploding in the freezer where we'd put them to chill nicely. We were sophisticated lads after all.

My mum blames my dad for introducing me to the link between rugby and beer. It all stemmed from my first visit to Twickenham in 1982.

England versus Australia with half-time entertainment laid on in the shape of Erika Roe taking off her top and streaking across the pitch. To be honest, this is slightly lost on me given that I was just ten years old and had only just managed to get over my confusion about why we had four tickets when Mum had dropped off three of us – me, my dad and a mate of his – at the station. It wasn't until we arrived at the ground and made our way to our seats in the North Stand that it all became clear. Dad opened his overcoat, produced a barrel of beer and proceeded to place it on the spare seat next to him.

I remember Dad roaring with laughter when Erika, whom I suspect had also taken drink, ran onto the pitch. 'I heard all this screaming and thought "I have to get off, the second half is starting," she later said. 'But I quickly realised the roar was for me.'

Yes and no, Erika. You did have some competition, although only my dad's mate noticed, looking at the wrong end of the pitch as he was.

'Who is this idiot, dressing up as a monkey!' he yells, laughing like a hyena in his slightly worse-for-wear state.

'What are you talking about?' Dad replies, his gaze fixed on the buxom intruder. 'That's a woman. Surely even you can work that out!'

Unbeknown to Dad – and, to be fair, all but the one bloke sitting next to him – at the same time as Miss Roe had revealed herself, a guy dressed in a monkey suit came on to the pitch at the other end. Funny how he didn't attract the same level of global media coverage as Erika. Still, Dad's mate thought gorilla-man was hilarious. Takes all sorts I guess.

The last laugh was on Dad, however.

We get off the train and Mum is waiting for us with a face like thunder. 'What are you thinking about taking our son to a game like that, Ron?!' she yells. 'He's only a child.'

If Dad is accused of being a bad influence that day – though I don't quite see it myself – my new rugby 'family' quickly pick up the baton and move things to a whole new level.

Take my first senior tour to Canada, with England B in 1993. We are in Victoria where the Commonwealth Games will be held the following year, providing golden memories for Linford Christie, Kelly Holmes, Sally Gunnell and Denise Lewis.

The only medal coming our way is for consistency in spending pretty much every night in a strip bar called Monty's. In this particular classy establishment scantily clad girls danced around poles in the main bar area, which is pretty standard in such haunts. Monty's, however, had introduced a clever twist: another pole built inside a clear-glass shower cubicle. Local custom demanded that if one of the girls was considered especially hot, the patrons would yell 'shower, Shower, SHOWER!!' and she would be obliged to head into the cubicle to cool down.

One night we are doing what we have done every other evening – necking bottles of beer and chanting, 'shower, Shower, SHOWER!!' at every girl we see – when suddenly there is a commotion. We look to the right and the cubicle is occupied. Yes!! Eh, no. The apparition before us isn't some curvy Canadian beauty but a scaffolder from Coventry called Darren Garforth (or as he liked to describe himself, a 'tubular technician'). Now whatever the correct job description for Darren's occupation may have been, it certainly didn't include the word 'dancer' as was all too clear to everyone enjoying Monty's hospitality that evening.

Sadly, I rip my hamstring in the first game of the tour so a few of the lads, including Steve Hackney, gallantly agree to accompany me to Monty's to help drown my sorrows. Steve is a top bloke, but quiet, until he's had a few beers that is. Anyway, we enjoy a cracking night and I successfully banish all thoughts of my injury. When the time comes to leave we say our goodbyes and all of us head back to bed. Almost all of us, I should say. At breakfast the following morning there is no sign of Hackers.

The story eventually comes out. Walking back through the park near the hotel Steve stops to say hello to a couple of tramps and, being the worse for wear, sits down for a momentary rest and passes out on their bench. Hours later he wakes up minus shoes, socks, watch, tie and dignity. You can probably guess the level of sympathy he received when he eventually walked, bare-footed, into the hotel.

Fortunately for him he is not the sole target of our banter. Enter Matt Greenwood, a second-row forward from Wasps. It's my last day before flying home alone and the tour has moved on to Vancouver, one of the great cities of the world. England are put up in the magnificent Pan Pacific Hotel on the harbourside, where the views are incredible and the rooms palatial. I cannot believe how unlucky I am to be going home.

On arrival we stream off the coach and traipse into the lobby where each of us is handed a key to a pre-assigned room. We head to the lifts and pile in. On either side of the doors is a panel with numbered buttons for each floor, which illuminate when pressed. Matt is on one side of the lift and I am on the other. Nearest to one set of buttons is Paul Grayson and he calls out, 'What floor boys?' We yell a range of numbers. He pushes the relevant buttons and each one lights up. Rocket science it is not. But the lift is full and we are all squeezed in tight and Matt, who is standing by the second panel, does not realise that Grays is doing the honours on his side. As each number is called out and immediately lights up in front of him, I can see him thinking, 'Voice recognition? That's amazing.'

Sure enough, later in the day I'm heading back down to reception with my bags and I walk into Matt standing in the elevator with the doors open shouting, 'Ground floor, GROUND FLOOR!'

Those early days with England B were a scream – a lot of young lads away together on trips with next to no media profile. There is no comparison with my first day as a British and Irish Lion.

'What is the form here,' I wonder as I walk around the Oatlands Park Hotel in Weybridge, smiling and greeting everyone I meet with a cheery hello. I'm in awe of the history and tradition of the Lions and of the great players around me. Should I be bold and brash when introducing myself and risk being seen as an English tosser by the Celts – or keep my head down and risk looking insecure and unsure of myself? The latter is hardly ideal for a prospective Lions scrum-half.

I try to pitch it somewhere in the middle but my nervousness is clear for all to see. At our first team-bonding session we are split into groups, given a flip chart and asked to select a spokesman to present our group's ideas on the way forward. The boys hand me the red pen and tell me to get on with it. This is not the moment for smart-arse wisecracks. I die a thousand deaths and quickly concede defeat. 'I can't do it, I really don't want to do it.'

The truth is I don't feel confident enough. It is like my first day at school or my first appearance on *A Question of Sport*, during which I'm so gripped with fear I can't even use a pencil. Sue Barker asks me my first question and my hands are shaking so much I'm unable to write on my notepad let alone come up with an answer.

'Calm down, breathe slowly,' I tell myself.

'John,' says Sue, directing the next question at John Parrott, the former world snooker champion. 'In which sport would you use a spider?'

I press my buzzer.

'Yes, Matt,' says Sue, the surprise clear in her voice.

'Er, snooker?'

I am right but John goes absolutely ape. He stands up and pretends to walk off, raging, 'Am I not even allowed to answer my own questions?' He is only messing about – I think – but I am mortified. I feel I've spoiled the whole show.

By its very nature a Lions tour has to hit the ground running. Four nations are thrown together with only a matter of weeks to build a team and a spirit capable of conquering one of the southern hemisphere's three rugby superpowers. That's why the first week together is spent flushing out shrinking violets, emboldening the less assertive and creating a sense of togetherness.

On day one Scott Gibbs did his bit to help me settle into my new surroundings, not so much by getting the creases out of my shirt but by making me feel I was as much a part of the show as he was. You cannot overestimate the benefit to an international rugby team of that sense of unity. Fifteen individuals will never win a bean in this sport, whereas a tight-knit unit can conquer anyone – in our case with South Africa in 1997, the champions of the world.

On that subject, it was no coincidence England were champions in my first Five Nations campaign in 1996, given the laugh we had as a squad on the night of my championship debut against France in Paris. The match was played at Parc des Princes, the magnificent old home of French rugby. France were overwhelming favourites against a young English side, yet we only went down to a last-minute Thomas Castaignède drop goal, helpfully deflected over the bar by the fingertips of Paul Grayson.

This was my introduction to Five Nations rugby and I loved it. I remember running out with Grays and Jon Sleightholme beforehand and Sleights dropping the ball as we ran around the pitch. You should have heard the abuse from the Parisian crowd. You'd think he'd dropped it over the line in the last minute to lose the game. We all looked at each other, everyone clearly thinking the same thing. 'Bloody hell, this is going to be some occasion.'

Despite coming up inches short, we changed into our penguin suits afterwards and headed to Versailles for the post-match banquet, amid priceless paintings and the sort of chandeliers you would not want to let Del Boy and Rodney loose on.

The starters arrive, a thick pea soup with accompanying bread rolls. Dean Richards, the vastly experienced Leicester No. 8 who would almost single-handedly beat Scotland at Murrayfield a month later, starts a food fight. The French lads fight back and the officials on both sides go completely bonkers.

As a cease-fire is called – well, demanded actually – Deano disappears outside with the intention of taking the team bus for a spin. He climbs on, starts it up but succeeds only in completely wrecking the gearbox. Not to be put off, he removes the 'England team' sign from the dashboard and swaps it with the one saying 'RFU Committee' on the adjacent bus. The dinner ends and players and alickadoos alike pour into the courtyard and clamber aboard what they think are their buses.

As we pull away, leaving the committee bus stationary and its driver shaking his head, someone from the back yells, 'Man down, Deano's not on board.' We screech to a halt, our driver sticks on his hazards and we wait. Still there is no sign of the big man. By now England head coach Jack Rowell is having a sense of humour failure.

'Leave him, we're off. He can find his own way back.'

We join the road heading towards the city with the flashing blue lights of a police escort in front and to the rear, and soon find ourselves approaching the team hotel. It's at this point I happen to glance out of the window to my right. I do a double take. The bike-riding gendarme is dressed in black tie, albeit with helmet and gloves, and bears a remarkable resemblance to a rugby-playing former policeman from the Leicestershire constabulary.

There is Deano, bold as brass, escorting the 'team' bus, with its cargo of players, back to the hotel on a police motorbike. We pull up outside our destination, file off the bus and make our way through reception into the bar.

'There you are boys,' booms a familiar voice. 'What are you having?'

This was a very different era of rugby from the professional world of academies and centres of excellence we see today. I'll let you into a secret: when I first broke into the senior England squad, I was enrolled into an élite drinking corps, known as the 'five before five' club.

The concept was simple. Those players selected on the replacements' bench would go up to the Roebuck pub on Richmond Hill the afternoon before game day and have to down five pints before five o'clock ahead of the 6.30pm team meeting. Remember, this was at a time when tactical replacements were not permitted. Substitutions were as rare as white rhinos.

At least that was the theory. Shortly before I was selected for the squad, England played Wales at Twickenham and during the eve-of-match 'five before five', replacement hooker John Olver was persuaded to wear nothing under the all-in-one quilted boiler suit that replacements in the early nineties used to be given. Well, nothing except socks and boots. You've got to look the part after all.

With two minutes on the clock England hooker Brian Moore went down and stayed down, which he never did. It's clear he is hurt. There is commotion on the home bench as a red-faced Olver jumps to his feet, turns on his heels and sprints off down the tunnel in search of underwear and playing kit. By the time he emerges, battle-ready, Mooro is up, the game has resumed and the rest of the lads are wetting themselves.

The 'five before five' club was in its pomp in the late eighties and early nineties. The arrival of professionalism changed things, though not completely to begin with. On Saturday nights ahead of international week we would all travel down to the England hotel after playing for our clubs and a small crack unit would go to the Sun Inn in Richmond for a late-night lock-in. It shows how 'professional' they were because I never noticed. Not once. They were never late for a meeting, they never shirked any training. And in that time England won three Grand Slams.

Still laughing at the memory of Dean and the motorbike, we won our next three matches, against Wales, Ireland and Scotland, and

England were 1996 Triple Crown winners and champions for the fourth time in six years. The question now was could that success be carried into Lions 'year' and on to a tour we are not given a snowball's chance in hell of winning.

Geech tells it to us straight – there is nobody on this planet, other than the people in this Lions squad and their families, who believe we will win this Test series. Pretty much everyone reckons we will be lucky to win a midweek game let alone any of the three Tests. The common consensus is we are going to get gubbed.

Joel Stransky, whose extra-time drop goal had made South Africa 1995 world champions, is typical of many. 'The South Africans play at a level above what the Lions are used to,' he said. 'If the Lions are lucky, they may get the last Test, but South Africa will win the first two because the Lions won't have had time to adjust to that level of rugby.'

It is hard to argue with that. This year had been a far from vintage Five Nations and the Boks are World Cup holders, a team full of very experienced players. From minute one it is all about how can we get the better of them tactically. The management are absolutely meticulous in working out what they can and cannot get away with. Primarily, we know we have to be defensively tough. Hence the selection of a fistful of players with top-level rugby league experience: Scotty Gibbs, John Bentley, Alan Tait, Allan Bateman and Dai Young. The physiques of these guys are way ahead of most of the union lads; they were also mentally rock-hard.

Next we set about combatting South Africa's areas of strength – the breakdown and scrum. It is widely assumed the Lions will go with the all-English front row of Jason Leonard, Mark Regan and Graham Rowntree as that is physically the strongest combination. Jim Telfer, our forwards coach, looks at the numbers. Our boys can push 600 kilos, but as the South Africans can shove 650k he recognises we will not be able to outmuscle them. So he decides we must beat them by being more mobile. Tom Smith, Keith Wood and Paul Wallace, a Celtic combo who could push 450k, get the call. What we lose in power we will make up for with technique.

That same principle is also applied to rucking where Jim and Geech know we need to push the boundaries of what is acceptable if we are to gain the upper hand. They identify that the referees in South Africa let players dive in and seal off the ball, which is illegal. Rather than moan about it, we get practising. Jim produces cargo nets and flag poles, holds them out, 'limbo' style, and we are drilled in adopting a lower body position by having to get underneath them. Again it is a case of brain trumping brawn. At least, that's the theory.

First, though, we have to get the team spirit right. A big night out at a local pub in Weybridge sets us on our way. We all wake with sore heads, which is hardly surprising since on returning to the hotel we joined in with a wedding party. We are friendly fellas, after all. In the morning we are split into teams of eight, each given four two-man canoes and the instruction to get out on the water and swap boats within our teams. It's all going well until John 'Bentos' Bentley decides to do a headstand on the seat of his canoe and ends up in the drink.

Bentos loves a laugh and is quickly appointed entertainments manager. His philosophy, spelt out in his book *Lions Uncaged*, is this: 'Touring is unique. It's not just playing rugby union, it's life itself. It's about people dropping barriers and becoming great friends overnight. On tour you eat, sleep and crap with people. A guy that you've only ever seen on the television or played against, you suddenly find yourself rooming with, following him into the bathroom and things like that. You see a completely different side of a bloke then.'

Mark 'Ronnie' Regan would certainly agree with that after being paired with Tom Smith, the Scotland prop better known as the 'Silent Assassin' on account of being very, very quiet. Tom would watch television into the middle of the night. Usually when you share a room it reaches a point when one of you says, 'Right, shall we call it a night now?' and you agree to flick the switch. Ronnie would hint, but Tom would quietly, but firmly, say he wanted to keep watching the box – and he'd continue doing so until the wee small hours.

One night Mark nods off, as usual with the volume blaring, only to be woken at 4am, TV still on, with a sleep-walking Tom standing over him with his hands out as though he's about to throttle Our Ronnie. Not surprisingly, it puts the fear of God into Mark, who can't get to breakfast quick enough to tell everyone and then spends the rest of the tour trying to get himself a single room. Tom is henceforth known as the 'Boston Strangler'.

Mind you, it makes a change for Ronnie not to be the butt of the joke. This is the guy who left Victor Ubogu open-mouthed as they travelled up a building in Durban in a glass-sided lift. Victor says what a beautiful clear blue sky it is and Ronnie replies: 'Of course it's clear, we're at altitude. That means we're above the clouds.'

One particular story Simon Shaw tells about Ronnie makes me laugh. It concerns another Bristol stalwart, Derek Eves, who after training one day tells the boys he is organising a charity greyhound race night to raise money for the Colts tour to South Africa. He asks his team mates if they will buy a dog for the event, which will then run in the races he has footage of. Your dog wins, you win. Usual race-night rules. Pretty straightforward.

Only Ronnie responds to being asked with the following: 'I'll have to think about that.'

'There's not much to think about,' replies Eves. 'You either want to buy a dog or you don't.'

Ronnie again says he needs to give it some thought and Eves turns on his heels muttering, 'Whatever.'

The following day Derek bumps into Ronnie before training and says, 'So, what have you decided?'

'I have spoken to my ma,' says Ronnie, 'and she said we've got an Alsatian and we don't need a greyhound.'

For all the stick that comes his way Ronnie has a wonderful ability to make people laugh. Take the day at England training when he was working with forwards coach Andy Robinson, who was known as 'The Growler' on account that he always seemed to be miserable and telling people off.

Ronnie was throwing the ball into a lineout but was not sure of the calls and hesitated. Out of the corner of his eye he saw Robbo stomping towards him with a face like stink and decided to get his retaliation in first.

''Ere, Babs,' he yelled. 'Call off the dogs!'

As the week at Oatlands Park Hotel progresses, my self-confidence grows. Paul Grayson and I had come up with this money-making idea of launching a new rugby ball, which we called '9210', as in scrum-half No. 9 (me) passes to fly-half No. 10 (Grays). In the boot of the car we travelled down in from Northampton we have stashed a big bag of these balls and I decide it would be a good way to get our business venture off the ground by getting the entire Lions tour party to sign them – just in case we are successful in South Africa.

Over the course of two days I ask everyone I see to put a squiggle on each of the ten balls. I'm thinking competition prizes, promotions, money, money, money. I'm guessing now that the players I asked were thinking something else. Something like, 'God Almighty, who is this chancer? We've only just met and he's getting us to sign stuff straight away.'

Of course, nobody actually complains or gives me a hard time because we are in full team-building mode but the fates conspire against me. At the end of the tour when I return to the hotel to collect my booty, I discover someone has nicked the lot. And it's not my mum, though she has been down to pick up a massive bag I left there before we departed for South Africa. In it I packed enough Lions kit and accessories to satisfy an entire rugby club.

What is it with free gear that brings out the kid in all of us? Look at the boys even in today's game. They're being paid to play, earning a really good wage, yet all the majority of them are after is a black card so they can walk into Nando's and get all their meals for free.

When it comes down to it, we are simple animals. If I could have wangled an extra pair of shoes that were three sizes too big but might fit my dad, I admit I would have done so. And boy, do the Lions get a lot of freebies.

Each of us in 1997 was assigned three giant kitbags, full to the brim with goodies. I had brought some pants to play in, my gumshield and my own boots, a couple of pairs of jeans and two or three T-shirts. I had some photos of my nearest and dearest, a laptop, a boxed set of *24* and a book written by Karin Slaughter entitled *Undone*, about a deranged killer. Everything else – sunglasses, watches, wash bags, suits, you name it – was provided by the sponsors.

MY FREEBIES XV

15) *Mobile phone (1995)*

14) *Swimming goggles (1997)*

13) *Diamond (1998)*

12) *Breathe Right nasal strips (1998)*

11) *Cuff links (2003)*

10) *Belt buckles and cuff links (1992)*

9) *Boots with name and lion embossed (2001)*

1) *iPod (Lions 2005)*

2) *Piss catchers (1997)*

3) *PlayStation games (2001)*

4) *Phone for Internet (1999)*

5) *Ball sack (1991)*

6) *Tempur mattress (2005)*

7) *Golf clubs (2004)*

8) *Dental check and gum shield*

15) Mobile phone (1995)

I'm not saying my priorities were wrong when I first came into the senior England squad in 1993 but what excited me most were the bundles of kit and associated loot dished out. With hindsight that may have distracted me from my performance and I was quickly axed for the more focused Kyran Bracken. What hurt the most was not losing my place, but missing out on the free mobile phone from then shirt sponsor Cellnet (now O2). Mobiles were a luxury item and texting didn't even exist – so imagine my joy at being recalled in 1995 and at last being given my very own phone, complete with special easy-to-remember number, which I still use today, and free unlimited calls! In those first, fledgling days of professionalism,

Mick 'the Munch' Skinner summed up perfectly what all sportsmen wanted out of professional sport when England captain Will Carling canvassed opinion from the boys about how things could be better on camp. The questionnaire went along the lines of: 'How can training improve? Do you like the food? What is the best thing about playing for England?' Mick's answer to the final question was not pride, honour or glory, but 'stash, wedge, flange!'

14) Swimming goggles (1997)

The first professional British and Irish Lions tour was bound to involve plenty of stash, and walking around Oatlands Park Hotel, the man you most wanted to bump into was not head coach Ian McGeechan or manager Fran Cotton but a guy called Huw. He was a lovely man with a broad Welsh accent but, to my shame, in my eyes his most endearing quality was that he worked for our sponsors, adidas, and had charge of the goodies – a vast array of sunglasses, watches, sweatbands, trainers, boots, flip flops, trunks, towels, caps and swimming goggles. Swimming goggles, on a rugby tour?! Not sure half the boys could even swim and these mirrored, wraparound goggles looked so ridiculous that only Will.i.am could carry them off. But hey ho, needs must.

13) Diamond (1998)

Just thinking about England's infamous Tour of Hell – one trip, taking in the three southern hemisphere nations with disastrous consequences – still sends a shiver down my spine, even if it gave me my first experience of international captaincy. Thrashed by Australia, New Zealand (twice) and South Africa, we were the laughing stock of the rugby world. I know the results didn't go our way – losing 18–0 to South Africa was far and away our best Test result – but, bloody hell, did we have a giggle. When the tour ended in Cape Town, the obligatory court session was held. Standard procedure: Josh Lewsey had his head shaved for being 'young', a prop who didn't play much got the 'unsung hero' award, and a few of us had a mischievous idea.

To thank us for at least turning up, the South African Rugby Football Union said they wanted to give each of us a small diamond. Well, that's what we told Ben Sturnham anyway. Ben, a Saracens back-row forward who joined Bath later that summer, was possibly the most gullible international on the circuit. We may also have chosen him in recognition of his tactical input before his debut against Australia, which amounted to, 'Don't worry about Kefu, Wilson and Cockbain or any of the Wallaby back-row moves, just give the ball to me and I'll make monster yardage.' We were battered 76–0. Goodness only knows how many we would have lost by had Ben not been there!

Unperturbed by his lack of 'monster' yardage, the Sturnhamator stood up in the bus afterwards to perform his 'first cap' song. Most people go for Sinatra's *My Way* or Tina Turner's *Simply the Best*. Ben chose *Ice Ice Baby* by Vanilla Ice. If nothing else, seeing the Sturnhamator attempting to rap put the smile back on our faces.

As captain I put together a small players' group (me, Ben Clarke, Matt Perry and, inevitably, Austin Healey) and we went into town to obtain the precious gem, or at least a fake stone that resembled a diamond. The presentation box probably cost more. Ben's face was a picture when I presented him with his 'gift' and I warned him that it should not be declared at customs on the way home as its value was in the region of £3,000.

Somehow we managed to keep a lid on the prank for the remaining days of the tour and throughout the journey home.

Summer came and went and we thought no more about it until word reached me that the Sturnhamator, as he liked to be called, had gone to a jewellers and had the plastic diamond set in an engagement ring. The thought of him down on bended knee, proposing to his young lady and handing her the sort of ring you might find in a Christmas cracker, never fails to amuse me.

12) Breathe Right nasal strips (1998)

Take yourself back to the late nineties and you may remember the world's sports élite taking themselves to their aerobic limits not by hours of training at altitude, or hundreds of reps in the gym. No. Their prowess was due to a small plastic sticky strip stuck to the bridge of their nose. Given the number of endorsements for this cutting edge technology from athletes, American Football players and Premier League soccer stars, it was inevitable that Clive Woodward, England rugby's innovative team boss, would follow. But there was a twist. We had Loughborough University develop a type of apparatus to increase our lung capacity and endurance to complement the fact that, with our prised-open nostrils, the air would be flowing in as though down a wind tunnel. The contraption looked like a futuristic pipe an addict from *The Matrix* may use. Incorporated inside was a type of resistance so the more you inhaled the harder your lungs had to work. You did feel faint and light-headed but that's where the narcotic simile ended. My chest burnt and I could taste blood in the back of my throat. Needless to say, after two seasons of believing we had the edge on our opponents, evidence was released to show that in extreme exercise a human switches to using solely their mouth to breathe – and not the nasal passage at all.

11) Cuff links (2003)

The build-up to the 2003 Rugby World Cup was the most ball-busting pre-season I ever experienced. Dave 'Otis' Reddin, our fitness guru, beasted us day-in day-out. In camp for five days a week drove us all to the brink as Otis set about maximising every last ounce of effort. After one such monstering, the entire squad was required to travel on a bus for three hours across London to attend a gala dinner. The boys were as low as I could remember as we pulled out of the England team hotel in Bagshot. 'Give us our beds and a power shake', seemed the general consensus, even when a smiling Clive got up from his seat at the front and walked along the bus handing out presents. Each of us was given a small gift-wrapped box in which was a set of pleasant, if not spectacular, cuff links with the English flag on.

'Hold on fellas, they unscrew,' yelled a voice down the back. 'Hey, that's quite cool.' Thirty rugby lads quizzically take another look at their cuff links and use their chubby fingers to undo the 'lid' and expose a tiny chamber in which is a neatly folded piece of paper no bigger than a stamp. The bus goes quiet as each player unfolds his find to discover either a picture, poem or phrase done by a family member with the aim of inspiring us. Mine read 'carpe diem', a favourite Latin phrase of Mum's, which she had written for me and which translates as 'seize the day'. It was an amazingly thoughtful gift, made even better by the fact that hidden in the other cuff link was a piece of material that turned out to be from the St George's flag that had flown over Twickenham. I don't mind admitting I welled up a bit, and I don't think I was the only one, at the realisation that, for all our pain and sacrifice, we were not doing it alone. Every step of the way we were supported by our families and the nation.

10) Belt buckles and cuff links (1992)

Even when playing for your club the beginning of the season means a new bag load of kit and associated accessories. Much of the stuff at Northampton wasn't of the highest of quality unless it was the shoes. Church's shoes are made in the town, so needless to say every September we always found a pair in the bag. Bloody hell, they were heavy. A classic brogue! But what really sticks in my mind in 1992, my first full season, is that our captain, John Steele, gave us all an early-season kick-up-the-ass by warning us not to think we are a decent side just because we are spoilt by generous local companies.

'Guys we f***ed up last season when we should have won the league. This year I don't want you lot getting carried away or distracted from the objective. Look at all the gifts we've been given. If we're honest, we don't deserve them. To win we need boots and gum shields not belt buckles and cuff links!' His military background shone through and some of us had a giggle at his turn of phrase. But not prop Gavin Baldwin, who was more pissed off that he hadn't received either a belt or cuff links.

9) Boots with name and lion embossed (2001)

What does any young aspiring rugby player want for Christmas? Simple – a new pair of boots. I remember getting my first pair like it was yesterday. Mum and Dad had wrapped up a few socks, some Top Trumps, maybe a Subbuteo – more than enough to keep me happy. As I started to clear the kitchen table to set up my new game, my folks passed over one last wrapped box, which could only contain shoes. Not just any shoes – a pair of Patrick Platini. I hugged them like a teddy bear, all but licking them with excitement. They fitted like slippers and I immediately unscrewed all the studs and started skidding about the house pretending to sidestep and dive pass like Gareth Edwards, before diving on my bed for the try.

Fast forward to 2001 and that childlike sense of anticipation is back as I head for the adidas kit room in the Lions' pre-tour hotel. By now I am an adidas athlete so the boots are not only fitted but personalised, with a gold lion embossed on the tongue and my nickname 'JarJar' (from JarJar Binks of *Star Wars* fame – apparently my ears stick out although I've never really noticed!) stitched on, too. Beautiful.

1) iPod (Lions 2005)

Sir Clive Woodward never did anything by halves. He prides himself on excellence and breeding élite performance, so when we rocked up at the Vale Hotel in Glamorgan for the pre-tour gathering in 2005, there was always going to be plenty of swag. But quite how much blew my mind. Aside from video cameras, belt buckles and cuff links, each of us received two giant kitbags containing the following:

2 red tracksuits
1 puffer jacket
1 windbreaker jacket
1 rain jacket
2 rain pants
1 fleece
1 crew-neck sweatshirt
3 polo shirts (red, white, navy)
6 training T-shirts (2 x navy, green, white)
3 gym shorts

1 Goretex jacket/trousers
1 windbreaker fleece top
1 retro rugby jersey
2 Lions tour dates T-shirts
2 adidas T-shirts
1 adidas swim shorts
1 adidas shorts
1 commemorative Lions/All Blacks T-shirt
1 commemorative Lions/All Blacks polo shirt
6 training shirts (2 x navy, green, white)
6 training shorts (3 x navy/red, 3 x navy/green)
8 running socks
8 training socks (4 x navy, 4 x red)
1 medium team bag
1 backpack
1 boot bag
1 gym sack
1 wash bag
2 caps
1 beanie hat
1 commemorative scarf
3 adidas boots
3 adidas training shoes

The star attraction for me was tucked inside our enormous red Lions playbook. Clive loved a Filofax, so for the Lions he commissioned the mother of all of them – loaded with pages of text on discipline, skills, training stats and analysis, all surrounded by motivational pictures of the greats from Britain and Ireland. There was also a rubber wristband (all the rage at the time) coloured

red, white, blue and green and embossed with the words 'the power of four'. Never mind that lot. I was too busy admiring the all-new white iPod attached to the inside cover. Engraved on the back with our name and Lions' crest, it was truly the business. More than that, Lions' manager Louise Ramsay had researched our favourite songs, downloaded them onto the playlist and created the perfect album. Epic!

2) Piss catchers (1997)

There are very few freebies us sportsmen would choose not to slip into the kitbag but shoes were always a funny one for me. It may have been due to my mother mentally scarring me at school by making me wear what could only be described as 'correctional' black Clarks. My mates slaughtered me for weeks until I 'accidentally' scraped them up the steps and the sole came away at the toe.

So when we were handed our casual shoes at the start of the 1997 Lions tour, I had a terrible flashback to my teens. The saving grace was that as we'd all been issued with them, we would share the embarrassment. We also had Mark Regan whose genius humour, often unwitting, was a joy. Returning from the toilet at the British Embassy in Johannesburg, he explained the reason for the footwear's design. The way the leather was stitched together meant there was a ridge on top of the foot, which created a kind of saucer. 'Ronnie', having splashed about in the lav, noticed the shoes were doubling up as a receptacle for his pee and announced them as 'piss catchers'. To this day I'd lay a wager any member of that tour would have that phrase in their vocabulary.

3) PlayStation games (2001)

A classic example of how I hoard. EA sports were great at supplying games so the England boys didn't get too bored. One night they came to the team hotel in Bagshot with a box load of treats. Sports games, beat 'em up, shoot 'em up, you name it we had it. I must have taken fifteen back with me to Northampton. That's bad enough, but I did not even have a PlayStation, Nintendo or Xbox. I found them the other day when researching this book and had to exorcise the guilt. I'm very sorry I denied a child all that fun.

4) Phone for Internet (1999)

Skype, text, email, Twitter, Facebook . . . it is no longer a problem keeping in touch with loved ones when abroad. In the nineties it was nothing like as straightforward, especially when rugby tours often visited remote parts of the world. I would not describe Australia as remote, but a tiny island off the coast of Brisbane called Couran Cove was. For two weeks prior to the 1999 Rugby World Cup, which felt like six months, it was England's training base. We were given computers by Elonex specifically for the use of viewing rugby analysis, but with nothing else to do with what little free time we had, the machine's potential could not be ignored. At that time the Internet boom was rocking our world. Clive Woodward certainly saw it as the future and was using email to inform us that we had been selected or dropped. What he didn't take into consideration was how quickly the lads would twig to the potential of connecting another gift, a phone, with our free computers. A quick trip to the mainland, to the Australian version of Office World, and bingo – we had mobile Internet. Just one lead from our Nokia 9110 to the laptop, a few fax-like screams and we were in. Naturally, I went straight to the sports websites, but not Bath prop Victor

Ubogu. Victor is a larger than life character who opted for larger-than-average files containing pictures and films. These took forever to download so he left his machine connected overnight. I think it may have been the £2,500 phone bill that prompted Clive to ban mobiles for the rest of our stay, though not before we had all got to see the 'analysis' on Victor's machine!

5) Ball sack (1991)

Some gifts are luxurious, some funny and some inspirational, but only a few are life-saving. At nineteen I was trying to establish myself as a Northampton Saint. I was a recently promoted youth player, given my chance by a Kiwi coach called Glenn Ross, and all of a sudden I found myself training twice a week with British and Irish Lions, such as Tim Rodber and Ian Hunter, not to mention All Black legend Wayne 'Buck' Shelford. Changing beside these rugby greats I tried not to draw attention to myself in any way, shape or form. When I dropped my shorts after training one cold winter's night and my new team mates began staring at my nether regions, you will understand that it was an uncomfortable moment. And then I noticed what it was that had drawn their attention. My right testicle was the size of a snooker ball.

That's odd, I thought. But it didn't hurt and as an indestructible youngster I told myself the swelling would go down overnight. 'Fraid not. The next day it had grown to the size of a tennis ball and was aching so badly it felt that someone was constantly kicking me. I panicked and went to the doctor, who gently 'cupped' me and said: 'You're a late developer. Don't worry, it will sort itself out.'

The next day it had not sorted itself out. It had ballooned to the size of a ten-pin bowling ball. I couldn't walk without impersonating John Wayne and my testicles were way too painful to touch. In a panic I sought out Phil Pask, physio for Saints as well as England and the Lions. Pasky is a former Northampton forward who, when he played, wore a special jock strap, which gave specific support to its contents. You will have to ask him why. Anyway, he still had it – all washed and perfectly clean in a drawer at home – and he agreed to lend it to me. It was thong-like in appearance at the rear with an opening at the front to put the little fella through and a comforting cotton-soft mesh basket for the swollen ones. Talk about a saving grace. Within two days Buster Gonad was no more, though if truth be told I wore Pasky's sling for quite a while afterwards. It was the most welcome freebie I ever received and one for which I am forever indebted.

6) Tempur mattress (2005)

When it comes to getting value from a giveaway, my Tempur mattress, a gift from England in 2005, takes the prize. To this day Mr and Mrs Dawson, sometimes joined by baby Alex, delight in a mattress that moulds around the contours of your body. Admittedly, it is not the easiest item to fit in the kitbag, but when the door bell rang and a delivery man asked me where I wanted this magnificent creation, I didn't worry too much about that. It has been so good that I have tailored my bed to fit the mattress.

7) Golf clubs (2004)

I am golf bonkers. That doesn't mean I am particularly good at it but I love the sport like no other. So it's not hard to picture my expression when TaylorMade sorted me out with a set of the latest clubs and more balls than Justin Rose hits in a year. They even invited me to a fitting session at their factory to customise the shafts and grips to my swing. In the room were an assortment of drivers and putters – which I drooled and pawed over and . . . well enough of that. They were there, that's all I am saying. I told you, it's like a disease.

8) Dental check and gum shield

Before every tour I ever went on with England and the Lions I was sent for a free consultation with Bill Treadwell, the RFU's dental surgeon, to make sure my teeth were up to scratch and to be fitted for the latest in gum-shield technology. How I could have done with Bill's assistance in the mid nineties when I agreed to a game of squash with Ian Hunter, my Saints team-mate and a 1993 Lion. We played at Dallington gym in Northampton on a Sunday after-noon and, leading 7–5 in the final set, I scented blood. But it was not his. In my rush to get back to the T after another lunge at the back wall I had ran straight into his follow-through. Hunt's racket cracked me straight across the mouth and knocked my right incisor clean out and onto the wooden floor. Cue blood everywhere and a mercy dash to an emergency dentist, who relieved me of £250. Check out any of the photos from the 2003 World Cup and you will see my toothless grin. Damn you, Hunter, I could have been a model!

As we say goodbye to the staff at Oatlands and the 1997 British and Irish Lions head for Heathrow, spirits are high among the boys. A week earlier few of us could have said, hand on heart, that we honestly believed we would win the series. Now we do. Not only have we come together as a group, adopting the motto given to us by Lions great Gerald Davies that 'whinging is the constant companion of losers', we have survived a potentially awful incident.

On the bus coming back from attending a Lions gala dinner one evening, the driver decides to reverse in and show off how good he is at parking. If he has seen the tree with the overhanging branch, it is not apparent. The bus catches the limb, which snags against the bus window, tauter and tauter until finally there is an explosion of glass as the build-up of pressure grows too much.

Shards fly everywhere, showering players and coaches. It's a very nasty moment yet remarkably, save for a few minor cuts, nobody is seriously hurt. Perhaps it's a sign. Maybe the 1997 Lions are going to be all right.

MY GREATEST LIONS XV

15) *Jason Robinson*
14) *Ieuan Evans*
13) *Brian O'Driscoll*
12) *Scott Gibbs*
11) *Gareth Thomas*
10) *Jonny Wilkinson*
9) *Rob Howley*
1) *Tom Smith*
2) *Keith Wood*
3) *Paul Wallace*
4) *Martin Johnson (captain)*
5) *Jeremy Davidson*
6) *Richard Hill*
7) *Martyn Williams*
8) *Scott Quinnell*

LIVING ON MY NERVES

15) Jason Robinson

Lions tours are always remembered for moments of brilliance – players at their peak making passes, scoring tries and kicking winning drop goals. I can recall Jason's try in the first Test of the 2001 Lions tour in Brisbane as if it was yesterday. Breaking down the left wing at a packed Gabba, the stadium a sea of red, the gasp of the crowd as he stands up Chris Latham and dances round him. Nobody in rugby union had really seen Billy Whizz at this level and certainly not Latham, Australia's very decent full-back. JR waltzed around him in a five-metre channel without Latham so much as laying a finger on him. It occurred right in front of me, sitting on the bench, and as we celebrated I turned to Jason Leonard who quipped: 'He'd have never done that to me.'

'Why so?' I asked.

'Well Daws, that is the benefit of being a fatty. With my girth I'll always get a hand on those speed weasels. No one can step that far left and right!'

14) Ieuan Evans

I know him as 'Grandad', simply because he was the oldest on the 1997 tour and I was one of the youngest. He had all the traits of a grandad too: thinning hair, a few false teeth and an inability to control his flatulence! Mind you, he was the speediest OAP I ever played with. Having watched the video of the victorious 1989 tour to Australia, which I have numerous times throughout my career, it was an absolute privilege to tour with the guy who capitalised on David Campese's blunder to score the decisive try and prompt the following immortal line from commentator Chris 'Buddha' Handy: 'You don't do this on your own line, you don't wear a green and gold jersey to pull out that sort of Mickey Mouse rugby.' To play alongside Ieuan was for me the equivalent of a back-row forward going to Northampton and packing down with the legend that was Buck Shelford. Ieuan epitomised everything that is good in the Lions: no airs and graces, no pre-conceived notions, he 100 per cent understood the power of a united Lions squad.

13) Brian O'Driscoll

A legend of a player, the 2005 Lions captain and scorer of a sensational try in the first Test against Australia in 2001. I can still recall my inner commentary as he bust the Aussie line – 'Go on Drico! Help him . . . someone help him . . . Ohh he's done Burkey . . . go on, my boy, go on . . . get in there!' For four years after that we licked our lips in anticipation of Drico taking the game to the All Blacks, only for a diabolical spear tackle very early in the first Test to bring an abrupt end to his tour. Happily, he claimed the series win his career so richly deserved at the fourth time of asking in 2013. Away from the rugby he'll always be in my Lions XV for knocking seven bells out of Austin Healey in a boxing contest (of which more later).

12) Scott Gibbs

Who will ever forget Scott's bulldozing charge on Os du Randt, the 20 stone plus South African prop, in the 1997 Test series; bumping him to the ground, running over him and winning a penalty. He then leans over the big man and whispers, 'Get up you fat bastard!' I'm not sure if that was brave or stupid but the whole squad thrived off that moment, puffing out our chests as if to say, 'No one is going to bully us!'

11) Gareth Thomas

When 'Alfie' stood up to deliver his team speech as Lions captain before the second Test in New Zealand in 2005, he had quite an act to follow. Twenty-eight years earlier, fellow countryman Phil Bennett had given this belter before a Wales-England match: 'Look what these bastards have done to Wales,' Phil said. 'They've taken our coal, our water, our steel. They buy our homes and live in them for a fortnight every year. What have they given us? Absolutely nothing. We've been exploited, raped, controlled and punished by the English – and that's who you are playing this afternoon.' Wales duly won the match.

Alfie has taken over as tour captain after Brian O'Driscoll is spear tackled out of the first Test and the series. We are getting battered in the press and the coaches are quite rightly on our cases. The day before the Wellington Test, during the Captain's Run, our new leader calls us into a huddle, stands in the middle and decides the time is right to say his piece.

'Fellas,' he starts, looking each of us in turn in the eye, 'as far as Saturday goes, you all know what's at stake. I'm not going to keep beating the drum about it. I've just got two words for you: don't f***ing panic!'

Counting was obviously not his strong point. This is the same Alfie who, a few weeks earlier, also in Wellington before we played the Hurricanes, came strolling round the corner with ex-Labour 'spin doctor' Alastair Campbell. I am sitting in the foyer chatting to my mum and dad and we bear witness to what unfolds.

Prime Minister Tony Blair is on the line and apparently wants to pass on his best wishes to the captain of the British Lions. Campbell hands him the phone and Alfie goes, 'Hello?'

Blair presumaby says, 'Ah Gareth. Hi, it's Tony.'

Alfie looks bewildered and quick as a flash barks back, 'Tony who?'

Campbell's face is a picture and, quickly realising his mistake, Alfie tries to rescue the situation. 'Oh for f*** sake,' he blurts. 'I'm so sorry, Sir.'

At that stage of the tour Alfie was the perfect man to step up. As much as we had a huge amount of confidence in the players around us, after the first Test, with tour-ending injuries for Brian and Richard Hill and the All Blacks looking pretty awesome, we all knew we had one hell of a task on our hands. We believed we could win but we knew we'd all have to play the game of our lives. It needed someone like Alfie to cut through the crap and say it how it was. He was never one to tread on eggshells. With him it was brutal honesty or nothing.

10) Jonny Wilkinson

Wilko in 2001 was a joy to play with. Watching him smash up the Aussie back row in Brisbane was a highlight. Unfortunately, he was plagued by injuries in both 2001 and 2005 so, to my mind, the Lions never saw the best of him.

The first time I came across Wilko was at an England fitness testing session at St Mary's College in Twickenham in 1998. While the coaches were setting up one of the tests in the gym, there were some basketballs knocking around and Jonny, who was a shy lad, quietly picked one up and started dunking it for fun. We all looked up and were amazed at how athletic and explosive this kid was. Everyone else was trying to do it – Austin Healey, bless him, could barely touch the net – but Jonny made it look as easy as shelling peas.

Yet he was so understated. He wasn't like, say, Paul Sampson who, when he was called up by England at the age of eighteen was so much quicker than everybody else that it was obvious to see why he had been given his opportunity. Jonny came highly recommended because of his association with Steve Bates, the former England scrum-half, first at school then up at Newcastle, where he was mentored by and then played alongside Rob Andrew. He wasn't desperately quick and I don't remember thinking 'this guy's going to be a superstar', but what you don't see straight away is his work ethic and his skill set and his accuracy, which later became his hallmarks.

Despite dropping the goal that decided the World Cup final in 2003, I felt he became weighed down with all the processes, calls and responsibility during that tournament. History perhaps remembers it differently but I don't feel we saw the vintage Wilkinson in Australia. That said, let's not forget the pressures that were on this guy. They were of David Beckham proportions. By 2003 he basically couldn't leave his room because he'd struggle to walk around the hotel unhassled. He had security escorts everywhere. I remember one day seeing him running along the Thames in Richmond around the time of the World Cup and he had security either side of him. When we played against Newcastle it was just a total frenzy. To be fair to Jonny, he dealt with it brilliantly.

My relationship with Jonny, for two half-backs, was actually very strange, unlike the way I was with any of the other No. 10s I played with, such as Paul Grayson, Paul Challinor, Austin Healey, Mike Catt and Ronan O'Gara. If I'm honest, Jonny and I couldn't have been more different. We would pretty much only communicate when we were on the rugby field, in training or during a game. We were rugby mates but didn't really have anything in common other than the sport. Outside of that it's fair to say there were times when we were at odds. This was partly me not appreciating his unique situation and partly, I think, him hiding a little bit too much. For example, not coming out with us after the World Cup win in Sydney. We should have all enjoyed those couple of days together, even if he did feel at the time it was the last thing he wanted to do. I wonder if he regrets that now. That said, if I had my time again, I would have dealt with my part of the relationship differently. More sympathetically.

9) Rob Howley

Rob and George Gregan were the two best scrum-halves I played against in an era when the world was littered with great No. 9s. Rob's fitness, decision-making, skills and preparation were second to none. There is no way I could have performed on the 1997 tour without his tutelage. I even copied him by taking my mattress off the bed because it was too springy. We shared a room in Pretoria and we both slept on the floor to save our backs. I was his understudy and the nature of being on the bench is that you are desperate to get on the field. But I can honestly say when Rob suffered his tour-ending injury in Natal playing against the Sharks, I was heartbroken for him. It was the one and only time in my career I felt that way when I replaced somebody.

1) Tom Smith

Can anyone picture him? I thought not! I know him a lot better now because of our time together at Northampton but on the 1997 Lions tour Tom did not say more than twenty words to me the whole trip. I even sat next to him on a long journey to Mpumalanga but all I got was a grunt, a 'No' or 'Mmmmm'. Is that classed as a word? Not that any of that matters because Smithy was a sensational

Lion. In all the months of pre-selection speculation nobody considered the Scotsman as a tourist never mind a Test starter, yet you always had the impression Tom's self-belief was greater than his rock-solid dynamic prowess as a loose-head. As the tour progressed his continued silence actually inspired me to focus more and find an inner strength in adversity I never previously had. Sometimes silence is definitely golden.

2) Keith Wood

Behaved like, and was known as, my father on the 1997 and 2001 tours. Keith kindly cropped my hair in Pretoria, causing me terrible sunstroke, and persisted in pinching the nerve in my neck as a paternal greeting every morning we met. But all that paled into insignificance when we were on the field. There are only a few forwards I've played with who would totally sacrifice themselves for their team mates no matter what the consequences. Martin Johnson, Jason Leonard and Keith Wood would probably be the top three. Woody's shoulders were attached to the bone by candy floss but he still insisted on smashing into rucks and mauls, making last-ditch tackles and scrummaging like a teenager in a county trial. His levels of enthusiasm and commitment were extraordinary and the amount of motivation he gave us all in the changing room cannot be overstated. I remember him screaming and shouting before the second Test in Durban in 1997 about how much this was going to mean to our families and friends. Inside, I grew a couple of inches and put on a few more kilos ready for the Bok onslaught.

3) Paul Wallace

Given the enormity of the task that the Lions front row faced in 1997, I would struggle to name a finer 1, 2, 3 combination in the history of the Lions. How on earth was a man of Paul's size able to overcome the trio of wardrobes with World Cup medals and a substantial advantage in muscle that South Africa picked in their front row? By bending the rules, that's how! Wally was genius and weasel in equal measure, a player the rest of us owed big time. The Goliath, Os du Randt, had his shoe laces tied together by Wally without the referee even noticing. The Munsterman scrunched himself into a little ball, spending most scrums viewing his own scrotum, but because he could hold that pose, Big Os could do nothing other than lose his bind and give a penalty away. Who said the scrummage is killing the game?

4) Martin Johnson

Captain fantastic. A true leader both at training and in a match. A players' captain and one whose man-management skills I greatly benefited from during Diary-gate on the 2001 Lions tour (I'll come to that little escapade later). I loved his frown, his enormous Kenny Everett-style finger-pointing and, most of all, his incredibly motivating team talks. An angry-faced 'COME ON!' in a huddle before running out pretty much summed them up but, my God, we knew what he meant. He is a rugby legend I will tell my grandchildren about when they ask their Yoda-looking grandpapa, 'Did you play with that Martin Johnson fella? Was he as scary as they say?' I'll reply, 'Scarier!' Absolutely nobody messed with Johnno. At club, country or Lions level, I never saw anyone take him on.

5) Jeremy Davidson

Aka 'Buzz Lightyear'. I struck up a great friendship with Buzz because we both found ourselves in the 'from nowhere to Test team' club on the 1997 tour. We tended to socialise together in midweek and we all know how the Irish like a gathering. I loved his dry wit and clumsy, gangly training methods. He's one of those men with a sharp everything, knees, elbows, backside, feet. You name it, it was going to hurt you if he connected. Saying that, he was incredibly athletic and had the engine of an Audi diesel. All day, every day. For a man with a chin to compare with Desperate Dan he was very popular with the ladies, too. Rather makes you sick.

6) Richard Hill

For my money, England's greatest-ever player, and a shoo-in for any World XV. I first met Richard on the plains of Wiltshire when Marlow took on Salisbury at Under-11 level. My party trick was to throw a dummy, break into the gap and feed the ball on to someone faster to score. Most teams fell for it at that age – as the 1997 Springboks did in Cape Town some years later – but not this lot in green and white hoops. The brains of their bunch was a back-row I would play with and against for the next twenty-odd years. No team with Hilly in its squad was ever stronger without him on the park. He never lost form, never missed tackles, rarely made errors, and was pretty much nailed on for man of the match. Yet he had the most incredible humility on and off the pitch. Australia won the 2001 series against the Lions only after recognising he was the key cog in our machine and 'put him out' of the second Test with a head injury. Until that point the Lions had not trailed. Two years later England limped their way through the World Cup until Hilly returned in the semi-finals against France. Remarkably, many sports fans forget to mention him when listing their greats. I urge you to watch a rerun of any game in which he played and just focus on him. He's a miserable sod most of the time, so don't expect to hear him talk himself up, but my goodness his rugby spoke eloquently.

7) Martyn Williams

Aka 'Nugget', Martyn is the oldest looking twenty-five-year-old I've ever known. Less hair than I have and, at a guess, only marginally heavier. But, as with Richard Hill, he rates as a master technician of his position. I've always been a fan of the natural footballing open-side flanker who has the ability to dog it out over the ball. Any team with a Neil Back or a Richie McCaw are always going to win trophies and that's the lofty bracket in which I would put Nugget. He had a better pass than I had and super-human strength, yet he resembled a hanky-on-head-wearing fair-skinned Brit on the Costa del Sol. Perhaps he isn't an Adonis but his rugby was a thing of beauty.

8) Scott Quinnell

Scott, Rob Howley, Scott Gibbs, Ieuan Evans and Rob Jones have three things in common. 1. They are Welsh. 2. They are Lions greats. 3. They are completely grounded lads, the very best of humankind. They never forget their roots, where they come from and who they are representing. I was thinking this while doing the Radio 5 Live commentary on the Wales v England 2013 Six Nations title decider. All Rob Jones, my co-commentator, wanted to talk about was that man-of-the-match Justin Tipuric was from the same village as him: Trebanos, population 1,400, in the Swansea Valley.

It's because the Wales boys tend to be so grounded that they have always been an integral part of Lions tours. And none more so than Scott Quinnell in Australia in 2001. The guy is as sensitive a bloke as I have ever met, both understanding and humorous, a real pussy cat. But when he crosses the white line all that goes out the window. Built like a brick outhouse, he was every bit as tough and uncompromising at the back of a Welsh or a Lions scrum. With the right team around him he was a world beater.

To think that Howley, Gibbs and Quinnell played in less-than-great Welsh sides, ones that didn't exactly stockpile titles and Grand Slams, but did lose regularly to the southern hemisphere, yet all three players were still World XV quality. That, in my book, puts them on even more of a pedestal.

I will never forget Scott's performance in the first half of the second Test in Melbourne in 2001. He battered the Wallabies black and blue and it was a complete travesty that we led only 11–6 at half-time. Sadly, I will also never forget what Graham Henry, our head coach, said to him at half-time. Henry, in his infinite wisdom, decided we were too predictable and told us to start using Scotty as a decoy. I couldn't believe my ears. I walked out of the changing room for fear of saying something I would regret. On reflection I wish I had said something as, in my opinion, that was the turning point in the entire series.

Scott terrorised them and we really should have been twenty points to the good. So what does Henry do? He tells us to stop giving him the ball and we go from that position of strength to suffering the biggest ever Test defeat by a Lions side in Australia.

I wonder what that tells us . . .

CHAPTER 2

LION CUB WITH A DUMMY

Some people say modern rugby players are a pampered lot – paid decent money to play the game, provided with the best medical back-up, showered with endorsement deals. Yes, I say, but the game is faster, the hits are much bigger. And as for the travel . . .

Take the 1997 Lions. Departure day is so hectic we barely have time to sit down and watch the FA Cup final, let alone savour a steak burger on the lawn of our luxurious country house hotel, during the barbecue laid on for the lads and family members who have come to see us off.

All too soon we have to lug our own bags onto the coach in readiness for the journey to Heathrow and an overnight flight to Johannesburg. Okay we travel Virgin Upper Class and each get an in-flight head and neck massage, a seat that transforms into a flat bed, and an invitation to complimentary drinks at the 'Upper Class' bar, but honestly . . . we're on that plane for hours.

Apparently, travelling with the Lions was once even more stressful. And I don't just mean no mile-high massage for the lads, in between watching the latest movie releases. I give you the first British Isles tour in 1888. Twenty-two guys selected and told to meet at Tilbury on 8 March where their boat bound for New Zealand will be waiting for them. Unlike us on our thirteen-match, six-week whistle stop tour of South Africa, they will not be home for summer. Nor autumn for that matter.

The *Kaikoura* steams out of Tilbury and makes its way to Plymouth, where it refuels with coal before embarking for Tenerife, the Cape and on to Tasmania, eventually arriving in Dunedin on 22 April, forty-six days later. That's just the start. They are then presented with a schedule that entails playing fifty-four matches in twenty-one days, thirty-five of rugby union in New Zealand and Australia, and a further nineteen of Aussie Rules. I'm serious. By the time they get home, 249 days after leaving Blighty, it is 11 November and they are without the captain of England, Robert Seddon, who capsized and drowned in a rowing accident on the Hunter River.

By 1908 things have changed. Barely. The voyage to New Zealand takes only forty-four days, the playing schedule has been cut to twenty-six games and the players receive a daily allowance of two shillings (10p). This is more than a century ago, of course, but as recently as 1950 the Lions are still travelling by sea. On that occasion they go from Liverpool to Wellington, at the southern tip of New Zealand's North Island, a five-week journey via the Dutch West Indies and the Panama Canal.

As with their maiden voyage in 1888, the players keep fit on deck, sprinting and running laps as part of a daily regime, though this time they do not have to abandon kicking and passing practice due to a loss of balls overboard. More balls are taken, and their 'refreshments allowance' has also been increased, to a whopping £2.50 per week.

That won't go far in 1997, particularly if we buck the odds and are successful. Cape Town and Durban, where the first two Tests will be played, are great party towns. Or so I'm told.

First things first, my barnet needs a trim. Having finally arrived in South Africa, after what seems like hours, I am assigned the first of my eleven different room mates on this tour. Keith Wood is as bald as a coot so perhaps I ask the wrong bloke to give my cropped cut a 'neaten up'. He's not exactly an expert on follicle matters. That said, I've bought some idiot-proof clippers so what can go wrong?

Woody as usual is babbling away as I throw a hand towel over my shoulders to keep the itchy bits off my back. He is lost in some anecdote about a bloke from Cork with a one-eyed dog and is unaware what his hands are doing. Sadly, I also fail to notice the guard coming off the clippers. He is wetting himself about the dog having walked into a lamppost when he suddenly goes quiet.

'Jeez, I've made a bollocks, Daws.'

I jump up and leg it to the bathroom. The light flickers then comes on, revealing what I can only describe as a reverse Mohican. He has cut a swathe through the middle of my hair. I wonder what the hell my mum will make of that, but there is nothing I can do about it.

As Woody apologises for the ninety-fifth time and leaves the room, allegedly for some physio – but I reckon to escape my death stare – I look into the mirror again. It is the first time I have been on my own since leaving home. In the quiet of my own company the magnitude of what I'm embarking on suddenly dawns on me.

'Can you believe this, Daws? You're a British Lion, son.'

Until 1989 the Lions were never on my radar. I mean never. Before then, when I saw footage of the Lions in action – always the great tours of the seventies – I had it in my head that I was watching Wales. For one thing they wore red shirts and white shorts, for another the majority of them appeared to be Welsh (sound familiar?). It's only when my mate Phil Chamberlain announces he is going to fly out and support the tour that I become interested. Up until that moment the cork board in my bedroom had pinned to it a distinctly tacky James Dean-themed mirror, which I won at a fair for throwing a wooden hoop over the neck of an empty Coke bottle, and random ripped out magazine pictures of pop stars – Wham!, Terence Trent D'Arby and Bros.

Phil's Lions trip changes all that. I am immediately jealous, though more that he is going to Australia than that he has tickets for the Tests. I have this thing about Australia. Of all the rugby jerseys stuffed into the drawer under my bed my favourite is a green and gold Wallabies number.

I realise this is a disturbing revelation, not least to the English journalist I tore a strip off for wearing an Australian Rugby Union centenary tie in England's team hotel in Manly on the day we played the Wallabies some years later. I can't deny it, though, I loved this shirt – which Dad had bought for me after we watched England beat Australia at Twickenham in 1988. Not surprisingly, nobody else had one so, of course, I wore it all the time, even when I trained with England Under-18s. Even more surprising is where it ended up. Will Greenwood, who, like me, would play in a World Cup final against Australia some years later, persuaded me to swap it for his brown Sedbergh school rugby shirt. Even now I can't explain why I agreed to that. I really can't.

As the tour comes closer I tear the front cover off a *Rugby World* magazine and pin the pictured roaring lion next to Terence Trent D'Arby. I then find other pictures of human Lions – Finlay Calder, the Scotland flanker and tour captain, Mike Teague and Jerry Guscott – and stick them on the cork board as well. The Test matches have afternoon kick-offs so I set my alarm for what to a teenager seems like the middle of the night to make sure I don't miss a second. What a series it is, the Lions coming from behind to win 2–1.

1997 BRITISH AND IRISH LIONS TOUR (P13, W11, D0, L2)

1) *Eastern Province, won 39–11 (Port Elizabeth, 24 May)*
2) *Border, won 18–14 (East London, 28 May)*
3) *Western Province, won 38–21 (Cape Town, 31 May)*
4) *Mpumalanga, won 64–14 (Witbank, 4 June)*
5) *Northern Transvaal, lost 30–35 (Pretoria, 7 June)*
6) *Gauteng Lions, won 20–14 (Johannesburg, 11 June)*
7) *Natal, won 42–12 (Durban, 14 June)*
8) *Emerging Springboks, won 51–22 (Wellington, 17 June)*
9) *1st Test, SOUTH AFRICA, won 25–16 (Cape Town, 21 June)*
10) *Free State, won 52–30 (Bloemfontein, 24 June)*
11) *2nd Test, SOUTH AFRICA, won 18–15 (Durban 28 June)*
12) *Northern Free State, won 67–39 (Welkom, 1 July)*
13) *3rd Test, SOUTH AFRICA, lost 16–33 (Johannesburg, 5 July)*

'These are not Lions but pussycats' runs a banner headline in one of the South African newspapers lying on the desk at reception in the hotel. The mind games are beginning. The pressure is being cranked up by our hosts. We don't need to be told we are up against it. What we do occasionally need, as the first match comes ever closer, is for that pressure to be relieved.

Not for nothing is John Bentley appointed entertainments manager. We all love Bentos for the way he wears his heart on his sleeve. With him a laugh and a joke is never far away. Take his relationship with Austin Healey, a guy he claims to find so irritating that by 4.30 every afternoon he has had his fill of the self-styled 'Leicester Lip'. Actually, they get on great but their knockabout relationship keeps us all amused for weeks.

The funniest moment, without any doubt, comes early in the tour. In week two to be precise. Bentos has been given a video camera by the makers of the official tour video, *Living with Lions*, which in years to come will be considered a classic and set the benchmark for fly-on-the-wall sporting documentaries. The producer tells him not to be shy and to feel free to point it at anyone and everyone.

This is a masterstroke on his part as Bentos enjoys the limelight and quickly realises that if he has hold of the camera, with accompanying microphone, he is going to get a lot of coverage. In no time at all he has slipped into his adopted role of tour chronicler and, given his northern humour and easygoing manner, it works brilliantly. Even if you don't particularly enjoy going in front of a camera, he has a manner that persuades you to think, 'What's the worst that can happen?' Then, just when he has put you at ease, he hits you with some jibe about how crap your dress sense is or what a rubbish haircut you have.

When Bentos goes out on missions, we look forward to his return, eager to see what he has caught on film. A favourite is the day he makes a nuisance of himself in the hotel gym, particularly when he spots an exceptionally fit blonde and wastes no time introducing himself.

'Hi, my name's Lauren,' replied his unwitting victim, a young lady in cropped top and skin-tight Lycra shorts.

'Lauren, how the devil are you?' says our dashing hero.

'Very well thank you.'

'You're obviously in great shape, Lauren. If I could just show the camera, Lauren.'

(The camera pans down, ignoring her smile and her finely tuned arms. Instead it scours her midriff, pauses for an indecent amount of time on her legs, then returning north, coming to a halt on her cleavage and panning in until it fills the screen.)

'Excellent. Great shape . . . !' says Bentos, all matter-of-fact. 'Now, do you have a message for the thirty-five boys in the squad?'

If she does, he is not listening. He is too busy working the zoom lens.

'Well, Lauren,' he says finally, long after she has finished speaking. 'Thank you very much for that.'

The footage brings the house down when it is shown that evening, though I think it is the front of Bentos, rather than the front of Lauren, that most makes us smile. And it gets funnier. Way funnier.

We are in East London, South Africa, and Bentos is rooming next door to his old mate Austin, who is renowned for wandering around naked because he likes the look of his own body. Bentos thinks it would be a good idea to clamber across onto Austin's balcony and video him, from behind the net curtain, parading around his room. He assumes he'll catch him making a cup of tea in the buff, or packing his bags or polishing his boots. Never in his wildest dreams . . .

We're on the bus bound for training later in the day when word gets round of what Bentos Productions has captured on film. It transpires that having sneaked across, SAS-style, onto Austin's balcony, his team mate's French windows are unlocked. Bentos takes a quick peer inside and the room is empty. You can hear the disappointment in his voice on the commentary that accompanies the footage. He tip-toes in, and hears a strange noise coming from the bathroom. Thinking Austin is in the bath, he hatches a plan. He will burst in and capture his cheeky grin peeking out above a sea of bubbles. The lads will love it.

The door flies open, the camera rolls and there is Austin, lying on the floor enjoying himself with a magazine, which I don't believe was *Rugby World*. Bentos can't believe his luck. He secures the evidence, thanks Austin for being so accommodating and legs it out of the room while our hero is adjusting himself.

Austin is nowhere to be seen on the bus. He has got wind of the fact some of the boys have already seen the evidence and is absolutely fuming – not so much because he's been caught in the act, but because he knows Bentos is providing the footage for the official Lions video and he's concerned his starring performance might play to a rather bigger audience.

He knows, at all costs, he has to get the tape back. Bentos knows it too and has removed the cassette from the camera and hidden it under his mattress in case Austin pays a visit. Sure enough, as the training session begins Austin is back at the hotel. He has thrown a sickie and is busy persuading the concierge to let him into the adjacent room. We arrive back to find the door to Bentos's room wide open. The place has been ransacked. Austin has found the evidence and destroyed it.

Was that a prank that went too far? I don't believe so. Have I ever been involved in one that did? You'd better believe it. And, sadly, I was the victim. It's 1994 and way back at the start of my representative career. The Barbarians, the sport's most famous invitation team, have asked me if I would like to join them on their three-match tour of Zimbabwe.

'Would I ever,' I say, without a second's hesitation.

I have a replica Barbarians jersey at home, the same black and white hoops Gareth Edwards wore to score that sensational try for the Baa-Baas against New Zealand in 1973. The prospect of wearing the No. 9 jersey he immortalised that day is reason enough to forego a rival end-of-season club tour to Chicago.

The fun-loving ethos of the Barbarians particularly appeals to me as at this time I am throwing myself head-first into the social side of rugby. Convinced that my natural talent will take me where I want to go in the sport, I am basically sitting back and letting it happen – with a bottle of beer in my hand.

That's the reason Kyran Bracken, my career-long rival for the scrum-half berth, has made it into the senior England team before me. That, combined with the fact I tore my hamstring on the England A tour in Canada the previous year and left the way open for him to make his debut – and become a national hero – in England's win over New Zealand at Twickenham in the autumn of 1993.

That was the game in which Kyran had his ankle stamped on by All Blacks flanker Jamie Joseph. I had been called into the senior squad for the first time a couple of days earlier and, remarkable though it seems now, because I was only named as a replacement, had not given it much thought. Nobody, but nobody, brought on replacements in those days.

Looking back, I can't believe how casual I was about my first appearance in a senior England match-day squad, but hey, that was me. I joined up on the Thursday, ran at scrum-half for thirty seconds in the Captain's Run the following day – one scrum, one lineout, that was about it – then pulled on the Red Rose on the Saturday. It did not seem important that I was totally ill-prepared until Joseph struck and Kyran stayed down. It was then England head coach Dick Best turned to me, nodded and said: 'Okay Daws, you know the moves, right?'

If only I had known at that exact moment what I know now, that there was not the first chance of Kyran coming off – not because the injury was not serious, it was, but because I was on the bench. I promise you, that was precisely what was in his head. I could read it in his expression as clearly as if he had said, straight out, 'I am not coming off this pitch and letting Matt Dawson have an opportunity to play in the No. 9 shirt.' There were no complaints from me, mind, as the full horror of my situation at last dawned on me.

'Dick, I don't know any moves or any calls. Honestly mate I haven't got a clue what's going on here,' I said, plunging into full panic mode.

What happened next you could not make up. Standing in the players' tunnel, the head coach of the England rugby team began going through the lineout calls for my benefit before realising how ludicrous the situation was, stopping himself and saying: 'Look, forget all that. Just give the ball to Rob Andrew.'

In the event, I did not come on, which, after the relief of escaping possible humiliation had subsided, gave me a second reason to resent Kyran. Never mind the great rivalry that history remembers us enjoying, he robbed me of my one shot at a Hollywood career. You think I exaggerate? I do not. Had I not been injured in Canada and left the door open for him, it would have been me, not Kyran, getting the big break.

LION CUB WITH A DUMMY

I refer not to England or Lions selection but to a guest appearance on *Friends*, the world's most popular sit-com, in which Kyran unwittingly starred. There was I, watching the episode in which Ross joins in with a game of rugby in the park to try to impress Emily, the English girl he is courting, when I found myself mouthing the words: 'You. Have. Got. To. Be. Joking.'

Ross has slotted a video into his machine in an attempt to get a feel for the alien sport he is about to play and up pops Kyran, making a break for England against Canada on the tour injury forced me to abandon.

So instead of appearing in *Friends* alongside Monica and Joey, or having a starting role for the senior England team, I find myself in Zimbabwe with a Barbarians squad made up mostly of Welsh players I have never met, plus Nick Beal. Bealer is one of my best mates and we spend most of our time together so, as is the way on rugby tours the world over, we are punished for being pals by the players' 'court'.

I assume that will mean drinking an evil alcoholic concoction of something that will have me retching and everyone else in fits of laughter. Or perhaps a go at the Circle of Fire challenge, where toilet paper is rolled up tight and lit with a match, and you have to clench it between your bum cheeks and run the whole way around the room before the flame reaches your skin. That's par for the course, and as I'm the youngest tourist I expect to be targeted. But there is no poison to neck, no flame to withstand. Instead I'm instructed to take down my trousers, bend over a chair and submit myself to being whacked by Bealer with a bloody great cactus leaf.

He takes a run-up and theatrically shapes to thrash me. Although he stops inches short of my backside I play along with the pantomime and howl out. I look round to share the joke with

Bealer only to see that Derwyn Jones, the giant Wales second-row, has relieved my mate of the cactus and is not only about to swing, but follow through. The pain as the sharp tips of the leaf cut into my arse makes me yell for real. There is no pretence this time. Blood drips from my cheek and as I let rip at Derwyn I swear to myself I will never again have anything to do with the Barbarians.

I'm deadly serious about this and years later I am still traumatised by the experience. So much so that on the 2001 Lions tour to Australia it comes back to haunt me when we are in the team room in Melbourne and Irish fly-half Ronan O'Gara comes up with a mass-participation form of table tennis, which, for some reason unclear to anyone, he calls 'Red Arse'.

'Right lads,' he says. 'One bat at each end of the table and the idea is we keep a rally going while running round the table and taking it in turns to return the ball. Cock it up and you're eliminated. Got it?'

What is there not to get?

Ronan starts the rally, drops the bat on the table and accelerates clockwise to join the queue at the other end.

'Oh, and by the way,' he says as he catches his breath, 'the loser gets a whack on the arse with the bat by every other player.'

Cue laughter from all but yours truly. My mind races back seven years to Derwyn and the cactus, and though I say nothing I feel immediately uneasy. A couple of minutes later and Ben Cohen, who is not having the happiest tour, having been given next to no chance to make his case for a Test place, nets his return and gets absolutely obliterated. The forwards, in particular, are merciless and his backside is left red raw. I refuse to contribute to his discomfort, telling the rest of the lads that on a point of principle I won't hurt a fellow Northampton player. It's a convenient excuse.

LION CUB WITH A DUMMY

Speeches

To mark one hundred days before the 2013 Lions tour an email pops up on my laptop with a link, purporting to be to the epic speech given by Jim Telfer to us 1997 Lions before the first Test in Cape Town. Curious about the relevance to the forthcoming tour of Jim's immortal words, spoken on a tour that took place on a different continent sixteen years earlier, I click on the link.

As the footage buffers then kicks into life I am transported back to the Holiday Inn at Newlands and the eve of my first – and greatest – day in a Lions jersey. We have arrived at the Test series in good shape as a team except at scrum-half where our first choice, Rob Howley, has been forced off tour with a broken collarbone sustained against Natal. I am the beneficiary, a guy who left home as, at best, third choice, behind Rob and Austin.

Back to the video. Telfer is prowling around the meeting room, taking me back to that evening in '97. He is rehearsing what he intends to say in whispered tones while arranging chairs in a circle. On the chairs appear to be the very cargo nets we used on the training field to dive and crawl under as we were drilled in the dark art of beating the Boks to the ball at the breakdown. 'Get your bodies down low,' Jim would demand. 'They are stronger than you, so you've got to be lower than them. F**k the rules, dive on top of people, seal everything off.'

The focus shifts to a group of men seated in a circle with Jim. At first glance they are players dressed in Lions shirts or training tops, awaiting final instruction before the biggest match of their lives. 'The easy bit has past,' starts Jim, as the camera focuses in on his audience. 'Convincing your mates to join you on the Lions tour to Australia is the easy bit. Now comes the hard bit: convincing your wives to let you go.'

A bald guy looks up. It's not Keith Wood. And his face is painted red. 'This is your Everest boys,' Jim continues. 'Where there's sand instead of snow, where the Sherpas wear bikinis. Very few fans ever get the chance to go for the top of Everest. You have that chance today. But you'll not do it unless you put your bodies on the line. Every one Jack of you.'

I recall that phrase, but not the big bearded guy dressed in a kilt, or the Irishman wearing a leprechaun hat. But Jim doesn't appear distracted as he impresses upon his men what they must do to be successful.

'The only way you'll make it to Australia is to outdo what they do,' he says. 'Out-argue them, out-nag them, out-logic them, out-guilt trip them, out-silent treatment them, until they're sick of you. You remember the pledges you made to her. Remember how you depend on each other, but most importantly, remember the time you knocked her electric toothbrush down the loo. She forgave you then, she'll forgive you again. Because pledges like electric tooth-brushes can be dragged through the toilet, rinsed off and come out as good as new.

'So will you be on that plane? Will you swap Swansea for Sydney, Bristol for Brisbane or Melrose for Melbourne? Isn't five weeks in tropical bliss worth one night in the doghouse? Nobody's going to do it for you boys, she terrifies your mates far too much for that. You have to find your own solace, your own inner strength. Because gentlemen, the moment's arriving for the greatest tour of your lives.'

The spoof video, created by Tourism Australia to encourage fans to fly out and support the tour, is not only amusing, it is uncannily faithful to the real event it sent up. I didn't know Jim before the 1997 tour, though his reputation as a drill sergeant went before him. Apparently, he is now slightly softer than he once was, but he still commands the sort of respect you have for your grandfather. If you were having breakfast with him, he would have a quick chat. If you were playing well or training well, he might give you half a smile. But if you didn't perform or you let anyone down, he completely blanked you.

I see him in action at close quarters for the first time in Pretoria where he schedules a scrummaging session for the forwards and me, as scrum-half. I'll never forget that day as long as I live.

We have this Predator scrum machine, a fearsome contraption on which Jim works the pack mercilessly. It's pneumatic, which means the man in control can either release pressure or add it. It appears more than a little dangerous to me, as in a human scrummage you can feel where the pressure is coming from and respond and adjust accordingly. On this beast, if you are in the wrong position when the button is pushed, with the pressure either added or subtracted, you are screwed.

Anyway, on this day the management have decided to open the session to the media so that they can see how hard we are working. While the forwards are being taken to hell and back, my job is simply to put the ball in and shout, 'Hit, two, three, four. One, two, three, four.'

Since the press are in attendance, Jim has been asked by head coach Ian McGeechan to calm it down a bit. He is wasting his breath. No sooner has the session begun than Jim goes bananas. One or two of the boys have been out the night before and though their efforts impress me – particularly given what I know they have been up to and how little sleep they have had – Jim disagrees.

He calls them together and in front of the media screams at the top of his voice, 'Right, you've got thirty to forty scrums to go.

I want you as tight as a duck's arse.' Or words to that effect! They scrummage for hours – and I mean hours – while the backs are just kicking or watching. It is brutal, the biggest beasting I've seen.

So this is Jim Telfer, who is about to address the '97 Lions forwards in Cape Town – it's 11 o'clock on the morning of the opening Test.

On my way to the backs meeting I walk past our team room, which has a partition separating the table tennis and snooker tables and the side where we have all our meetings. This morning the forwards will be congregating here. The door is open and there is Jim in his tracksuit mumbling to himself.

'We are as sharp as a f***ing knife. There's no way we go back,' he whispers as he arranges the cargo net between the chairs. 'We take every step forward. Nothing, nothing stops us hitting our f***ing maximum.'

What the hell is he up to? Surely this lunatic is not going to get them down on their hands and knees, crawling around under the netting in a corporate room in the Holiday Inn, before they get on the bus? He's bonkers, absolutely bonkers.

At our gathering Geech is calm and precise. We come out and their door is still closed. Jim is still hard at it. When finally the forwards emerge – the starting eight plus replacements – it is as though they have been hypnotised. They seem to be in a trance, a completely different space, eyes glazed over. It is no time to crack a joke.

It's only later I discover what went on in that now famous meeting. Jim looked each of them in the eye, then started to speak. Slowly and firmly. 'The easy bit has past. Selection for the Test team was the easy bit. You have an awesome responsibility. This is your Everest boys. Very few ever get the chance in rugby terms to go for the top of Everest. You are privileged. You are the chosen few. Many are considered but few are chosen. It's an awesome task you have, an awesome responsibility.'

To his immediate left sits Rob Wainwright, Richard Hill, Jeremy Davidson, Tom Smith and Barry Williams; to his right, Paul Wallace, Keith Wood, Tim Rodber, Lawrence Dallaglio and Jason Leonard. Straight ahead, directly in his eye line, is Martin Johnson, wearing a dark green adidas T-shirt.

'To win for the Lions in a Test match is the ultimate. But you'll not do it unless you put your bodies on the line, every one Jack of you, for eighty minutes. Defeat doesn't worry me. I've had it often and so have you. It's performance that matters. If you put in the performance, you'll get what you deserve. No luck attached.

'They do not rate us. They do not respect us. They don't respect you. They don't rate you. The only way to be rated is to stick one on them. To get right up in their faces and turn them back, knock them back, out do what they can do, out jump them, out scrum them, out ruck them, out drive them, out tackle them until they are f***ing sick of it.

'Remember the pledges you made. Remember how you depend on each other. Every phase, teams within teams. Scrums, lineouts, ruck balls, tackles. They are better than you've played against so far. They are better individually or they wouldn't be there. So it's an awesome task you have and it will only be done if everyone commits themselves now.

'That was written yesterday about us,' Jim says, pointing to a white flip chart behind the circle. 'Read it silently, take note of it and then make a pledge.'

On the paper he has scrawled the following quotes: 'Their weak point is the scrum'. 'The Boks must exploit this weakness'. 'The

Boks must concentrate on the eight-man shove every scrum'. 'Scrummaging will be the key'. 'Their weakness is the scrum'.

'They don't think f*** all of us. Nothing. We are here just to make up the f***ing numbers. Nobody's going to do it for you. You have to find your own solace, your own drive, your own ambition, your own inner strength. Because the moment's arriving. For the greatest game of your f***ing lives.'

For what seems an age nobody moves. Jim's words hang in the air. Finally, Jason Leonard rises, followed by Martin Johnson and Tim Rodber. Then Richard Hill and Barry Williams, who pats Woody's bald pate as he files past him – exactly as the guy in the spoof video does sixteen years later.

From the moment we assembled in Weybridge everyone told us we were going to get battered up front in the forwards. Quite rightly, Jim took the view that all that really matters is redressing the balance. I only see the video much later, once victory is in the bag. When I do, I nod knowingly. I understand. No wonder it went the way it did.

MY TOP-TEN MOST MEMORABLE SPEECHES

1) *Ian McGeechan (match day, 2nd Test, 1997 Lions v South Africa, Durban)*
2) *Jim Telfer (match day, 1st Test, 1997 Lions v South Africa, Cape Town)*
3) *Ian McGeechan (match day, 1st Test, 1997 Lions v South Africa, Cape Town)*
4) *Martin Johnson (changing room, 2003 World Cup final, England v Australia, Sydney)*
5) *Martin Johnson (red carpet pre-match, Grand Slam decider*

2003, Ireland v England, Dublin)

6) *Lawrence Dallaglio (match day, 2005 Lions v New Zealand Maori, Hamilton)*

7) *Phil Bennett (match day, 1977 Five Nations, Wales v England, Cardiff)*

8) *Willie John McBride (match day, 1st Test, 2001 Lions v Australia, Brisbane)*

9) *Jack Rowell (England team announcement, Australia 1997)*

10) *Sir Clive Woodward (ahead of 1st Test, 2005 Lions v New Zealand, Christchurch)*

1) Ian McGeechan (match day, 2nd Test, 1997 Lions v South Africa, Durban)

Jim Telfer's rallying call to the forwards was special, but the speech that moved me more than any other in my rugby career was given by Ian McGeechan – later to be knighted for his immense services to rugby – a week later, hours before the Test match that would decide the outcome of my first Lions series.

'There are days like this that many rugby players never have. Never experience. It is special. Jim and I have been involved in rugby a long time. I can tell you these are the days that you never believe will come again.

'It has. I've given a lot of things up; I love my rugby and I love my family. And when you come to a day like this you know why you do it all and why you've been involved. It's been a privilege, it is a privilege. Because we're something special.

'You'll meet each other in a street in thirty years' time and there'll just be a look. And you'll know just how special some days in your life are.

'We've proved that the Lion has claws and has teeth. We've

wounded a Springbok. When an animal is wounded it returns in frenzy. It doesn't think. It fights for its very existence. The lion waits and at the right point it goes for the jugular. And the life disappears. Today, every second of this game we go for the jugular. Every tackle, every pass, every kick is saying, "The f***ing Springbok, you're dying. Your hopes of living in this Test series are going."

'And on that field sometimes today, all it will be between you is a look. No words, just a look, that will say everything. And the biggest thing it will say is, "You are special, you are very, very special." It has been, and is, a privilege. Go out, enjoy it, remember how you've got here and why, and finish it off. And be special for the rest of your lives. Good luck. Go for it.'

2) Jim Telfer (match day, 1st Test, 1997 Lions v South Africa, Cape Town)
See pages 74–6.

3) Ian McGeechan (match day, 1st Test, 1997 Lions v South Africa, Cape Town)
In case anyone thinks Geech was a one-speech wonder, I can tell you the words he spoke to us before the first Test of the 1997 tour were pretty special, too. Remember that we were given no chance at all, yet ended up triumphant.

'That badge we've always said represents four countries. I think it represents something else. You carry one on your own jersey. That is a very personal thing. What goes into that is your own country and three others. But what also goes into it is you.

'You should be carrying that badge for people who have put you in that position. It might be a schoolmaster, mother, father, brother, sister, wife, girlfriend. Whatever's special to you, the

LION CUB WITH A DUMMY

people who have brought you to this place, that's who you should be wearing it for. That's who you should be playing for. Because in the end they're the ones who matter. They matter to you. And if it matters to you, it will matter to all of us. And if it matters to all of us, we will win.

'Go out, enjoy it, but play for everything that's in that badge. For you personally, for all of us collectively. Good luck. Let's have a win, let's frighten them to death, eh? Let's go.'

4) Martin Johnson (England changing room, 2003 World Cup final, Sydney)

On reflection, an extraordinarily special moment in my life. At the time, the England changing room inside the Olympic Stadium was a well of anxiety, excitement and fear. Fear, not of the opposition, Australia, nor of the occasion, but of not doing ourselves justice.

'Right, come into a huddle,' said Martin Johnson, minutes before we left the changing room and headed up the tunnel. 'Everything we've done is for today. All the f***ing work. Everything. You're whole life is down to now. Here and now.'

Johnno had never been one for Churchillian speeches. A classic example of Johnno the orator had come in Wellington earlier in the year when England were playing New Zealand and faced a scrum on their own line with two men in the sin-bin. The captain called the remaining five forwards around him and delivered the immortal line: 'This is it, lads. Just bend over and push!'

This being the World Cup final he realised he needed to have something a bit more special. 'Our country is a long way away and everyone there is watching us,' he continued. 'We always produce. Every game we f***ing produce. Push them round the field. Make it fast and furious but keep control. They're going to have the ball at some stage, they're going to do something with it. Just respond. Don't get out of position. Keep working. Look them in the eye and keep f***ing working.

'They think they're going to be inspired tonight. They think that's going to be enough for them. That is not going to be enough for them. We're going to take these boys to the cleaners. Work hard for it and it will come. It will come in that last ten minutes. Okay? Don't think you have to do anything special, but don't get inhibited either. Just play. Go out and enjoy it, but enjoy working hard. No regrets. One massive performance, boys. You can only live this hour and a half once, boys. You can only live it once. Do it right.'

We headed out of the changing room in our red tracksuits and walked onto the pitch and into another huddle. Now Johnno was pumped up. Everyone else pulled in tight and squeezed the player either side of him, but not him. He never put his arms around his team mates. He had to be animated. This was his way of getting to where he needed to be. You could sense he was going to put his body into a physical place none of us were ever likely to visit.

By that stage in the huddle, everyone was chipping in. It was all effing and blinding. Anger and angst so close to the surface. It was on-the-edge stuff. Any phrase that came to mind to hype up the confrontation got an airing. It wasn't a time to think about the future, or even the next hour and a half. It was all about that first kick-off, first opportunity, first scrum. 'We're going to nail them, smash them, hit them,' said the skipper. So we did and, a little bit later than we anticipated, we became world champions.

5) Martin Johnson (red carpet pre-match, Grand Slam decider 2003, Ireland v England, Dublin)

Unquestionably the greatest captain's speech ever made without the use of language. It was all about what Martin Johnson did, not what he said.

Standing in the tunnel at the old Lansdowne Road in Dublin, Johnno turned around to me and said, 'Go on then, Daws, lead us out.' It was my fiftieth cap, and what an occasion for it. England and Ireland both unbeaten, both shooting for the pot: Triple Crown, Six Nations Championship, Grand Slam.

'No mate, I don't want to do it. Let's just get on with it.'

Johnno nodded, then turned to an Irish Rugby Union official and asked which way we were standing for the pre-match protocol. 'Out and right,' came the reply. I distinctly remember that.

Johnno grabs a ball and starts walking and we duly follow our leader. Nobody is thinking about pissing anyone off. We just want to get the game started and won. Out of the tunnel we walk and, as instructed, turn right, forming a line along the edge of the red carpet laid for dignitaries, including Irish president Mary McAleese.

The Ireland team follow us out but rather than turn left they also turn right and line up the other side of us, beyond the end of the red carpet. None of us have any idea what is going on. Frankly, we have more pressing matters on our minds, like a first England Grand Slam in eight years. All of a sudden there is this tiny little fella with his head cans on – a TV guy or stadium facilitator, I don't know which – who comes up to Johnno and says, 'Guys, you're on the wrong side, you've got to move.'

Johnno refuses.

All along the England line everyone has clocked what's going on and we all start adding our tuppence worth.

'That's right, Johnno, tell him to f*** off. We're not moving.'

By his actions Johnno has set the tone for the afternoon. We will not be moved, we will not be pushed around. I do feel a bit for the little fella, who scurries away with a flea in his ear, only to be sent back by his boss, clearly messing his pants, to ask Johnno again.

This time he gets it in the ear from the entire team. Replacements, too. We have no idea what sort of commotion this is causing in the wider world, how big a diplomatic row this will be spun into. We're in our own little world. We could have been in England or Australia or on Mars. Two hours later we are in heaven. We have won the game 42–6.

6) Lawrence Dallaglio (match day, 2005 Lions v New Zealand Maori, Hamilton)

Everyone gets emotional but with Lawrence it was always clear for all to see. Whether it was the chin coming out, his state of over-animation or actual tears, he seemed to understand, better than most, the emotion of the group. The difficulty with this occasion was that he had sustained a tour-ending injury in his very first match against Bay of Plenty. He was heading home and, naturally enough, he was upset. It's difficult to give a speech when you're not playing in the game, but Lol delivered a blinder on this day in Hamilton before the 2005 Lions faced the New Zealand Maori.

'From my point of view I think it's important we start to realise what it means for us to be in this room,' he started. 'We all work incredibly hard as rugby players, we play so many games for our clubs and our province and, if we're lucky, which many of us are, we get to put on our national jersey. However, if we're truly special, and this is special, we get to be in this room now.

LION CUB WITH A DUMMY

'When I got my letter through the post a couple of months ago, it came with a questionnaire. The first question was: What does it mean to be picked for the British and Irish Lions. For me, I put down it's the greatest honour I could ever receive as a rugby player, it is the pinnacle of my career and I know if I go round the room and ask you the same question, the answer will be the same. It may not be the same words, but it'll be pretty damn similar.

'Now, for me, this game of rugby is more than just a game, it's our life: you live it, you breathe it, you make huge sacrifices to be in this room. Your family make huge sacrifices, your parents, your coaches, your girlfriends and your wives. They all make sacrifices to allow you to be in this room and you've got to bring that out tonight. It's not just about you, it's about all the people who make you the person you are – that's what goes into that shirt. Whatever it takes, you've got to find a little bit extra for them. Whether they're alive or dead, they're there watching and you've got to make it happen.

'This tour is now about stepping up to the next level. We've had these two games, we know what they've been about and now it's time to turn up the heat on these boys. In order to do that we're going to have to take ourselves out of the comfort zone and put ourselves in a totally different environment. It's a place we've been before, not many times, but it's a place you've all been before in your life at international level and you've got to take yourself out of the comfort zone. It's going to hurt but you've got to be prepared to suffer.

'I was in a hotel room similar to this four years ago when Graham Henry got up and spoke. The words he said will live with me for the rest of my life. He said: "In this part of the world they do not respect you. They do not think you're good enough, they do not think you're skilful enough, they do not think you're fit enough and they do not think you're strong enough. And I should know because I'm one of them". Not my words, his words, and you know what? He's right, they don't respect us. But when they come off that pitch tonight they're going to know how good we are, they're going to know how strong we are, they're going to know how skilful we are and they're going to respect us. When they wake up tomorrow and they're eating their breakfast, they're going to know that we're here to win a Test series.

'When you take this shirt tonight, I want you to look at the number on the back and I want you to think about all the great players who have worn that shirt. And when you come off that pitch, having given absolutely everything and having won the game, you can add your name to that list of great players. You've got a great captain here and I'd love to be running out with him tonight. Get behind him and do it, let's get some emotion into this game. Let's take it to another level.'

7) **Phil Bennett** (match day, 1977 Five Nations, Wales v England, Cardiff)

A classic of its kind. An example to all of how to inspire an international team, drawing on every prejudice and stereotype you can find – and even some truths.

'Look what these bastards have done to Wales,' says Benny to his Triple Crown-chasing team moments before they run out to play their greatest rivals. 'They've taken our coal, our water, our steel. They buy our homes and live in them for a fortnight every year. What have they given us? Absolutely nothing. We've been exploited, raped, controlled and punished by the English – and that's who you are playing this afternoon.'

Final score: Wales 14, England 9.

8) Willie John McBride (match day, 1st Test, 2001 Lions v Australia, Brisbane)

A perfect way to start a day that ends brilliantly for the Lions, who upset the odds to pummel Australia, but goes disastrously wrong for me. The *Daily Telegraph*, containing my tour diary, rolls off the presses back home and all hell breaks loose.

Willie John is a Lions legend. End of. How many British Isles records does he hold? Most capped player (seventeen), most consecutive Tests (fifteen), most tours (five) and, not surprisingly, given that his Lions career spanned thirteen seasons, the oldest of all when he won his final cap fifty-one days into his thirty-fifth year.

Yet he stands up and says he is humbled and honoured to be asked to speak to us. He says he does not know why they chose him to deliver such a momentous speech and that he just wants to let us know what it would mean for the Lions to win, not only for us but the whole of the British Isles.

He sits with us in a circle and speaks softly. Gentle words from a bear of a man. 'It will be tough. It will be painful. At times you'll feel you don't want to continue. But you must push yourself through the pain barrier because the reward will make it all worthwhile.'

At no time does he raise his voice but the passion in his words is unmistakable. We hang on his every syllable. When he is finished, he thanks us once again for the honour. We are ready to play rugby. We head to the Gabba and thump Australia 29–13.

9) Jack Rowell (England team announcement, Australia 1997)

The 1997 Lions tour has finished and we are de-mob happy. But English rugby being what it is, the Rugby Football Union have decided that, rather than flying home for a couple of weeks of recovery before the start of a new season, we should fly from Johannesburg to Sydney to join up with England, who have come off their own tour to Argentina, and play Australia for the Cook Cup.

Jack Rowell is head coach and the team is captained by Phil de Glanville, who was overlooked by the Lions. Now he's about to captain a side in which only he and fellow centre Nick Greenstock are not Lions. It is, to put it mildly, a strange situation.

We arrive in Sydney on the Tuesday of Test week and file into the team room for the selection meeting. Jack is standing waiting for us beside an overhead projector. Not for him a Powerpoint presentation. Jack is old school. He places the acetate on the projector, turns to the screen and has started talking tactics when a fly settles on the image he is referring to. Of course, although it appears to land on the screen, in reality the fly is on the projector, but Jack doesn't clock that and begins swatting it. 'Ballsy fly', he presumably thinks to himself as it stands its ground, despite his best efforts. We all look at each other. 'Is he taking the piss?' I ask Mike Catt, my half-back partner in a game we will lose 25–6. He isn't. It's one of the most hilarious perform-ances I have ever witnessed.

Jack has not finished. It's time to announce the team. Jack is a smart bloke, a guy I have some time for as he gave me my first cap in 1995, even if he did immediately bug the hell out of me by issuing instructions to abandon the fast and furious brand of rugby, which I was told had earned me selection in the first place, and instead just 'pass and kick'. Anyway, the fact he does not have the team and replacements bench written down does not surprise me.

He rattles through the forwards then starts on the backs. 'Scrum-half: Matt Dawson. Fly-half: Catty. Wings: . . . er . . .' He pauses, looks at Les Cusworth, coach of the backs, and says, 'Les, who did we pick there?

'Bentos, Jack.'

'Of course, John Bentley. On the other wing . . . er . . .'

'Nick Beal,' says Les.

'Right, yes,' says Rowell. 'Les?'

'Yes Jack.'

'Tell them the rest of the team will you.'

That was Jack's last game in charge. He had been the right guy at the right time to steer England through the transition from amateur sport to professionalism. Clive Woodward, his successor, would take us to the next level.

10) Sir Clive Woodward (ahead of 1st Test, 2005 Lions v New Zealand, Christchurch)

Forgive me for not remembering the exact words but one of the most extraordinary speeches I was privy to, came from Clive, who had by now won a World Cup and got a knighthood for his troubles. Clive was head coach of the 2005 British and Irish Lions and ahead of the first Test he announced that we were going to perform a response to the All Black haka. In New Zealand.

There was a sharp intake of breath and we looked at one another as if to say, 'Is this April Fool's day or what?' Poor old Brian O'Driscoll, Clive's choice as captain, had to try to sell this barmy idea to us. Clive said he had received an email from a Maori elder detailing how we should go about showing maximum respect to the haka. This, he said, was to line up across the pitch in arrowhead formation with the youngest member of the team, Dwayne Peel, at the point. To finish with, Clive went on, Brian should formally accept the challenge by plucking a blade of grass from the pitch, while keeping eye-contact with New Zealand captain Tana Umaga, and tossing it to the wind.

Talk about best intentions backfiring. The effect was akin to pouring petrol on a bonfire. At least that's how it seemed. How did Brian put it in his post-tour book *A Year In The Centre*? Umaga, he said, looked 'extremely agitated' as the blades of grass blew away in the night air. We were later told that other All Blacks and locals felt we had insulted them. The game kicked off, the clock ticked to forty-one seconds and Brian was spear tackled out of the tour by Umaga and Keven Mealamu.

STRICTLY TERRIFIED

It's showtime in telly land, the moment I have dreaded more than any other in my working life. 'Live from London,' says the announcer as my partner Lilia and I are led into position behind the curtain and a cold shiver shoots up my spine. 'Welcome to *Strictly Come Dancing.*'

The first show of the 2006 series has begun and I am a quivering jelly. 'Our next couple, performing the cha-cha-cha to *I Can't Get No Satisfaction*,' continues the booming voice on the Tannoy, 'Matt Dawson and Lilia Kopylova.'

Cue applause, a thumbs-up to us from the floor manager and a signal to step out into the spotlight in front of God only knows how many people. We muddle our way through the routine, albeit with the lowest score of the series for our allotted dance. When the music stops, Lilia smiles. My face is as pink as the shirt I've been persuaded to wear.

I hate every moment of it, including all the razzmatazz surrounding the show. It's so far removed from the sports environment I know. I didn't go on *Strictly* to be made to look a fool – but in my mind I feel that is what's happening.

Sports fame is one thing, *Strictly* something totally different. It's claustrophobic. Whether you're sat in a coffee shop or filling the car full of petrol, it feels like everybody knows who you are – all ages, all backgrounds.

It is quite daunting because everywhere you go people would just talk to you about *Strictly*. I remember turning up at Twickenham for an England–All Blacks game a year after I retired from playing. A load of kids ran up to me. They didn't want to talk about rugby. They were saying: 'OMG you're the guy who did *Strictly*.'

Back in front of the judges and the votes are registered. Two out of ten from Craig Revel Horwood, five from Arlene Phillips, and six each from Bruno Tonioli and Len Goodman, who quips that it was a 'Matt' finish when it needed to be gloss. I smile, wishing the floor would open up and swallow me.

Nicholas Owen's waltz spares me elimination. He gets slaughtered by the judges, I get saved by the viewers and am condemned to dance another day. I curse Nick for prolonging my ordeal and get straight on the phone to my agent.

'Get me out of the show. I don't want to do this.'

'Be rational, Daws, calm down,' he replies.

He's right. What can he do? He can't fix the results so that I'm eliminated. It is down to me either to walk or to zip up my sequined one-piece and grin and bear it.

I think back over my rugby career to occasions of extreme anxiety. Trawling through my memory I recall school games and trials for county and country. Kicking for goal at Twickenham, leading England out on strike, receiving hate mail as England captain. Nothing I can think of compares to this feeling. Then I remember Neil Jenkins.

We are in the changing room at Newlands Stadium in Cape Town. We've had the knock on the door. 'Two minutes gents please, two minutes.' We are in a circle, metal studs tap dancing on the concrete floor. The first Test is upon us, a match for which we are rated 5/1 underdogs. No-hopers, as the locals put it. Time for a few last key motivational phrases.

Martin Johnson, our captain, starts to speak but is interrupted by this primal sound. It is a cross between a groan, a belch and a retch. 'Like a walrus humping up the beach in search of a mate,' as Will Greenwood puts it.

'F***ing smash 'em,' says someone. 'This is the day we've lived for,' says another. 'We get stuck into them from the fir . . .' somebody else begins to say. He stops mid-sentence because in the huddle, his arms wrapped around team mates either side of him, is Neil Jenkins, chucking up his boots, belching up all his bile and Lucozade. Right in the middle of everyone.

I have known plenty of players down the years who have suffered badly from pre-match nerves. You wouldn't be human if you didn't feel anxious before playing an international rugby match. It's not unusual for guys to go into a corner of the changing room and have a little bit of a retch; but not the full works.

Jenks to me sounds like a mother bird regurgitating food for her chicks. It is understandable he's shitting himself as he is playing out of position at full-back, is sure to be targetted, and he suspects, as we all do, that if any one of those giant Springboks gets him one-on-one he will bulldoze over, or more likely through, him. But that's not what happens. Neil has an unbelievable game with the boot.

For an hour he keeps us in the game. That and some fantastic defending. Os du Randt barrels over early to put them in front but three penalties from Jenks sends us into half-time leading 9–8. More of the same follows. The Boks score their second try within four minutes of the resumption, but we cling on by our fingernails and, with twenty minutes left, Jenks' fifth penalty pulls us back to within a point.

According to the scoreboard the contest appears finely balanced, but the two-nil try count is a better indicator of South Africa's dominance. We cannot get close to their goal line. Our gameplan revolves around Tim Rodber setting close targets with 'pick-and-go' runs, but he is getting battered, so with seven minute remaining, he turns to me and says the words that will change my life.

'Daws, just go, mate. I'm getting bashed. Do a Solo. Do a Solo.'

A 'Solo' is a move we have rehearsed in training and involves the scrum-half going on his own down the blind side with the option to pass to the winger outside him or the No. 8 or No. 6 on his inside.

The ball goes into the scrum and I look at their blind-side flanker, Ruben Kruger. He has been breaking his binding on the short side all afternoon and I have made referee Colin Hawke aware of it. Perhaps sensing Hawke paying closer attention to him this time, he holds firm. I see my chance and go. Before he can react I am past him and their captain and No. 8 Gary Teichmann. Ieuan Evans cuts inside from his wing in support but by the time I see him it's too late. That leaves me with precisely no option but to go it alone and that can only end badly for me. Unless, of course, they buy my ridiculous dummy.

Theatrically, I feign to throw an overhead pass inside to a Lions-free area of Newlands, while slowing down, pretty much resigned to my fate. But rather than pile into me the Boks take the bait and stop in their tracks. I can't believe my luck and, thinking it rude not to accept their hospitality, help myself to the try line.

Not only does this moment decide the match, which we win 25–16 following a last-minute second try scored by Alan Tait, it shapes the series and becomes a 'where were you when . . .' moment for Lions fans everywhere. For weeks, months, perhaps years to come, people will tell me where they were and what they were doing when I went over.

Believe it or not, I am quite an introverted bloke at this point in my life. So the final whistle blows and rather than soak up the sights and sounds of our glory moment I head straight to the changing room. My comfort zone is the company of my Northampton club-mates within the squad, not yet the other Lions. Back in the changing room I discover that the way people regard me has altered.

My performance and, I guess, my try has brought me up to the level of the others. Doubtless there had been an air of worry from the rest of the squad when I was given the shirt for the first Test. Some of the lads must have thought, 'God, we haven't got Rob Howley, we're in trouble.' I think that's why, in the run-up to the game, a lot of the guys looked after me, put an arm around me, took time to talk to me. And when I did deliver, I think that gave them all confidence, reassured them that I actually was up to the challenge.

The best example of this transformation is that I have my first real conversation with Jeremy Guscott. I played with him for England but he had never spoken a word to me other than to bark,

'Pass the ball!' or 'Get on with it!' If I went for a break and got tackled, he'd tut and whinge at me. If I made a wrong decision, he'd highlight it. I honestly never got the impression he rated me as a rugby player, and for a young lad, being snubbed by this hugely influential England and Lions legend made life difficult.

I was not the only person to experience this. Not for nothing was Jerry's nickname Jack, as in, 'I'm all right Jack' (and before you think I'm picking on him, he had 'JACK' written on his gum shield).

Take the third week of the tour. We are in Pretoria, a little over a fortnight from the first Test and the pressure is beginning to crank up. The way the games are being refereed, our opponents are being allowed blatantly to dive in, off their feet, to secure ball. We decide there's no point moaning about it, and we might as well just follow suit.

So Neil Back, the Leicester open-side flanker once described as a 'pocket battleship', and a master at the breakdown, is instructed to take a session with the backs to show us the method we need to employ.

'Listen,' he says. 'When you're presenting the ball, or one of your team mates is, you need to go in like this.'

Having talked us through it, he asks Jerry to demonstrate. Jerry casually goes down to his knee, then onto his side and presents the ball. It is textbook stuff but Backy is looking for rather more intensity.

'More like this mate,' he says.

We look on open-mouthed as the pocket battleship steams in. Rather than gently bending into position to show the bridge over the ball, Backy gets into character, puts in a little sprint and dives down onto the ball to secure it. In the process he accidentally butts

Jerry and, much to the amusement of the rest of us, splits his eyelid wide open.

'For f*** sake, Backy, what the f*** are you doing?' explodes Jerry, blood pouring from the wound. The doctor rushes on, inspects the damage. 'Sorry Jerry, we're going to have to go away and stitch that.'

Jerry, already a Lions series winner in 1989, looks at him incredulously. 'There is no way you're f***ing stitching that. I'm not having a scar there. Put a couple of steri-strips on. I want no needles.'

Before we know it there are three little butterfly stitches above Jerry's eye; the sort you get when you are nine years old. I am surprised he hasn't gone the whole hog and had a Mickey Mouse plaster slapped on it as well.

I make light of the fact he never said much to me other than 'give me the ball', but as it turns out it is Jeremy Guscott's economy of words that probably decides the series in our favour. That and his surprising ability to drop a goal.

I'll let you into a secret: we have no pre-arranged drop-goal routine. Not like six years later when England would coolly execute the last-minute move that allowed Jonny Wilkinson to win us the World Cup with a swing of his right boot. That night in Sydney, when we manufactured field position, every player wearing an England jersey knew exactly their role in the play.

Role play for the '97 Lions revolves around scrummaging and defending, to combat the power game of South Africa. Never mind the trimmings, physicality is what we're about, first and last. Such delicate extras as drop goals are rather left to chance.

Before the game, Fran Cotton, our team manager, reads us a note sent by Phil Larder, the Great Britain rugby league coach, in which he says the Lions have won the respect of his team. Fran says he never thought he'd hear such praise from a rugby league man. He then uses it to emphasise the fact that respect for us has been in short supply from our opponents.

'All they've talked about is that they didn't play too good,' he says. 'No credit to us. We never get any f***ing credit here. Well, we're going to earn their respect today because I'm sick to my back teeth of hearing about Springbok pride and how that's going to win this game. I tell you, pride only takes you to certain levels in this game. There's a hell of a difference between pride and morale. When it comes down to the bottom line, pride doesn't win it.

'Napoleon said, "Morale is to the physical as three is to one." In other words, when morale is high in the camp one of ours is better than three of theirs. That's what we've got and it doesn't f***ing evaporate. They think they're going to beat us with power and by beating us up. We said from the first moment we met there's no way we're taking one step back from any situation. I don't care when it starts, we're in there and we're in their faces for eighty minutes.

'We've got to control, control, control. Concentration. That's the difference between world-class performance and not. When the heat's on – and it doesn't come any heavier than this – for eighty minutes you retain that concentration. The final thing is patience. This is an eighty-minute game. The last twenty minutes is our time. Every single game on this tour we've finished more strongly than the opposition.'

Fran is not wrong. We turn in one of the greatest defensive performances of all time yet enter the final quarter down by six points. South Africa have scored tries either side of half-time, through my opposite number Joost van der Westhuizen and centre

Percy Montgomery, who is in the team primarily as a goalkicker after their woeful kicking display in Cape Town. Andre Joubert, their full-back, adds a third on fifty-four minutes and we have not got close to their try line.

Yet because we have Neil Jenkins, we are still in the game. Sick to his boots beforehand he might have been, but he has kicked every goal, and from quite ridiculous distances. South Africa can't believe we are not dead and buried and two further infringements by the home forwards enable Jenks to tie the scores at 15–15 with seven minutes remaining.

If the score stays like this we will be guaranteed at least a share of the series and suddenly I think of Ian McGeechan's words at the start of the tour.

'The mantle that you carry and the challenge that you have is to put a marker down in South Africa about the way we play rugby. A Lion in South Africa is special. The Lions are special. The legends go with it.'

Four minutes remain and it's all hands to the pump. All game former rugby league boys Alan Tait and John Bentley have chased my box kicks down the touchlines and smashed into the receivers. Apart from when Scott Gibbs has been blasting the ball up the middle. In their frustration the Boks are time and again being penalised for slowing down the ball. Meanwhile, Tim Rodber is punched in the eye because he's held someone back. It's chaos. We stick at it, kick to touch, then drive upfield into kicking range from the set-piece and wait for French referee Didier Mene to blow again.

For the second successive Test the Springboks are sick of the sight of Jenks but they keep coming at us and we have to defend for our lives. So when our fly-half Gregor Townsend gets the ball and drives deep into the home 22, we welcome the respite as much as anything. The ball comes back to me and my first thought is to get it out wide. Nobody mentioned drop goal at the previous set-piece and Gregor has not put me on alert that he is looking for a pot shot.

So I'm looking for a wide ball to play in somebody on a flat pass but there's nobody suitable. There is no option for me other than to pass back into the pocket where someone is screaming for the ball. It is not Gregor because he is my team-mate at Northampton and I would recognise his Borders accent anywhere. And it can't be Jerry because he never talks to me. Only, it is.

Just in time I clock it's him. And because Jerry has been whinging all tour about not getting the ball I reckon I'd better give it to him. 'Right you have it, you deal with it.' With no set routine in place, not with Townsend let alone with Guscott, it's very much a decision Jerry is taking on the hoof. Thank heavens for that. He pops the ball between the sticks, as coolly as you like, we win the match and with it the series.

The final whistle sounds and Lions fans and players alike go berserk. 'Test match rugby is about taking your chances,' Ian McGeechan tells the media. He is not wrong.

CHAPTER 3

THE PENNY DROPS

'How many drop goals would it take to win a Test match?' Clive Woodward, head coach of the England rugby team, asks the question and scours the room in search of an answer. We are in a team leaders' meeting on the Australian island resort of Couran Cove, off the Queensland coast, during a summer training camp shortly before the 1999 World Cup.

We stare at him quizzically. 'Look,' says Clive. 'We've got Jonny Wilkinson in our team who's brilliant at drop goals. We are spending so much time trying to work out how to score tries, why can't we just use Jonny to kick drop goals?' There is silence. I'm not a big fan of drop goals and I know I'm not alone.

I enjoyed the one I landed to win a game for Northampton against Harlequins the first time I played opposite Will Carling. I admired the forty-five yarder All Blacks No. 8 Zinzan Brooke knocked over against England in the World Cup semi-final in 1995, though only because it was an outrageous piece of skill by a big forward. And of course I am a big fan of the one Jeremy Guscott landed to win the 1997 Lions' Test series. Those apart, I would far rather run with the ball.

'Well?' says Clive, irritated by our obvious lack of enthusiasm. Finally, Mike Catt speaks, replying to our leader with a question of his own.

'How many Fs in bothered?'

Clive looks non-plussed. He doesn't get it, but we all do. It is a dig at him for the 'How many Fs in . . .' teaser he posed when he first took charge in 1997. To reinforce the point he was trying to make about the importance of attention to detail – in this case how lazy the human brain and eye are – he instructed us to read the following passage and then answer his question.

'Finished files are the res-
ult of years of scientif-
ic study combined with the
experience of many years'

Everyone got it wrong except Jason Leonard who, at a stroke, dispelled the notion that props are not the sharpest knives in the drawer. We all said three, Jason correctly counted six, and gleefully pointed out to the rest of us that, 'the Fs in "of" do count you know?!' Clive and Jase wore the smiles that day. Now it's our turn.

Except that not for the first time Clive is absolutely spot on. The drop can do enormous damage, as we are about to learn to our cost. A couple of months later England are eliminated in the quarter-finals of the World Cup in Paris when South African fly-half Jannie de Beer, almost unbelievably, helps himself to five of the damned things.

It's a painful lesson and one we really should not have needed to learn, given that Jerry Guscott's Lions 'drop' is still pretty fresh in the memory. But learn it we do and that 44–21 loss to the Springboks means Clive's words come back to haunt us. There is an upside, however. We, the England players, finally wise up to the power of the drop goal. Come the 2003 World Cup, and extra time in the final against Australia, we have a well-rehearsed move to get us upfield to put Jonny in position to do what he does best. The contrast with the chaos that surrounded Jerry's kick six years earlier could hardly be greater.

In Durban in '97 pandemonium reigned. In Sydney in '03 there is relative serenity from the moment Australia draw level from the penalty spot, leaving us just time for one last attack from a lineout thirty-five metres from the posts. We know precisely what we're going to do.

The move is called 'Piss Flaps'. For public consumption it is known as 'Zig Zag' but on the field, when Elton Flatley kicks the goal to bring the Wallabies level, Jonny and I turn to each other and we don't mention zig or zag. Why, you may well ask? Well, 'piss flaps' was a name coined at Northampton by fly-half Paul Grayson, who reckoned that in any arena, no matter how loud the noise, you could always pick out those two words and the call could not be confused with any other. That was certainly true and, if I'm honest, there was also a naughty pleasure in getting Jonny Wilkinson to scream 'piss flaps' at the top of his voice.

We had rehearsed the move numerous times in training. Kick long at the re-start to pressure the opposition into kicking into touch, throw long then take the ball directly to the line before working Jonny into position to pull the trigger. It works like a dream. Steve Thompson hits Lewis Moody at the tail of the lineout, I feed Jonny who hits Mike Catt on the crash ball. Catty takes it into contact, lays the ball back and it's in my hands again. I spot a gap in Australia's ruck defence and am away . . . five, ten, twenty metres upfield. The Wallabies are in a flap but we have cool heads. I go to ground and we are within Jonny's range, but with no scrum-half to pass to him Martin Johnson calmly puts his head down and takes the ball through another phase to allow me time to get back onto my feet. Now I'm up and in position. I check Jonny is ready then spin him the pass. We all know what happens next. As the ball leaves his boot to spark the mother of all parties, I am struck by a thought.

'I love a drop goal.'

MY TOP-TEN DROP GOALS

1) *Jonny Wilkinson (extra time, 2003 World Cup final, England v Australia, Sydney)*
2) *Jeremy Guscott (2nd Test, 1997 Lions v South Africa, Durban)*
3) *Rob Andrew (1995 World Cup quarter-final, England v Australia, Cape Town)*
4) *Matt Dawson (1993, Courage League, Northampton v Harlequins, Twickenham Stoop)*
5) *Zinzan Brooke (1995 World Cup semi-final, New Zealand v England, Cape Town)*
6) *Stephen Larkham (1999 World Cup semi-final, Australia v South Africa, Twickenham)*
7) *Joel Stransky (extra time, 1995 World Cup final, South Africa v New Zealand, Johannesburg)*
8) *Jonny Wilkinson (2007 World Cup semi-final, England v France, Paris)*
9) *Thomas Castaignède (1996 Five Nations, France v England, Paris)*
10) *Jannie de Beer (1999 World Cup quarter-final, South Africa v England, Paris)*

Back in South Africa there is still a series to complete, even if the third Test has become a dead rubber. But we're not yet ready to think about the final Test in Johannesburg. There is some serious partying to be done.

This has been a good tour for letting our hair down. Unlike the 2001 Lions tour to Australia, where the management would get the balance hopelessly wrong between work and play, we are afforded plenty of opportunity to chill out between matches.

One memorable night in Pretoria sticks in my mind. Neil Back, Jeremy Davidson and myself somewhat unwisely visited a bar off the beaten track and must each have downed twenty-five shots. We stayed so long that the barman went home and asked us to lock the door when we left! It was not the smartest move on our part, not least because we got lost on the way home in a country where you just don't do that sort of thing. We ended up seeking sanctuary in a petrol station, where the owner called us a taxi while giving us a bollocking for being out alone in that neighbourhood at that time of night.

No such dramas in Durban after the second Test where the whole squad go to a bar called TJs and I am introduced to Tequila 'Body Slams'. Now everyone has heard of Tequila Slammers, right? This is a variation on that theme and involves drinking lemon from the mouth of one waitress, licking salt off the midriff of another, then slurping Tequila from her belly button. Nice. The night quickly descends into a wild after-party. I remember John Bentley having his shirt ripped off by Backy and Keith Wood. But not much after that – until I am woken by a loud banging sound.

'Daws, Daws!'

'Er, what, what's that?' I mumble. 'Who is it? What's the matter? . . . Wait a minute.'

I force my eyes open. I'm lying in bed beside my then girlfriend Natalie, who is still out cold. I reach for my watch, which is in my right shoe on the floor just within reach. Seven o'clock. Jesus, it's early.

'Come back later please,' I yell. The violent hammering continues. I slide out of bed, stand on a cufflink, yelp, then hop to the door ready to give the maid a mouthful for wanting to change my towels at this ungodly hour.

'All right, Daws?'

Scott Gibbs is standing there, still dressed in his post-match glad rags, a crate of beer under one arm and a duvet under the other.

'We're heading to the beach for a beer, you coming?'

I pause, look round at Natalie, who has not stirred. 'What the hell'? I pick up a blanket, pull on some shorts, a Lions polo shirt and flip flops, being sure to shut the door quietly as I leave. The team room is open downstairs and I help myself to a crate of the sponsor's brew and five minutes later we are sitting with Bentos watching the sun rise over the Indian Ocean. It is a perfect way to celebrate what we have achieved.

There is nothing planned for the day save for needing to be ready for an afternoon bus journey to a place called Vereeniging, an industrial town in the middle of nowhere, which the management thought, in their pre-tour planning, would be perfect to focus ahead of the Test decider. Of course, the series is done and dusted and it's now the last place on earth we want to be. The town smells of chemicals and the hotel is near an abattoir.

A couple of lads have stuff stolen from their hotel rooms and in the final midweek match Kyran Bracken, who broke off his Caribbean holiday after just one day to join the tour as a replacement, badly damages his shoulder on his first appearance. It is difficult because mentally we are thinking 'job done'. Yes, there is another Test to play, at Ellis Park in Johannesburg, but our mission is already accomplished. We hadn't come to win the series three-nil, we'd just come to win the series.

For the record, I score our only try in that third Test, in which South Africa finally field a recognised goalkicker and Jannie de Beer kicks the Boks to a 35–16 consolation victory. Sadly, I don't get to be on the pitch when the final whistle blows to end an amazing series as I have, to my surprise, been replaced by Austin Healey.

Oh well, I figure at the time, you can't have everything. That is not what I think now however. The little bastard.

Healey did me in cold blood that night. With ten minutes left in the game and the Lions twelve points behind, the substitution was an obvious one. Neil Jenkins, whose goal kicking had secured us the first two Tests, had run himself to a stand still at full-back and we were in need of a fresh spark if we were to rescue the match.

Back then the practice of using replacements was very different from today, where everybody seems to get a game. The bench was rarely deployed other than in the event of injury. Prior to a match the nominated replacements would be made aware of which position they were covering and, over the course of the week, get the opportunity to rehearse the 'what-if' scenario. But more likely than not, come the event they would be left kicking their heels.

Austin, though, was a useful man to have in reserve as he was so versatile, a player who during his career represented England in pretty much every position in the back line. He possessed the speed of a back-three player (unless of course that back-three player was New Zealand's Jeff Wilson against whom he didn't look quite so clever!). He also had the creative mind and the passing and kicking skills of a half-back.

So there we are at Ellis Park in the dying moments of the series when play stops and the Lions shape to make a change. I look across and there is Austin stripping off. He has been in the coaches' ear all evening.

'They must have cracked,' I think to myself.

I now know the instructions given to him were as follows: 'Warm up, Healey, go on for Jenks and show us how good you are!'

These days the procedure for making a replacement involves a member of the team management formally advising the fourth official who is going on and who is coming off. Not back then. Austin wanders up to the official and says calmly, 'I'm on, Sir.'

'Who for?'

Austin glances briefly back at the bench, smirks to himself, and replies: 'Dawson, Sir. Number nine!'

When I hear this story at a dinner years later, I don't believe it. Surely nobody, not even Healey, would pull that stunt. But then I trawl through my memory back to that night, to how I felt as I trotted off the field. Right enough, I was a bit bemused. Neil Jenkins was gasping for air, I wasn't. And Austin did laugh as he ran past me. One day, Healey. One day.

Had I known then what I know now it would be him trussed up the following day, rather than the Welsh hooker Barry Williams. Barry is getting married straight after the tour; what better excuse to have a long lunch and a skinful of beer. Emotionally exhausted and a little inebriated, I stagger back to the hotel for an afternoon kip, thinking the action is over. How wrong I am. In my absence Barry is stripped naked, taken outside the restaurant and taped to a lamppost, with only a jock strap to preserve his modesty. Another reason never to forget this tour of a lifetime.

CAPTAIN FANTASTIC

The 1997 British and Irish Lions tour is a personal triumph for one man in particular – a former bank clerk from Market Harborough in Leicestershire. Despite no experience of international captaincy Martin Osborne Johnson was appointed skipper by team manager Fran Cotton for the simple reason that he would 'terrify the opposition when he went in for the coin toss'. To do that in South Africa, the land of the rugby giants, is a measure of the man, in every sense.

He will go on to become the only player ever to captain the Lions in two separate tours; to lead Leicester to back-to-back Heineken Cup triumphs and numerous other trophies; and, of course, to skipper England to the 2003 Grand Slam and World Cup.

What is it about Johnno, I hear you ask, that made him the leader he was? In a nutshell, every team he led respected him and every team they came up against feared him. You could sense the opposition was never going to mess with him. It was a presence, a look, the way he went about his business. He never got involved in stuff he considered unimportant. So when he did intervene, we all knew it mattered. And if it mattered to him, it mattered to all of us.

LEADERS WHO SHAPED MY CAREER XV

15) *Martin Johnson*
14) *Lawrence Dallaglio*

13) Will Carling

12) Tim Rodber

11) Pat Lam

10) Wayne 'Buck' Shelford

9) Keith Wood

1) Gary Pearce

2) Ron Dawson

3) Colin Tattersall

4) Chalkie White

5) Paul Volley

6) Budge Pountney

7) Phil Tufnell

8) Lilia Kopylova

15) Martin Johnson (my captain with England 1998–2003 and Lions 1997–2001)

The toughest England player I played alongside and a leader who always put the concerns of his men first. There were no frills or spills with Johnno, simply an incredible work ethic on and off the pitch. His presence alone gave us an advantage. I never met a player, coach or official who did not take note of the mono-browed expression he wore in the heat of battle.

Well maybe one, and it coincides with the only time I get on the wrong side of that look – during the 2003 World Cup final. Johnno, like the rest of us, is starting to lose patience with South African referee Andre Watson. To say we are not exactly getting the rub of the green at scrum time would be understating it some-what. We have the very real sense that Mr Watson is letting the Wallabies back into a contest we are dominating through a series of debatable decisions.

THE PENNY DROPS

Having twice taken issue with calls without success, Johnno has had enough. He makes a beeline for the man with the whistle, clearly meaning business. Then I open my mouth.

'Johnno, stop! Don't do it! Your body language is appalling!' I shout, in my poshest Home Counties accent. 'I'm not sure Andre will appreciate your manner!'

Johnno swings round and gives me a look I have seen somewhere before . . . Got it! The trance-like death stare Ka the snake gave his prey in *The Jungle Book*. 'Your body language is appalling!' 'Appreciate your manner?' What am I on?! I laugh about it now. I didn't at the time.

For all his fierce façade there is a softer side to Johnno. During the time we played together he was never happier than when he was at home watching *Countdown* with his feet up on the sofa and a cup of tea in those big mitts of his; or playing *Madden NFL* on PlayStation (he is a massive American Football fan, and played for Leicester Panthers); or organising the sports quizzes in the England camp. I answer sports questions for my day job on *A Question of Sport* and like to think I have a pretty decent breadth of sporting knowledge, but even now I suspect it is no better than Johnno's, back when we were playing. And I know for sure that I don't take it as seriously.

That is not to say he can't enjoy a good laugh. I've never known a dryer sense of humour. Take the day he and I were sitting in the bar at the England team hotel, Pennyhill Park, having a coffee with Jonny Wilkinson before we headed off to the 2003 World Cup. At the time we are being flogged to death on the training field and I say to Johnno, 'Mate, you've got to speak to Otis [England conditioning coach Dave Reddin] because while we're loving the work, we're struggling when it comes to game time.'

Johnno nods in acknowledgement. I think he knows where I'm coming from. He is suffering along with the rest of us. Then Jonny piped up.

'Don't let him in, Daws. Don't let him in.'

'What?! Don't let who in?'

'Don't let Mr Tired in! The window is ajar and he's knocking on the door. You mustn't let him in.'

Johnno looks at Jonny, then at my disbelieving expression. The faintest hint of a smile flickers across his face. It looks like he wants to laugh and take the mick out of Wilko but then thinks better of it.

'You're right, Jonny,' he says. 'Stay strong, Daws . . . even if Mr Tired is banging the crap out of the door.'

He was not always quite such a diplomat. During the England players' strike in 2000, he played hardball on behalf of us all. You might think he was difficult to budge on the red carpet at Lansdowne Road three years later but that was nothing to the way he stood his ground against the Rugby Football Union in our quest for what we considered a fairer pay deal when away on international duty.

Our beef was that the balance was wrong between match fee and win bonus, tilted too heavily in favour of us winning when if we lost by a point we were giving exactly the same commitment and effort. There was also an issue over our image rights, but the whole thing still amounted to no more than £250 per game, a ridiculous sum considering the fuss it caused. Still, it was a point of principle and as a squad we unanimously agreed Johnno should handle the negotiations with the RFU.

There was a lot of flak flying around, the media were largely critical of our stance (telling us we should walk over broken glass to play for our country, which we felt rather missed the point) but through it all he was very matter-of-fact. He was animated when he needed to be but never lost the plot. He remained cool, calm and collected, aware always that he was there to represent all of us players. I grudgingly tip my hat to Francis Baron, the RFU's then chief executive, for holding out for as long as he did. Even dealing with a reasonable Martin Johnson must have been an intimidating experience.

He was a proper players' captain, was Johnno, able to crack jokes in times of extreme tension, or simply adopt the 'less-is-more' approach. The Friday night meetings before a Test match would be the last chance for the coaches to get stuck into us, then there would be a motivational video, then the captain would take over. When I was skipper I used a flip chart to go through a number of points. Johnno didn't. He'd just say something like 'Let's batter these pricks!' get up and leave.

Before extra time in the 2003 World Cup final Clive Woodward came down out of the stands and approached us. Johnno spotted him, turned round and said firmly, 'I've got it Clive, don't worry.' Clive backed off and went and found Jonny instead to tell him that if we get a penalty, he should kick it. Bet Jonny hadn't thought of that.

Several times during my England career we had interminably long meetings with the coaches about how we should play against the opposition. We'd then get in a huddle on the training field and Johnno would say, 'With all due respect to the coaches, you lot know what to do. Don't worry about what they're saying, I want this out of you Matt, this out of you Lawrence,' and so on. He wasn't telling us a different message from the coaches, he was just translating it into more player-friendly language.

A question I'm often asked is whether he feels his spell as England team manager, and events – particularly off-field – at the 2011 World Cup damaged his legacy. I can only speculate but in my opinion, no. For one thing his England team won a Six Nations title, in 2011 – the first since he himself held aloft the trophy in 2003. For another, because of the figurehead he was and continues to be now that is behind him. Johnno took the job with no concern for his legacy or ego. How do I know that? Because he told me so when I hosted a Q&A lunch with him and Will Carling about a week before he was given the post.

There were rumours he was going to do it and we were chatting away on the stage when he said, 'There's no one else who's going to do it. They've asked me. If I can help England at all, that is what I want to do. I'm not bothered about ego or reputational risk. I'm not in this for that.' I honestly think that if they'd asked him to be the kit man and he thought that by doing so England would be successful, he'd have agreed. He always put England's best interests ahead of his own. He was a one-off and I'm honoured to have played alongside him.

14) Lawrence Dallaglio (my England captain 1997–99 and 2004; my Wasps captain 2004–06)

The most openly passionate England captain I played under. Emotion was what sparked him off. He played his best rugby with bottom jaw out and tears in the eyes. You could feel Lol wanted others to get to that same level. He would build it up through the week. Softly, softly, into medium, then just before the first whistle we'd be ready to explode.

Lol was very good at pitching his team talks at exactly the right level. He understood which buttons to push on which individuals.

He was excellent at reading up on what the opposition were saying and using that as motivation. Now and again we'd catch him out quoting something we had all read in the papers but it didn't matter. On a Friday night, while it was Martin Johnson's captaincy style pretty much to sit there, looking round the room and saying something only if it needed to be said, Lawrence would have a four or five-page flip chart presentation on what we're going to do, how we're going to attack and where. And he would drum it into us.

As captain he was the Red Rose on the shirt, the figurehead that got fans and team mates alike pumped up. He had a little bit of the Will Carling about him – in his personality and back and front-page news potential. He liked to be seen around London town. His town. Above all, he cared passionately about English rugby.

He was as tough as there was. As he got older, because he knew the game so well, he didn't need to have that hard-man tag, but in his pomp – I'd say between 1998 and 2003 – he was uncontainable. He was so fast off the base of the scrum no one could get anywhere near him. The bookies even had a spread bet for how many yards he would make in an international, which they hilariously called 'Larry's Carries'.

I joined Wasps in 2004 after he collared me and spoke about it during the previous year's World Cup. I was impressed with how the club was run, how professional the set-up was, and playing again under Lawrence's captaincy appealed to me. With him there was always a bit of bravado involved. There had to be when he referred to himself as 'The Lol' in the third person. The Wasps boys gave him stacks of banter but that kept his feet on the ground. And if we're honest, he invites it. I can say that when I think of the stick he gave me and Austin Healey about doing *Strictly*.

'You'll be doing it one day, don't you worry about that,' we replied.

'I don't think so,' he countered. 'I don't go on TV to be famous.'

The next thing we know he's cycling from Greece to London with Freddy Flintoff in a high-profile charity challenge, appearing on every media platform along the way. Lawrence, of course, made light of it when I next saw him. He has that priceless ability to laugh at himself.

My favourite story about him comes from South Africa in 2000 while I was at home recovering from a shoulder operation. I was asleep one night when my phone rang. It was Austin.

'You won't believe what Lol has just done,' he said, going on to explain that, after being controversially beaten in the first match of a two-Test series, a few of the boys had gone into Pretoria to drown their sorrows.

'There was me, Neil Back, Jason Leonard, Martin Johnson, Leon Lloyd and Lawrence,' said Austin, taking up the story. 'Shortly after midnight we were in a club when Lawrence disappeared. All of a sudden over the speakers came: "WhoooaaaaaAAAAA!" It was the start of *Nellie the Elephant* and there, in the middle of the dance floor, right in the spotlight, was Lawrence wearing orange pants.

'As the song played he raised his arms higher in the air until it reached the chorus, "Nellie the Elephant packed her trunk . . ." at which point Lol began jogging furiously on the spot and going berserk.'

Austin was doubled up laughing as he relived the moment and he obviously retold it a few times when he got back to the hotel. The following day, when head coach Clive Woodward got up to speak in the team meeting, all the lads gave it, 'WhoooaaaaaAAAAA!' at the height of which Lawrence jumped to his feet and started bopping about again.

Six days later England bounced back to beat the Springboks in Bloemfontein with a victory that we still look back on as being crucial to us going on to win the World Cup three years later. As Austin put it, 'That was classic Lawrence, a magnet for people around him to attach themselves to in times of anxiety. He can inspire confidence in players and sometimes that can be enough to change the mood of a team.'

13) Will Carling (my England captain 1995–97)

The first time I went to Twickenham to watch England play was Will's first game as captain. We were playing Australia and I remember thinking what an absolute legend this fella is to be captaining his country at the age of twenty-two. A few years later, as I've mentioned already, I played against him in the centre for Northampton against Harlequins and dropped the winning goal as he tried to block it. That's all I remember about the day. Not who else was in the team or that we won, just that I was up against Will Carling. I couldn't believe it.

Fast forward to 1995 and he is my England captain. Paul Grayson and I have both been given our debuts against Western Samoa, as they were then, and are sharing a room at the Petersham Hotel in Richmond. It's match day and we have *Grandstand* on the television. The programme is coming live from Twickenham where in a few hours we will win our first caps. I am getting more and more anxious when into our room walks Will.

'You all right Matt?'

'Yeah I'm fine.'

'Oh, I thought you'd be crapping yourself on the toilet at the thought of the game.'

I was. I was bricking it. Him telling me that I should be messing myself has always stuck with me. It was his way of getting across to me that everyone's going to be nervous, don't worry about that. But rather than say, 'Is everything all right?' as some captains do, and then be all serious about it, his way was to make light of it, crack a bit of a joke and lighten the mood.

Will was amazing to play alongside because I grew up watching him. He was playing for England when I was still practising passing to my dad in the back garden. Yet we ended up winning a Five Nations Championship together. And now he's a good friend. Why was he a good captain? People say he was lucky. Right place, right time, great set of players. I don't buy that. To do what he did at that age with that group of senior players, who had been around the block, took some balls. Brian Moore, Dean Richards, Peter Winterbottom, Mike Teague – they would never have suffered a fool. The thought of a twenty-two-year-old going into that team room and being captain is just ridiculous. There was no faffing around with him, no hype. He had that shouting and screaming military side to him, but also a great ability to put his arm round you and talk very softly and eloquently about what you needed to deliver. He would be absolutely crystal clear about what he wanted to see and what had to happen.

I see a bit of that calm authority today in Chris Robshaw, another Harlequin who was awarded the England captaincy despite having precious little experience. The difference is that Chris just gets on with the job and his example is such that the players around him raise their games because they don't want to let him down.

When you're in the backs it's very different, particularly when you've got Jerry Guscott outside you abusing you for not passing him the ball. Will had to manage that scenario as well as tactically try to get the team into the right areas of the field. You have to be a special player to do both, which is why midfield captains, such as Carling and Brian O'Driscoll, are such a rare breed.

12) Tim Rodber (my Northampton captain 1998–2001)

My old mucker and fellow 1997 Lion won't mind me giving away some of his trade secrets. Now that he is a successful businessman and out of the Army it's about time the dirt was spilt. Captain Tim Rodber of the Green Howards in Yorkshire is one of the toughest men I ever met. Let me give you an example, and I have a few. I once had a running race over the length of a pitch on the old training pitches at Northampton Rugby Club.

Rodders was quick on his toes for a blind-side so it was never going to be a stroll in the park. Even so, I would comfortably win with a bit to spare. He knew it, I knew it and the gathering crowd after training knew it. He needed to find an edge, so he bullied me into agreeing that he could say, 'Ready, steady, go'. Naturally, he bolted at 'steady'. It gave him a head start of six or seven metres and despite my best efforts my little sparrow legs just couldn't close the gap. It was my turn to pull a stunt. I wasn't close enough for an orthodox round-the-legs tackle but I reckoned I could tap his trailing foot. Down he went and with fifteen metres to go I went past giving the V's and telling him not to cheat next time.

It worried me that he didn't see the funny side. In fact he wasn't even angry. Instead he gave the impression he was hurt. 'Pathetic,' I said as I trotted back to where he was writhing on the turf. 'Pathetic?' He repeated to me quizzically, removing his hand from his knee to reveal a gash about five inches long and at least one inch wide and deep. Shit.

We rushed him to the physio on the back of groundsman David 'Piggy' Powell's tractor and called for the doc. In he came with a needle, thread and nail brush! He proceeded to scrub the dirt out of the cut without any anaesthetic, then insert twenty-eight stitches, eight of them internally. To rub salt into this horrific wound, Tim was due to play for England against Wales ten days later. He had to withdraw. I felt dreadful.

Tim was tough as teak and, unfortunately for Northampton team-mate David Dantiacq, he expected the same from his players. The Rodber leadership style was naturally fairly military, but what he did to Dantiacq would not be found in the Sandhurst manual. Saints were playing a key European match against Narbonne and the French boys had just scored a try to take the lead, courtesy of a missed tackle by our Frenchman. This incensed captain Rodber and as we huddled around one another under the posts he gave us an almighty bollocking, reminding us of our duties as Saintsmen and the importance of winning in front of our home fans. Then he noticed Dantiacq not paying attention and eyeing up someone in the crowd.

Whack! Tim lurched across the huddle and kicked David, studs and all, right in the chest. 'Oi, that was your fault they scored. Now get a grip and show us you've got the balls to play for this team!' If the ref had seen it, I reckon he would have sent Tim off for a high tackle. There was shocked silence and I really did think David was going to cry but, to his credit, he took it virtually on the chin and had a blinder for the rest of the match.

11) Pat Lam (my Northampton captain 2000–01)

Pat was a warrior leader who captained Northampton to European Cup glory in 2000. It was the club's first trophy in 120 years and although due to injury I missed the Twickenham final – a 9–8 win over Munster – I was still involved in the build-up which, under Pat's leadership, meant a pre-match prayer involving the whole squad.

Trying to introduce a spiritual dimension into a rugby team made up of lads from all walks of life was fine by me, though praying in this way before a game had never been part of my mental preparation. He prayed for power and strength and for the support of our families and the fans – and generally for the welfare of the club. For him it was a prayer in the spiritual sense. Others, I suspect, used it more as mental preparation for a massive game.

I wonder whether he also thanked his lucky stars. For there had been a real chance he, too, would miss the game because his wife Stephanie was due to give birth to their fourth child on the day of the final and Pat insisted on being present. Happily, little Josiah arrived three days early.

I would be lying if I said I don't ever pray. I do, but those thoughts tend to be for others, people who are ill or need a bit of help. Not for myself and a game of rugby. The times Pat had us sitting head bowed, I certainly wasn't seeking divine intervention out on the pitch. It was more getting my head straight for the game with a moment's quiet reflection.

Pat captained Samoa and represented them in three World Cups (two when they were Western Samoa) before going on to become assistant coach of Scotland. He was very strategic, very thorough and very influential in his leadership style. He was captain of the club when I was captain of England and there were lessons I learned from him, notably the importance of ensuring everyone had a voice in the changing room.

His spiritual beliefs didn't stop him bringing one of his children to an end-of-season booze-up. The little lass could not have been more than four months old. He brought her in a basket, which he sat on the bar, while the rest of us drank and danced and generally had a right good time. Before you ask, Pat behaved impeccably. As club captain he knew he had to turn up, but he also knew he had a parental responsibility that night. He enjoyed a couple of beers, the baby didn't wake once and at midnight he lifted the basket off the bar and the two of them headed home in a taxi. Class act.

10) Wayne 'Buck' Shelford (my Northampton team mate and one-time second team captain 1991–93)

This fella would make any rugby player's list of top captains AND hard men and it was one of the great privileges of my career to snap at his heels during his time as Northampton No. 8 and skipper. He came to us with a legendary reputation, not only as a World Cup winner but for what happened in a Test match against France in 1986. The match became known as the 'Battle of Nantes'. In three separate incidents he lost three teeth when kicked in the face at a ruck, was knocked out cold by a blow to the head, and had his scrotum ripped open, leaving one of his testicles hanging free.

'It bloody well hurt at the time,' Buck told ESPN some years later, 'so I just chucked the old proverbial Jesus water down the shorts to make it feel better. That didn't do a lot, so we just played on. I went off the field with twenty minutes to go not really knowing where I was, let alone what day it was. As history shows, we lost the game, and it was not until I got changed that I realised that my scrotum had been torn, and that the testicle was hanging a good four or five inches out of the scrotum. It was all put back into place and stitched up nicely.'

With a hard-as-nails reputation like that who would not jump at the chance to play alongside him? Not me, that's for sure. Having Buck around meant I could get away with pretty much anything on the pitch. Then, at the slightest hint of trouble, hide in his shadow.

His philosophy was that if he could do something, he expected you to follow suit. If he could play with his hamstring falling off, for example, so should you. I remember him coming in on the afternoon of a game and taking his shirt off. At first glance he resembled a roadmap. All these horrific gristles, twenty to twenty-five one-inch gashes on his back and arms. He'd been to the doctor that morning, had them stitched up, then turned up as normal to play.

After winning twenty-two New Zealand caps between 1986 and 1990 Buck was controversially – some would say inexplicably – ditched as captain in favour of Gary Whetton and chose to come to England to end his playing days at Franklin's Gardens. The All Blacks' loss was most certainly our gain. Rugby union was still an amateur sport but, with the help of local businessman Keith Barwell, Buck took on a none-too-taxing job and played at the weekends. I, of course, had watched him on TV in the World Cup and although I knew him a little from Northampton, which I had joined in 1991, I had no idea just how revered he was in his homeland until I visited New Zealand on a rugby exchange in 1992.

England B were also there on tour at the time and when they came to Hamilton I went up to give them a bit of support against the Maori. I arrived in good time and tucked myself towards the back of the stand. Two minutes before kick-off, a deathly silence fell over the ground. I looked down to the touchline and there was Buck making his way into the stand. The crowd burst into spontaneous applause, which quickly turned to, 'We want Buck. We want Buck!'

He acknowledged the adulation with a wave then wandered up the steps of the old stand in my direction. I looked at the free seat next to me and thought, 'He's not, is he?' He did. Wayne Shelford parked his enormous backside right next to me then shook my hand and embraced me like a long-lost son. Thousands of eyes looked on in awe at the legend from North Harbour while presumably quietly thinking, 'Who's the skinny little pale-faced Pom with the curtains haircut?' I didn't care. At that moment I felt like rugby royalty.

9) Keith Wood (my Lions captain v Mpumalanga 1997)

My midweek Lions captain in 1997 and the first captain to scare the life out of me. I'll explain. It was week three of the tour and Woody was appointed captain for our game against Mpumalanga. We had just beaten Western Province with our best performance since arriving in South Africa and the locals, particularly national hero James Small, had not liked it one bit. (Small refused to shake hands with John Bentley at the end and falsely accused Bentos of gouging him.) Anyway, we expected some sort of backlash four days later when we took on Mpumalanga in Witbank. We needed to be right up for the challenge, primed for the battle heading our way.

Woody did not need too much of an excuse to get emotional. That was the type of character he was. But this day he was so wound up he was spinning like a top. Inside that tiny cream-rendered-walled changing room, next door to a load of nutters ready to kick the crap out of us, he let us know in no uncertain terms that we needed to meet fire with fire. By the time he had finished nobody was in any doubt what was at stake and the responsibilities that went with wearing the Lions shirt on that particular day.

Not to put too fine a point on it, he went completely bonkers, talking so quickly I didn't understand half of what he was saying. It was just this tirade of passion and enthusiasm, punctuated only by Neil Jenkins as usual retching in the background. I liked to prepare quietly for a game, get into the zone my own way. Woody had other ideas. He came over to me and pressed his forehead on mine. I tried to stay calm but he started shaking me around, not butting me but pushing his forehead against mine, sweating all over me, shouting at me, spitting in my face. 'Do you know what, Keith?' I thought. 'This is scaring the crap out of me. I really don't need this right now.' But it served a purpose. Although Doddie Weir had his tour ended by a disgraceful incident of foul play on that bone-hard pitch, we ran out easy 64–14 winners.

In all my playing career I did not encounter a more passionate individual on and off the pitch than Woody. The fact he was a hooker, by definition right in the thick of everything that is going on, and was able to display an ice-cool temperament, made him all the more remarkable.

1) Gary Pearce (my Northampton captain 1991–92)

Come with me, if you will, back to my very first senior appearance, for Northampton Saints in a friendly against Headingley. I had played a couple of second-team games at centre and Saints coach Glenn Ross thought I deserved a shot with the big boys. My captain was Gary Pearce, a well-respected, seasoned England player, who would go on to play more than 400 times for Northampton. As I sat in the dressing room that day my eyes were opened to what lay ahead in the years of amateur rugby. Cheating! Whatever you could get away with seemed to be fair game and if you did get caught, a simple apology was sufficient.

Take my captain's boots. The referee came into the changing room to toss the coin, chat to the coach and check every player's studs. I guess sometimes the odd stud may have been frayed or even missing but more often than not a quick swipe with the palm of the hand on the soles was all that was required. It was no different that afternoon. Pearcey got the all-clear, shared a joke with the ref, then waited for him to leave the room before throwing his boots in a bag and pulling out an almost identical pair – save for the six twenty-two-millimetre nail-like pieces of metal sticking out from the underside. These were the days when if you were on the wrong side at a ruck, you got a shoeing. And by God you would only do it once when Gary was about.

2) Ron Dawson (my dad and first coach 1972–83)

Behind every successful sportsman or woman there are always un-sung heroes, people without whom you could never have achieved your dreams. I am no different and it would be remiss of me not to mention a few, especially my dad, Ron, who coached me from the age of five at the Esso Rugby club in Southampton. Even before that I have vivid memories of watching him play at Old Rockferrians in Birkenhead. I even recollect him sitting me on his knee, letting me believe I was driving the car up the club's gravel path (I didn't realise his knees were steering!). Most of my youth rugby was at Marlow RFC, a fabulous club steeped in mini rugby history with a nationally famous tournament held every April, for which teams came from as far afield as Wales, Scotland, the Isle of Wight. Even Maidenhead.

I'm sure my parents could recite plenty of tales of my running about causing havoc, or the day I was sawing around the corner flag post in the empty sheds and accidentally sliced open my mate Mark Davis's eye. But my undying memory of Marlow Minis is of my dad as the coach. There are thousands of fathers across the country like him, I know that. Guys who sacrifice their Sunday mornings, who pull on five layers of clothing in the winter, who wait patiently for latecomers to arrive, who get abused by the other parents for not picking their sons or daughters, who hold a tackle shield for the freakishly huge lad that smashes into their ribs while everyone else falls about laughing.

Without them there is no grass-roots rugby, yet did Dad get any credit? Only grief. My issue with him was that I felt picked on. My dad is always fair, but I took his criticism personally. If he singled me out for a bad pass or a loose tackle, I would stomp about like a baby – 'stop picking on me . . . Leave me alone . . . I hate you . . . You're not my real dad!' – you know, all the classics. I'd often run the half mile back to the clubhouse and sulk in the shower.

What a fool! How did he put up with me?! Mind you, he was no angel himself. When I started to play a little more seriously at school, and county trials were on, he was shown the odd red card himself for being too loud. In my early days at Northampton I could actually hear his voice in the crowd. That was until Mum, who would get so embarrassed when he piped up, issued an ultimatum. 'Ron, either quieten down or you can drive yourself to games and forgo a beer afterwards.' That did the trick.

3) Colin Tattersall (my school rugby coach 1983–88)
If Dad set me on the road to a career in rugby, Colin Tattersall, head of PE at RGS High Wycombe, made sure I completed the journey. Not only did he coach me at rugby, cricket and basketball, he was responsible for me being able to stay on at school to take my

A-levels. I hadn't done as well as I should have in my GCSEs and the school thought I should leave. Colin knew he needed me in the first team for the next two years, and was confident I would make the England Schools' team, so he persuaded the then headmaster, R P Brown, to let me retake and progress further.

It was a life-changing moment. I was picked by England and played the entire season, including a match against France at Franklin's Gardens. Northampton were impressed by my performance on their home ground that day and invited me for a trial. The rest is history.

4) Chalkie White (my England development coach 1984–85)
The first person to identify my England potential, Chalkie was one of my development coaches when I was twelve and thirteen. He was also the person who taught me not to spit, and this story illustrates why I thought so much of him. Most people in rugby condemn spitting as a filthy habit, loutish behaviour. 'The sort of thing you see in football – we don't need that behaviour in rugby.' Quite so, but not necessarily the best way to persuade youngsters, who also love their football, not to gob. Chalkie suspected he would meet with more success if he came up with an explanation based solely on sports science.

So there we were in the middle of a game at this summer camp for decent rugby players, where you were earmarked for representative teams (or so my parents were told before they parted with the not inconsiderable participation fee). One of the lads let go a massive greenie and Chalkie immediately blew his whistle to halt play. 'Here comes the lecture,' I thought. Wrong.

'Listen,' Chalkie said, putting an arm around the culprit's shoulder. 'You're going to sweat it all out and you're going to struggle to rehydrate, so why would you purposely lose fluid? Trust me, you're going to need every drop of saliva.'

The kid looked at him and nodded in agreement. No apology was required, no embarrassment was felt. Not only did I never see him spit again, whenever I see someone do it I always think of Chalkie. He was an absolute gentleman and in that schoolboy environment, where there were a lot of egos among the best of England's young talent, he handled us very well. Oh, one other thing. My best friend there was Magnus Batey from Cornwall. For some reason I can't recall, he was known as Master Batey.

5) Paul Volley (my Bucks Under-18s captain 1989–90)

Paul Volley, formerly of Wasps and an all-round nice bloke, was my Buckinghamshire Under-18s captain. He was a promising open-side even back then but I can't speak quite so highly of his captaincy as he had the job for only a handful of games and my recollection is all but lost in a haze of cheap beer and 'Pernod and black'.

What I do remember about Paul is the warm-up he gave us at Aylesbury Rugby Club before we played the RAF. It was a Sunday morning and, as we were sixth formers, naturally most of us had hangovers. Not me, though. I was desperate to impress as England selector Chalkie White was at the game. As we circled the back pitches swapping from stretches to more dynamic moves, the nerves started to show. I'm sure I am not the only one who when slightly apprehensive tends to yawn. Volley did not buy the 'nerves' excuse, not after yawn number two. 'Daws, for f**k sake pull yourself together. This is a massive match, one we've all been waiting for. Stop yawning. Were you on the piss last night? This is unacceptable.'

We beat the RAF by sixty points and I scored four tries.

6) Budge Pountney (my Northampton captain 2001–03)

There is much debate these days about the importance of a captain. I've heard arguments for and against, but I firmly believe it remains a vital role in any team. Why? Because at all levels of sport, inspiration can be the difference between success and failure. Some captains, Martin Johnson being the most obvious, prefer to lead by example. To use a military analogy, every one of Johnno's troops would have followed him over the top without hesitation. We had seen his dedication on and off the field for years, so when he asked for the extra effort, we could always find it.

There is then the more vocal style adopted by the likes of Lawrence Dallaglio and Keith Wood, who mixed fire and brimstone with a gift of the gab and would have you convincing yourself there was nowhere in all the world you would rather be than standing shoulder to shoulder with them on the field of rugby combat. Those two, in particular, also enjoyed a fabulous relationship with management and were adept at delivering messages to the team via coaches so that it didn't seem too managerial.

Another category of captain is the world-class player who is so good on the field that the coach assumes he can captain the team as well. This always baffled me, and I use Jonny Wilkinson as an example. Jonny was a total phenomenon between 2000–2003. The rugby press worshipped him and the global media held him in such esteem that they would follow him on his holiday to Mauritius to pap him and his partner from boats as they lay on the beach. Why then would you want to heap even more pressure on a lad who had no captaincy experience and was just back from injury?

Finally, you have the coach's favourite. Come on, you've all seen it. Whether it's just in selection on a Sunday morning or the football team you support, you wave your arms in frustration and wonder,

THE PENNY DROPS

'How on earth is that bloke wearing the armband?' My example of this was at Northampton. I played under the captaincy of Scotland flanker Budge Pountney. Now I could certainly not dispute his playing credentials as he was a cracking open-side and very unlucky not to get on the Lions tour in 2001, but as far as captaincy – hmm, not so sure.

The year was 2002 and we were up against London Irish in the final of the Powergen Cup. It was a beautiful day for running rugby at Twickenham and we were favourites by the slimmest of margins. The Irish were coached and captained by Brendan Venter, a hard-nosed, no-nonsense South African. He was physical and verbal and someone I had to keep my eye on, as we had a chequered past.

Without wishing to rake too deeply through the ashes of one of my worst rugby days, we were beaten long before the game finished. In fact we trailed 24–0 at half-time. To add injury to insult Mr Venter had 'tackled' me high on a number of occasions and referee Steve Lander had seen nothing untoward. (The clue, Steve, was that every time I had my hands on the ball Brendan had coached his team to scream, 'Kill him, kill him, kill Dawson!' It worked 'cos I shat myself!)

My frustration built and I'm not proud to say that when we didn't get a decision from the referee right on the opposition's goal line, I turned to Steve and gesticulated. In stepped my captain to cool me down. As Budge put his arms around my shoulder to talk to me I shrugged him off. 'For f*** sake Budge, he [Lander] is giving us nothing. You've got to speak to him!' Now that is verbatim. I thought nothing of it and we played the rest of the game. We narrowed the gap slightly but there was no way we deserved to win and quite rightly London Irish lifted the trophy. Afterwards we went out as a team and drowned our sorrows before being asked to regroup on Monday at the club for a debrief. Come Monday morning John Steele, our then Director of Rugby, summoned me to his office and handed me a sealed envelope containing a letter he had written. The note, on official Northampton Rugby Club paper, was a request to attend a disciplinary hearing for bringing the club into disrepute. Unbeknown to me, Sky Sports commentator Stuart Barnes had decided to cite my conversation with Budge at the end of the first half as the sole reason for us losing by twenty-odd points.

I was numb. A club I had sacrificed everything for over a ten-year period was doubting my integrity. I decided to take it up with my captain as surely he would tell the powers-that-be exactly what had happened. I drove straight round to Budge's house and knocked on the door. His dog barked but no one answered. I thought that a little strange as his dog was nuts and they rarely left him home alone. I tried again but once more there was no response.

As my head was spinning I popped next door to where John Leslie, another of my team mates, lived. John welcomed me in and I explained my predicament. Without hesitation he said, 'Mate, you should definitely speak to Budge about that. I remember it, it was nothing.'

'He's not in,' I replied.

'That's funny,' said John. 'I heard him in the garden about five minutes ago.'

I peered out of John's window over the garden fence and sure enough there was my captain in the kitchen. I went out back, hopped over the fence, catching him a little off-guard I admit, but all very smiley and non-aggressive. I explained the letter and the hearing and asked if he could quickly phone our boss to clarify the situation before it ballooned into a major issue. In one fell swoop he cut our working relationship off at the knees. He stated that he didn't want to comment on it and it was a matter for the club to deal with.

I understand there are always two sides to a story and some may read this and say that I undermined him when I shrugged him off during the game. Indeed one of Irish's players, Glenn Delaney, later said the sight of the two of us, 'having a bit of a scrap was great because we knew we'd got them.' In defence, it was a highly charged domestic final that I was absolutely desperate to win.

Compare Budge's response to that of Martin Johnson in 2001 after the Lions' first Test against Australia in Brisbane. Now this is a moment of which I most certainly was not proud. I'd given the *Daily Telegraph* the opportunity to write some juicy headlines that may indeed have rocked our Lions ship. And yet Johnno's response was unequivocal. 'If Matt gets sent home, I'll be on the plane with him.' Different class.

7) **Phil Tufnell** (rival captain, *A Question of Sport* 2004–)

I am at the airport waiting to fly to the United States to watch the 2013 US Masters golf tournament when my phone rings. It's Phil Tufnell, my sparring partner on *A Question of Sport*.

'What you up to mate?' he asks.

'I'm at Heathrow, pal,' I reply. 'I'm going to the Masters.'

There is a slight pause. 'Really. What you doing there?'

'I'm going with a few lads to watch the golf.'

Silence. 'Do they have golf courses in Damascus?'

'You what? . . . THE MASTERS, you muppet!'

Phil Tufnell, aka 'The Cat', is a character like no one I have ever known. Hilariously funny, intelligent and sensitive in equal measure. He was a bloody good cricketer, too.

He plays the fool and sometimes is the fool. Like the episode when we both had to write on a white board the answer to the question: 'What made you most nervous: your first cap or appearing on *Strictly Come Dancing*?' We both had the same answer but Tuffers spelt it 'Strickley' and brought the house down.

'Why you laughing?' he asked, slightly bewildered by the audience's reaction. 'It was bloody terrifying.'

That was a rare occasion of people laughing at him. I can't think of too many others, as the laughter and affection is invariably with him; a guy who deep down is bright, always engaging and occasionally deep-thinking. He has his own art collection for example, he paints and sells his work. The first time he told me I assumed he did them in crayon, but no, he uses oils.

When I first met Phil there was an obvious question I had to ask. 'Why do they call you "The Cat"?'

'Well Daws,' replied Tuffers, 'out all night, sleeps all day. No seriously . . . the Middlesex and England lads always used to find me curled up in a corner of the changing room having a little snooze.'

'Makes sense,' I said.

'Oh, and I can lick my own balls!' he added. 'And I've been caught next door urinating in the neighbour's garden.'

For as long as I've known Phil he's been extremely genuine, up-front and honest; never too big to ask questions and seek advice. Just a really lovely guy to be around. He's also quick-witted and sharp as a tack, as Sue Barker found to her cost when she responded to a compliment he paid her by saying, 'Ah Phil, are you trying to butter me up?'

Quick as a flash he came back with, 'Ah Sue, I'd love to see that.'

He hears things like a comedian. I'm absolutely sure he could do stand-up. On the *QOS* tour he holds the whole thing together. When he's on the stage, he's just incredible, which brings me to my favourite Tuffers story.

The 'Greatest Knight of All' was a star-studded tribute evening, organised by David English and the Bunbury's Club, to mark Sir Ian Botham's knighthood. It was held at the Grosvenor Park Hotel in March 2009 and the great and the good from the sport and entertainment worlds pitched up. Off the top of my head I remember seeing Allan Lamb, David Gower, Bob Willis, Jeff Thomson, Rodney Marsh, Allan Border and Dennis Lillee from cricket and Martin Johnson, Lawrence Dallaglio and Jason Leonard from rugby. Peter Kay and Piers Morgan were also there. So was Tuffers.

Each took their turn to say a few words and when it came to Tuffers' turn it was apparent that he, like many of us, had had a good night. He rambled a bit and slurred the odd word but he was, as ever, funny and we got the message loud and clear that he thought Beefy was a legend. Then the stage cleared and one of Beefy's old pals came onto the stage with a guitar in hand.

'My God, it's only Eric Clapton,' I said to no one in particular.

He too said a few words about Sir Ian, then broke into strumming those immortal first chords of *Layla*.

'What an absolutely unbelievable night this is,' I thought. Clapton starts singing and I'm loving it.

He gets to the chorus and we're all waiting for that brilliant line 'Layla, you've got me on my knees' when who appears at the back of the stage with a microphone in his hand and beats him to the words . . . Oh yes, Tuffers.

'Laaaaaaayla!' he screeches.

There is this stunned silence for a moment around the room. Then pandemonium. People either in hysterics or not at all impressed.

Me? I have never laughed as much in my life. For a moment I struggled to catch my breath. Tuffers eventually has his mic switched off and is 'encouraged' off the stage leaving Eric to continue.

What I find especially funny about Tuffers is the way he says what he's thinking. I guess I like to work things through in my mind before committing them to the spoken word. I'm not sure that applies to Phil.

In one episode he was asked this question: Who won the 1995 Rugby World Cup? Not the toughest one for me as I very nearly made it to that tournament in South Africa, where England beat Australia in the quarter-final through Rob Andrew's late drop goal, before being buried under an avalanche of Jonah Lomu's tries in the semi-final. New Zealand were the class outfit that year and should never have lost the final to the Springboks and Joel Stransky's extra-time drop goal – unless, of course, their food *really* was poisoned by the mysterious waitress, Susie, as conspiracy theorists would have us believe.

'I know the answer to that one,' declared The Cat confidently. 'I'm sure that was the President Nelson Mandela final in South Africa, at the end of apartheid. Didn't Mandela come on the pitch with the blond fella, you know their captain ... François ... François Pienaar. Yeah, that's right. Now who were they playing against? Oh it was the All Blacks wasn't it? That Lomu guy? He scored four tries, ran over everyone, didn't he?'

Phil's two team mates weren't rugby players and he had no help from them, so he continued working through his thought process for the benefit of the BBC's however many million viewers.

'It was the All Blacks. Yeah Jonah Lomu won it that year with the All Blacks. No, wait a minute, didn't the All Blacks get food poisoned? Yes, that's right and South Africa won and Nelson

Mandela, wearing Pienaar's No. 7 jersey presented him with the trophy. Yeah, that's right. And the jumbo jet buzzed the top of the stadium.'

'So,' said Sue, 'have you got a final answer for us?'

'I have Sue,' replied Tuffers proudly. 'Australia.'

Uh? What did he just say?

'Australia. I've just had this sudden flash of inspiration. The Wobblies won it that year.'

The place fell about laughing, but I'm pretty sure his team still won the game. Typical. Lulls me into a false sense of security with that I've-got-no-idea act then wham, The Cat pounces.

He did that to me another time when we had a challenge on the show that required me to face him in cricket nets at the National Sports Centre at Lilleshall. Phil likes a drink and a smoke and whenever we do these physical bits on the show he always says, 'Go easy on me, Daws.'

'Yeah, yeah,' I laughed this time, but secretly I did fancy my chances, having played quite a lot of cricket before rugby took hold. Also he'd not fared the best in two recent challenges.

In the first we were required to pass a rugby ball through a hole in the midriff of a dummy or throw a cricket ball at a set of stumps. The idea was that if you got your question right, you got to go at your discipline, and if you got it wrong, you would attempt the other's. Phil answered all his questions correctly – and I don't think he hit the stumps once, from all of five metres away. He ended up going underarm and still missed.

That was funny enough but the show's producers then set up a coconut shy with, instead of coconuts, six heads of famous footballers, five of whom had won the Ballon d'Or (the annual world's best player award). The aim of the game was to hit the one you thought hadn't. The answer, surprisingly, was Maradona but Tuffers was convinced it was Karl-Heinz Rummenigge (who actually won it twice and was runner-up on another occasion). Aiming at the German, he knocked three other heads off their perch. In fact he did well even to keep the ball in the coconut shy itself. When the carnage was eventually over, there was one head left. Diego Maradona.

So there I was, pads on and taking my guard.

'Show me what you've got, pal,' I shouted out. 'What was it you bowled, a bit of slow left-arm spin?'

'Something like that, chum,' he replied, moments before my bails came off. He had the ball spitting and kicking all over the place. He beat me for fun, absolutely took me to the cleaners. He could still produce real spin and movement across the line, and a little bit of bounce as well. When I made contact, it was more by luck than judgement. He ended up taking pity on me and dollied one up for me to smash. I skipped down the wicket after it . . . and pulled my hamstring.

8) Lilia Kopylova (dance partner, *Strictly Come Dancing* 2006)

Moscow junior ice-skating champion at the age of nine, Lilia grew up to be an incredible dancer and teacher. She also drew the short straw when landed with partnering me on *Strictly Come Dancing*. Dave Reddin, England's conditioning coach when we won the 2003 World Cup, was a tough taskmaster, but no more than Lilia and her 'just get on with it' approach to training. I spent the first month of lessons standing on her feet, kicking her in the shins and, on one awful occasion, dropping her on her head. There were no tears. Not from Lilia anyway.

THE PENNY DROPS

The core strength of these dancers is as good as any rugby player I have known. Then there is the mental strength required to train novice dance partners to perform on *Strictly*. To keep going for six or seven hours a day in front of the camera, remaining patient and largely good-humoured, while trying to turn dancing's equivalent of water into wine, takes a special type of person.

I'm sure Lilia, when she first saw me dance, must have thought, 'Oh my God, what have I got myself into? He can count, but that's pretty much it.' Did it deter her? Did it hell. One week we were working on the pasodoble, which contained a move I just couldn't get right. I turned up for training on the second morning to be greeted by Lilia demanding, 'Right, we're doing this move a hundred times until we crack it.'

'Yeah, yeah, whatever,' I said.

'Matt, I'm serious. We nail this today.'

After forty attempts at the sequence I had it, no problem.

'I said a hundred.'

By the end of that day I decided her favourite phrase in all the world had to be, 'Do It Again!' Heading home I had a vision of Cold War athletes behind the Iron Curtain training day and night. This is what I had let myself in for.

Her commitment to teaching me was total. The professionals on *Strictly* don't get a lot of recognition and they're not paid a huge amount of money. Every day Lilia would take two buses and the underground to Chiswick in west London, where we trained (round the corner from my house), and she would still have a half-mile walk to the gym. She never missed a session.

It was my great fortune to be paired with her on two counts. 1. She was reigning champion, having won the Glitter Ball with England cricket legend Darren Gough the previous year. 2. We got on so well, even if I was somewhat intimidated by her turning up for our first lesson wearing white cowboy boots and a white leather mini skirt.

She was my rock through the whole series. She knew I didn't really enjoy it, particularly those first three or four weeks. It was so far from the world I knew of team sport and being with the lads. *Strictly* existed in an alien world of showbiz glitz and West End glamour where everyone air-kissed. 'What the hell was I doing there?!' I suppose at least I never succumbed to fake tan. They all do it now. Even Michael Vaughan, England's former cricket captain. Dear lord.

Lilia kept my spirits up by tolerating a bit of mickey taking. I think it worked in my favour that she had spent a series dancing with Goughie, who was not averse to going out and having a few beers and rocking up on a Saturday morning smelling of his night out. She just got on with it because she is so professional. She would spend every Sunday night at home with her husband and fellow *Strictly* dancer Darren Bennett, devising our routine for the next week. I hope our second-place finish behind Mark Ramprakash made her feel it was worthwhile.

CHAPTER 4

Sliding Daws

Manly Pacific Hotel, New South Wales
24 November 2003

There is a knock on the door, followed by the sound of footsteps heading rapidly along the corridor to the lifts.

'Daws, we're late,' a voice yells. 'The bus is leaving. Get your arse in gear.'

I look into the mirror one more time, straighten my light blue polo shirt and smile to myself. How does that saying go? He who laughs last . . . laughs longest? Yeah that's the one.

I tap my back pocket to check my wallet is there, scoop up my phone and keycard off the table and flick the light switch.

'Oi lads, wait up. I'm coming.'

The lift door opens on the ground floor to a scene of bedlam. The reception area of the hotel, with its spectacular beachfront view, is a sea of humanity. And that is only media, security and hotel staff. Outside, hundreds, maybe thousands, of England rugby supporters swarm around our team bus and line both sides of the road. White shirts and flags of St George are everywhere, just as they had been all over Sydney on this, the greatest weekend of my sporting life.

I don't remember much about the journey to the airport. My head is spinning. For one thing the size of what we have achieved is still registering. For another, I've been drinking for twenty-four hours solid. Ten years earlier I had played in England's World Cup-winning sevens team at Murrayfield, and family and friends had a bit of a party. Landing the 2003 World Cup is off the scale. We've been catapulted into the sporting stratosphere.

Sydney Airport and more of the same. England fans everywhere, wisecracking Aussies strangely conspicuous by their absence. Two years before it had been so different. I left Australia with my head bowed. A beaten Lion, and a shamed one, too.

'Not now, Daws,' I tell myself as conflicting emotions collide, well up inside me and threaten to break the surface. 'There's something you've got to do.'

We enter the terminal and a cheer goes up from a good number of the 50,000 English supporters who had seen the final, acclaimed Jonny Wilkinson's drop-goal match winner and accompanied me as I sang *Wonderwall* by Oasis on the pitch afterwards. We make our way slowly through the crowd, signing autographs and posing for photos as we approach security. My head is starting to thump. It has been a hell of a party.

'Laptops, phones, keys in the tray please gents. Any change in your pockets?'

The guy on the other side of the X-ray scanner beckons me

forward. I take one step, then a second, and the alarm goes off. I feign surprise, and wink at the supporters looking on.

'Ah that will be my watch. Sorry.'

I take it off and step forward again. Off goes the alarm and this time a cheer goes up from the onlookers. I feign bemusement.

'Any loose change, sir?'

I put my hands in my pockets, feel a piece of shrapnel and fish it out. Apologising insincerely I retrace my footsteps – and off goes the alarm again. The security operative looks at me, his patience running out, not helped I suspect by the increasingly boisterous crowd milling around. He reaches for his electronic detection wand and is just about to wave it up and down me when I turn to my audience and smile, then turn back and theatrically lift up my shirt.

'Oh, I'm sorry,' says I to a massive cheer and raucous laughter. 'Do you want me to take off my World Cup winner's medal as well?!'

The Gabba, Brisbane
30 June 2001

Martin Johnson is sitting in the away changing room at the Gabba. This stadium is one of the temples of Australian cricket. But not tonight. The Lions have taken over the joint. There is a sea of red in the stands, Lions shirt-wearing fans outnumbering the home support by, I reckon, six to one. On the pitch we have just given Australia a hiding, winning 29–13. Only once before have the Lions ever scored more points against the Wallabies. I come into the changing room and head straight to Johnno. I've got something for him. It's the match ball.

'You deserve this, mate,' I say to him. 'Something with which to remember this unbelievable night. That was f***ing epic.'

'Appreciate that Daws, really do,' says Johnno, and he looks genuinely touched. He raises the ball above his head, just as he will the World Cup two years later, and clears his throat.

'Great effort lads, every one of you.'

Some of the boys cheer, a couple clap. It is one of those special moments in life that money can't buy. I feel a tap on my shoulder. It's Alex Broun, our media manager. His is the only non-smiling face in the room.

'Matt, Donal wants a word.'

'Yeah okay, in a mo . . .'

'Matt. Now.'

Donal Lenihan is our team manager. He's a former second-row forward who won fifty-two caps for Ireland and went on three Lions tours as a player. I can't think why he wants to talk to me, unless it is to explain why I did not get off the bench, which I did find strange. But would he really be bothering to explain that to me now? Unlikely. Then I think of the match ball.

At the final whistle I'd gone up to the nearest ball boy to ask him for it. Remembering Mike Teague doing the same on the 1989 tour of Australia, the kid not giving it up and it all turning a bit messy, I thought I'd employ a different tactic.

'Can I have that ball a minute?' I asked politely. When the ball boy looked at me in a way that suggested his reply was going to be either 'No' or 'Why?' I took the decision out of his hands. I grabbed the ball and legged it. I wasn't very proud that I'd stolen a ball off a thirteen-year-old lad but Johnno deserved a souvenir of his team's win and I knew he'd never think of getting it for himself.

It can't be that, I tell myself, opening the door into a boot room where I am greeted by an apoplectic Donal.

'I've just been grilled on *Sky Sports* about your column,' he rages, referring to my tour diary, which has appeared in the *Daily Telegraph* back home this very day, to coincide with the first Test. 'What have you said?'

'Um . . . Well . . . You know . . . Nothing controversial.'

'You joking me?' he snaps back. 'You've said this, that and the other. It's all over the news. Everywhere.'

The *Daily Telegraph* column on that fateful day, 30 June 2001

Lions in turmoil as walk-out threatened

By Sam Lyon

The British and Irish Lions are in turmoil ahead of their vital first Test against Australia in Brisbane on Saturday.

Along with the injuries to key players, the tragic death of their liaison officer Anton Toia and the intimidation tactics by Australia both on and off the pitch, it has now been revealed that many of the players have had to be talked out of quitting the tour in fury, as oppressive training conditions and the lack of respect for the coaching staff takes its toll.

Matt Dawson, writing exclusively for the Telegraph, *has launched an astonishing attack on the tourists' harsh regime and poor preparations. The England scrum-half claims that Graham Henry has failed to inspire trust and that he treats the players like children.*

'*It's official – some of the boys have decided to leave the tour. We said at Tylney that if this should happen we would implement peer pressure, but to be frank with so many young players it is hard to avoid,*' claims Dawson.

Following the 28–25 defeat to Australia A, players became '*hacked off with the post-match comments of Donal Lenihan. Treated us like kids. As if we wanted to lose. They have flogged us in training day in, day out and defeat was waiting to happen.*

'*Every day consists of mindless training. The coaching staff are taking it too far. Boys are not enjoying themselves. No energy for bonding. What's the point of all that work and expense at Tylney Hall if the boys never have time or energy to get to know each other when it counts.*

'*Seems like the coaches have forgotten what a long season the boys have had. Yes we're up for a Lions tour but there's only so much that is good for you.*

'*There are lots of unhappy people here, which is a shame because I think there's a better bunch of individuals than in '97.*'

Along with the oppressive training conditions, it has also been revealed that training sessions are badly focused, and that crucial back-ups, such as recovery fluids and post-training food, is not always available.

'*Training before match days has been mindless,*' claims Dawson. '*We get a talk from Andy Robertson, Phil Larder want, to say and do his bit, then Graham Henry does his pre-match speech, which doesn't inspire me at all. Too much shouting and screaming. Picks out individuals to wind them up but it's all very childish.*

'*I get a vibe that there are too many voices, saying stuff they know nothing about.*

'*To compound it all, we are expected to train like maniacs and recover for the next day, but there are no recovery supplements or specific nutrition to help. It's shoddy.' claims Dawson.*

Dawson's comments will rock the English support back home as the country builds to one of the biggest Lions tours in recent history.

Following the Lions series win in South Africa in 1997, expectations are high, but it appears that preparations for the opening match, could hardly have been more disrupted and divided.

Dan Luger, Mike Catt, Phil Greening and Lawrence Dallaglio have all had to leave the squad through injury, and other rumours around the British and Irish Lions camp suggest that some players have lost heart as it becomes clear who is favoured and who is not for the Test teams. Colin Charvis for one seems particularly upset by the fact he has not been selected in the team, despite proving his form throughout the tour. His selection as potential 'impact sub' has done little to appease him.

All in all, therefore, it seems that all is not well in the tour camp. However, as Matt Dawson concludes, 'No doubt, though, that when the Tests are upon us, everyone will be fully focused.'

Everyone at home will hope so.

Let me start with an admission. I was pretty mixed up in June 2001. My personal life was a mess and I was frazzled from non-stop rugby. Mix in the philosophies the Lions' management brought to running the tour and I was a ticking timebomb waiting to go off.

It disappoints me hugely that I could not see that for myself at the time. I was part of an England team that had broken all records in the Six Nations, before an outbreak of foot and mouth disease forced the last round of the tournament to be suspended until the autumn. I had captained England to the Championship the previous year, finally establishing myself as first-choice scrum-half in the process. Above all, I was a victorious Lion from 1997 and, as such, could not wait to pick up from where we had left off in South Africa.

As it turned out that was the problem. We had the same captain, in Martin Johnson, and many of the same faces from four years earlier, but the tour could not have been more different. For a start, where before there had been the relaxed but focused leadership of head coach Ian McGeechan and team manager Fran Cotton, there was now the tetchiness of Graham Henry and Donal Lenihan.

The pair created a completely different atmosphere, which might have worked had they done everything their own way. Instead, having obviously watched *Living with Lions*, the fly-on-the-wall access-all-areas documentary of the 1997 tour, they cherry-picked aspects of '97 and tried to lay them onto their own template. The whole tour became a box-ticking exercise.

A perfect example of this is the get-to-know-you night out at the pub, which had been so influential in getting the 1997 tour off to a flying start. I can almost hear Graham and Donal saying, 'Ah we've taken them to the pub, like they did in '97, we can tick that box.' They didn't have a clue and even now it winds me up just thinking about it. Why? I'll tell you why. In '97 we all got tanked up and came back to the hotel and rampaged about the place. There was a wedding party going on and some of the single lads were trying to fire in with the wedding guests. It ended up resembling some kind of stag do, but absolutely no harm was done.

As unprofessional as that might sound it did wonders for team bonding. All of a sudden there were stories to tell, notes to compare, memories to share. You could sit next to anyone in the squad, whether you knew them or not, and you had ready-made material for a conversation. Four years on I'm expecting a similar experience. Instead, we rock up at this pub and before we can get the first round in and start the getting-to-know-you process, word reaches us that Ed Morrison, one of England's top referees, is coming into camp first thing in the morning to ref a live 15-on-15 session.

We look at one another, push our untouched pints away and re-order soft drinks, which we don't finish. This is a Lions tour, the pinnacle, an adventure in which every opportunity to impress has to be taken if you are to earn selection for the Test series. Nobody wants to jeopardise their prospects by turning up the worse for wear at the first training run. There should not have been that session. What we gained from it paled into insignificance compared to what we lost from aborting the social. In morale terms I'm not sure the tour ever really recovered.

Maybe it would have worked had they duplicated 1997 to the letter. We will never know. But just taking bits and making a mish-mash of it all was a policy destined for failure. They created an atmosphere that didn't motivate enough of the players, as you can see from my *Telegraph* diary, which amounts to 'training-sleeping-game, training-sleeping-train some more'. We were too knackered to do anything else.

The crying shame is that 2001 was a stronger Lions squad than its predecessor. I'd go so far as to say it was one of the great Lions squads. Look at the way England were playing. We were on fire. Look at the individual brilliance from some of the other nations. And then factor in those guys who performed above themselves because they were playing with great players – Martin Corry was a giant in that first Test, Scott Quinnell absolutely massive in the second; Dafydd James looked like the world's second-best winger, behind Jason Robinson. It was an incredible collection of talent. Yet Australia won the series.

By the time the first Test came around a number of the players had had enough. It was quickly apparent the management had ear-marked the Test team early in the trip and saw the rest of us as little more than tackle-bag holders. Look at my tour. I was involved in nine of the ten matches but started only four. Bitterness and resentment grew. And please let's not be selective with our memory on this point. It was not just me. It culminated with a rare night out for the midweek workhorses during which Rob Henderson, the Irish centre, who ironically would make it into the Test team alongside Brian O'Driscoll and become such a success, rewrote the lyrics to the Travis hit *Driftwood* – which became our anthem – and labelled us 'The Drift'.

Australia's an island
a long long way from home
we're touring with the Lions
and feeling all alone

Big games at the weekend
with nothing in between
except training until sunset
trying to look keen

Do you know what I mean!

SLIDING DAWS

We're driftwood
touring with the Lions
playing on a Tuesday, Tuesday, Tuesday . . .

So I put pen to paper. I had been asked by the *Telegraph* prior to the tour whether I would keep a diary of my experiences in Australia for publication in two parts: immediately before the first Test and following the end of the three-match series.

'I'm up for that.'

Without shifting the blame in any way, it was probably my misfortune to be rooming with Austin Healey when my frustration was at its height. And not just because Austin had this bizarre game he played whenever he was not the centre of attention. He was like a ten-year-old. If I was chilling, listening to music, reading a book or watching the TV, he'd lift up the end of my bed, as if it was a foldaway, press it up against the wall and dump me on the floor. After the first couple of times I couldn't relax. He would hover at the end of the bed and I would have to take direct action to get my retaliation in first, resulting in a constant string of WWF-style wrestling competitions. The most disturbing occasion was the time he decided to try to tip me up having literally just come out of the shower.

Anyway, for all this japing around Austin shared my frustrations and talking it over only fuelled our bitterness. It was the only conversation in our room. Maybe if I had been with someone else it wouldn't have loomed so large. I can think of certain individuals who, had I been in their company and read my diary out loud, may well have said, 'Hold on a minute, that could be a bit tasty.' However. Austin was spouting similar mutinous sentiments in his newspaper column and to his ghost writer, who was putting together his autobiography. In comparison to what he was saying, my observations seemed relatively tame. At least, until the balloon went up.

2001 BRITISH AND IRISH LIONS TOUR
(P10, W7, D0, L3)

1) *Western Australia, won 116–19 (Perth, 8 June)*

2) *Queensland Pres XV, won 83–6 (Townsville, 12 June)*

3) *Queensland, won 42–8 (Brisbane, 16 June)*

4) *Australia A, lost 25–28 (Gosford, 19 June)*

5) *New South Wales, won 41–24 (Sydney, 23 June)*

6) *NSW Country, won 46–3 (Coffs Harbour, 26 June)*

7) *1st Test, AUSTRALIA, won 29–13 (Brisbane, 30 June)*

8) *ACT, won 30–28 (Canberra, 3 July)*

9) *2nd Test, AUSTRALIA, lost 14–35 (Melbourne, 7 July)*

10) *3rd Test, AUSTRALIA, lost 23–29 (Sydney, 14 July)*

I handed my manuscript to *Daily Telegraph* rugby correspondent Mick Cleary a few days before the start of the Test series. We were in Coffs Harbour, up the coast between Sydney and Brisbane, for a midweek game against a New South Wales Country XV. There were whale-watching opportunities for the travelling supporters, and a tidy little golf course laid out around the hotel. It was all very relaxed. Mick took it away, said he'd give it the once over and get back to me. Sure enough, the next day his text arrived.

'You're absolutely sure this is what you want to go in?'

I looked at the text and was mildly surprised by what I read, but no alarm went off in my head. No part of me thought that I was handing them something juicy. As far as I was concerned

I'd been asked by the *Telegraph* to keep an honest diary of the tour and that's what I'd done. I'd told it how it was. No gossip, no exaggeration, no untruths. Just a faithful account of our day-to-day existence.

I texted Mick back. 'All good, thanks.'

'Fine. Just double checking.'

With that I stuck my phone back in my pocket, threw on a clean top, and headed out to yet another training session. I would not give it another thought until an hour or so before we left for the game, when Austin Healey bounded into our room and told me I was in 'deep shit'.

'Yeah right, Aus.'

I reached over to the desk, picked up my diary and skimmed through it again.

'What's wrong with that? I've said that Henry doesn't inspire me. Well, he doesn't. Come on, we've got to go.'

MY AGAINST-ALL-ODDS XV

15) *Lions v South Africa*, won 18–15 (2nd Test, Durban 1997)
   Amazing defence and Jeremy Guscott's late drop goal wins series for Lions.

14) *Lions v South Africa*, won 25–16 (1st Test, Cape Town 1997)
   Lions trail 15-9 with fifteen minutes left but rally to win Newlands opener.

13) *Lions v Australia*, won 29–13 (1st Test, Brisbane 2001)
   Given little chance by the experts, the Lions race 29–3 ahead before late Aussie flourish.

12) *England v South Africa*, won 27–22 (Bloemfontein 2000)
   The game where England's 2003 World Cup bandwagon began

to roll. Jonny Wilkinson kicks all twenty-seven points in famous win on highveld.

11) **England v South Africa**, *won 13–7 (Twickenham 1998)*
England foil world champions' bid for an historic eighteenth straight win. I kick two second-half penalties to see us home.

10) **England v New Zealand**, *won 15–13 (Wellington 2003)*
Down to thirteen men at one point, England win in New Zealand for first time in thirty years to confirm No.1 ranking ahead of 2003 World Cup.

9) **England v France**, *won 15–9 (Paris 2000)*
Unbelievably good defensive display by England team I have the honour of captaining seals win at Stade de France.

1) **England v Australia**, *won 22–19 (Twickenham 2000)*
Dan Luger scores from Iain Balshaw's chip in last play of game, eight minutes into injury time, to floor world champions.

2) **England v Scotland**, *lost 13–19 (Edinburgh 2000)*
Credit where it's due. We had won all our games, the Scots had lost all theirs. They deserved this one. It cost us the Grand Slam.

3) **England v Australia**, *won 12–10 (Marseille, World Cup 2007)*
Sensational scrummaging display by England produces a huge upset and sends England through to semi-finals.

4) **England v New Zealand**, *drew 26–26 (Twickenham 1997)*
Paul Grayson's late penalty seals a draw in one of Twickenham's greatest games, ending All Blacks' hopes of winning every game in 1997.

5) **England v Australia**, *won 25–22 (Cape Town, World Cup 1995)*
Rob Andrew drops a goal with last play of game to topple world champions and send England into World Cup semi-finals.

6) **England v France**, *won 14–9 (Paris, World Cup 2007)*

Jonny Wilkinson's late penalty and drop goal knock out hosts and put England into second straight World Cup final.

7) **England v Australia**, *won 32–31 (Twickenham 2002)*
   Aussies lead 31–19 in second half but England hit back to extend winning streak at Twickenham to seventeen matches.

8) **England v New Zealand**, *won 31–28 (Twickenham 2002)*
   Ben Cohen's brilliant tackle on Ben Blair preserves England's fifth ever win over All Blacks.

The 2001 Lions might have been a joyless tour for me and The Drift, but there were notable exceptions to our rule – and none more notable than Jason Robinson. Robbo was on the tour despite not having started a match for England. He had come across from rugby league only months before, not received a single pass on his England debut and been selected for the British Isles on the basis of three appearances off the England bench.

Concern that he might be out of his depth disappeared within moments of him taking to the field for his tour debut against a Queensland President's XV in Townsville. It was the opposition players who were out of their depth as Robbo helped himself to five tries.

It embarrasses me now to think that initially I questioned what Clive Woodward was doing bringing him to union. I had great respect for league but I didn't buy into the notion that these guys being great players in the thirteen-a-side code necessarily meant they would be any good at union.

I quickly revised my view. No sooner had he made his debut, a brief cameo against Italy, than I was crying out for him to start. I was struck by how quiet he was yet how hard he worked. This guy who had achieved everything in rugby league was utterly focused on learning how to play rugby union from scratch. Take for example his kicking game. When he first came across he could not kick out of hand, to the extent that you wouldn't know if he was left or right-footed. Yet he worked tirelessly to learn how to punt and became brilliant at it. He was professional with a capital P.

I had played with and against some great footballers but none had his ability to beat people with the ball in hand. I would say he was the best winger I played with for England, along with Ben Cohen in his absolute prime. Robbo didn't need to know all the rules. Give him the ball in space and you knew he would get you some go-forward at the very least. It makes such a difference when you know that if you give your wingers the ball in certain areas, they will bust the line and finish it off (like Alex Cuthbert and George North do these days for Wales). The confidence that instils is incredible.

Nonetheless a Test match for the British and Irish Lions against the world champion Wallabies was a considerable step-up from anything Jason Robinson had known. Having been beaten by Australia's second string eleven days earlier we were given no chance of victory. And while as a professional player you never recognise a lost cause, we awoke on match day knowing it was a tall order.

Between breakfast and kick-off two factors combined to change our perspective. One was the sight of Lions supporters filling the stadium and turning it into a home fixture for us. The other was the sound of Willie John McBride.

For all my criticisms of Donal Lenihan it was an inspirational decision by him to ask The Greatest Lion Of All to address us hours before kick-off at the Gabba. Even I didn't know it was coming and, remember, at that time I knew everything! The most-capped Lion was already in the team room when we filed in with our game faces on.

With Rob Howley rightly picked at scrum-half, I was named on the bench. I sat spellbound as Willie John spoke, absorbing every syllable he uttered. He was eloquent and passionate, emotional yet focused. It was unscripted, unrehearsed and it was magnificent. It's very easy for former players to come in and bang on about how they used to play, what it was like in their day and this, that and the other. That isn't in any way motivating. What lifts you is what is around the corner and specific lessons of history that can aid your performance going forward.

So while there was romance in Willie John's message, it was built on a foundation of hard-nosed reality, which we could use. On the one hand he spoke of what it would mean to us and our families to look back on this day in twelve years' time should we be successful, on the other he gave us the tool of belief with which to go out and actually make that happen.

'This is your time,' he finished. 'Good luck, boys.'

There was silence, followed by a collective shiver up the spine, followed by Graham Henry's voice dragging us kicking and screaming back into game plans and structure. Nobody said anything but I sensed the mood of the room. I don't speak for anyone else on this matter, but this is what went through my head at that moment. 'Oh you've got to be joking, please don't go into rugby now. Absolutely don't.' I'm sure Graham would have learned from that and not repeated the mistake with the All Blacks, but at the time it was a real horror show. I was thinking, 'You can't possibly be saying these things now. Why would anyone talk at this precise moment in time?'

In the book he wrote after the tour, at one point Graham says, 'And then it was time to leave the team and let them get on with it.' That never happened. Graham was constantly ticking boxes in his mind. Whether it was in the dressing room before we ran out, or at half-time, he felt he needed to say something. He was wrong. Sometimes there is nothing more powerful than the sound of silence.

Happily, the wall of sound created by what seemed like 50,000 Lions fans as we emerged into the Gabba flushed out any negative thoughts. As they lined up for kick-off the boys seemed visibly to grow in stature. Especially the little guy on the left wing with the dancing feet.

The game kicked off, play quickly moved left towards Jason Robinson and in an instance he left the Wallabies in no doubt why his nickname is Billy Whizz. Right in front of where we were sitting on the bench, there took place the greatest standing-up of a player I've ever seen. We knew that Robbo had the weapons in his armoury to cause problems but there was a 'what-the-hell?' moment of disbelief from the whole bench as he played now-you-see-me, now-you-don't with Chris Latham, one of world rugby's great fullbacks. He made him look like a third-string club player, dancing around him, in a space not big enough to swing a cat, and touching down in the left corner.

As Jason went over I was up on my feet, celebrating wildly, but not so wild, I didn't think, that it should command the attention of every touchline snapper. They all pointed their camera lenses at me rather than at the hero of the moment. I couldn't work that out. It made even less sense when the roaming TV camera was right in my face, getting a close-up of my reaction, as Jonny Wilkinson dinked over the conversion.

It was only later the penny dropped, after tries by Dafydd James, Brian O'Driscoll and Scott Quinnell had completed the rout; after I robbed the ball boy; after I had the tap on the shoulder from our media manager and assumed Donal Lenihan wanted to explain the decision about my omission to keep me sweet.

'What have you said in your column?'

'Um . . . Well . . . You know . . . nothing controversial.'

Donal stomped out of the room, leaving me alone in a shell-shocked state. I stood there for a moment, my head spinning, then headed back to the changing room, quickly showered and dressed and joined the squad on the bus back to the hotel. The lads were in high spirits, as they fully deserved to be. One or two were on their mobiles doing newspaper columns, but the rest asked me what was up. I explained that Donal had been interviewed by *Sky* who told him that I'd said all the players were unhappy and that twelve were leaving the tour. I told them I had not said that, which is what I also said to Donal. What I'd actually written was only that people were unhappy. Okay I did write 'some of the boys have decided to leave the tour' but it was just an expression; they hadn't literally left the tour. My team mates knew the situation already, of course. It was the management who were in denial.

The last question Donal had asked me was a straightforward one. 'Are the words in the article yours?' Having replied that yes, they were, I was keen to get back to the hotel and check that was still the case; that they had not been changed. The lads were in either the 'that's exactly how I feel' camp or the 'I'm not really bothered' one. Nobody gave me a hard time. Not one player said, 'Wind your neck in pal, what do you think you're doing? You're not helping.' But I had to live with myself, so I logged on to the

Telegraph website and saw that yes, the article was indeed faithful to the original.

I reread it and still didn't see anything wrong. Nothing. I was oblivious to the offence I had caused, not least as pretty much everyone else in the squad was talking about the same thing. My thinking was clear. 'There is nothing new in what I've said here. Everyone already knows this.'

That shows how mixed up I was at the time because years later it reads very differently. It smacks of a frustrated young lad who didn't recognise what was best for the team and who certainly didn't know where to draw the line between what should be made public and what should be kept in-house. I remember afterwards saying, 'I don't take any of it back, it's a timing issue'. Well that's no longer the case. I do regret putting it out there. It's too late now of course. Unfortunately, my relationship with the Lions, particularly in Australia, will always be remembered for that diary column, which is terrible for me because I am very proud of playing for the Lions. But it's where I was in my head, in my life, in that summer of 2001, and I can't pretend otherwise.

I'll tell you how messed up I was. The same night that my life turned on its head, my mum passed out in the hotel lobby. Told of the trouble I was in she fainted out of stress and worry for my situation. Mum and Dad had only recently arrived in Australia to support me. She thought I would be sent packing in disgrace. Yet did I immediately drop everything to go and find my mum? No I did not. I picked up the phone and called her to make sure she was all right, but then dealt with a few things before going to see her. My priorities were completely wrong.

Looking back, I firmly believe that moment was a defining point in my life. Absolutely massive. It finally made me realise I was in an enormous bubble, one I needed to burst bloody quickly if I was not to lose the people who mattered most.

One man stood tall with me throughout my ordeal and I will be grateful to him to my dying day. Martin Johnson came to my room that night and assured me of his support. He told me I'd been a complete prat but that because he knew there was a lot of truth in the article he would stand by me.

I've already quoted in this book what Johnno said to the media, but the significance of his words, to me, justifies the repetition.

'If Matt gets sent home, I'll be on the plane with him.'

BRITISH AND IRISH LIONS TEAM CAPTAINS

1888: Robert Seddon
1891: Bill Maclagan
1896: Johnny Hammond
1899: Matthew Mullineux
1903: Mark Morrison
1904: David Bedell-Sivright
1908: Arthur 'Boxer' Harding
1910: John Raphael
1910: Tom Smyth
1924: Ronald Cove-Smith
1927: David MacMyn
1930: Doug Prentice
1936: Bernard Gadney
1938: Sam Walker
1950: Karl Mullen
1955: Robin Thompson
1959: Ronnie Dawson

1962: Arthur Smith
1966: Mike Campbell-Lamerton
1968: Tom Kiernan
1971: John Dawes
1974: Willie John McBride
1977: Phil Bennett
1980: Bill Beaumont
1983: Ciaran Fitzgerald
1986: Colin Deans
1989: Finlay Calder
1993: Gavin Hastings
1997: Martin Johnson
2001: Martin Johnson
2005: Brian O'Driscoll
2009: Paul O'Connell
2013: Sam Warburton

The morning after the nightmare before I woke feeling shattered. I had hardly slept, my stomach was churning. I lay there looking up at the ceiling, trying to devise an exit strategy. But there was no escape. I had to take the bull by the horns. I threw on some clothes, brushed my teeth, and went looking for the management. One by one I knocked on their doors and told them how sorry I was, not for the content of the article but for the timing, which was unforgivable. It was then Graham Henry admitted to me that he felt unable to inspire himself let alone the rest of the squad. In other words, he was basically agreeing with what I had written in the paper. Now wasn't the time to get into a philosophical debate, however. The management said they felt I should formally apologise to the whole tour party. I said I would appreciate the opportunity to do so.

So there we were, in the very same room where twenty-four hours earlier Willie John had inspired me to do the Lions proud, attempting to explain why I'd done the opposite. The stage had been carefully prepared with a circle of chairs and one in the middle. I later discovered Austin Healey had done the seating plan. The same Austin who, when I stood up to speak, shouted, 'Stone him, stone him!' and, 'He's a very naughty boy!' Great film, *The Life of Brian*, but I really wasn't in the mood for Monty Python.

The one saving grace was that the three biggest wind-up merchants – Healey, Jason Leonard and Lawrence Dallaglio – were all seated together, so I was able to avoid eye contact with them and instead face the management. When I had finished my apology, I sat down and Donal asked if anyone had anything to say. The room went quiet, then, inevitably, one hand went up.

'Yes Austin,' said Donal.

'Does that mean the public stoning is cancelled for tomorrow?' he asked.

'Yes Austin I think it does.'

'Oh shit. 'Cos I've already bought a bag or gravel and two flat rocks.'

Being serious for a moment, I don't know how I would have coped had Austin not been around. Without his presence people would have been slitting their wrists. Seeing him getting a bollocking from Graham Henry provided light relief for everybody else. He knew that. He knew the mood needed to be changed and he took it upon himself to do it. The previous night had been a case in point. As I sat in the room we shared with my head in my hands he began throwing stuff into my bag.

'What the hell are you doing?'

'Packing,' came his matter-of-fact reply. 'I thought I'd do this for you because you'll be off tomorrow.'

I smile about it now but at the time I was in the eye of a media storm and feeling very much alone. Every paper was writing about me, every broadcaster was talking about me. I felt very very isolated. Thank God they didn't have Twitter then. It would have been a car crash. As much as the players said they agreed with me, I felt I'd let the Lions down, be that the 2001 Lions or the Invincibles of 1974. It was not only the brand I'd betrayed, it was the whole heritage. That is an enormous personal regret I carry around with me today because nothing in rugby makes me more proud than to have gone on three tours, played in seven Test matches and contributed a little to the 1997 triumph. Yet I feel there is a negative asterisk against my name when it comes to the Lions. It is something I have to live with.

Just as life goes on, so did the tour. Next stop Canberra, capital city of Australia, and a midweek game against the Brumbies. I was told I would be both starting scrum-half and first-choice goalkicker. I was allotted a room with Irish fly-half Ronan O'Gara, who had himself been caught up in a controversial moment, though one not of his making. Against New South Wales ten days earlier he had been pinned to the turf and had his lights punched out by their full-back Duncan McRae in a totally unprovoked attack. That gave us something to talk about but I still wasn't really in the mood. I didn't leave the room other than to do one analysis session with Keith Wood.

Woody is a man for whom I have boundless respect. He was something of a father figure to me in South Africa in 1997 and his opinion matters to me enormously. Put simply, he said I had been an idiot. 'We all feel the same Daws, but you should know better than to come out with that sort of stuff in public. You have got to buck your ideas up.'

It was the sort of wake-up call I desperately needed – and could have done with a lot earlier. Woody slapped me around a lot verbally. He didn't say I'd let others down. He focused on the fact I'd let myself down and it was time for me to change.

'But you know that, don't you Daws?'

The truth of course was that I hadn't, until it was too late.

I looked around for self-justification and took comfort from Austin writing in his column in the *Observer*: 'Everything Daws wrote was true. The only problem was the timing of the article. Other than that I think a lot of players respected him for sticking his head above the parapet.'

Dan Luger said much the same in his column. 'Is life with the British Lions as black and torturous as Matt Dawson made it sound? I can honestly say YES,' he wrote in the *News of the World*. 'Daws was right – Graham Henry has trained us to a standstill. My legs have never been as tired, even in pre-season training, but that is Henry's decision. He's the man and he simply wants to get the job done.'

Dan went on to point out four 'huge' differences between the 2001 tour and its 1997 predecessor. 1. In '97 rugby union had only been a professional sport for two years and there were still a lot of the amateur ways. 2. That side played 15 matches, 10 in the build-up to the first Test, whereas we had 10 in the entire tour. 3. The 1997 Lions were firm underdogs whereas we were expected to give Australia, as Luges put it, 'a good run for their money'. 4. Henry is the first foreigner to coach the Lions and is under far more pressure than was Ian McGeechan on his fifth tour in 1997, knowing there are people waiting for him to fail.

All valid points, but I had not factored them into my thinking before firing from the hip with an outburst that would cost me a third of my tour fee. Woody was able to see both sides of the argument and form a balanced view. Listening to what he had to say to me – and the way he put it – brought me back to reality and set my mood for the Brumbies' game. It was time to show what the British and Irish Lions really meant to me.

There were bigger games in my career, Test matches for England and the Lions, one with a World Cup resting on the outcome, but none that at the time seemed as important as the Lions against the Brumbies in front of 20,093 spectators at Bruce Stadium on the third day of July 2001. For all the hullabaloo I had caused, we were one-up in the Test series and it was the responsibility of the midweek boys to maintain the momentum through to the second Test in Melbourne four days later. At 19–3 to the home side, shortly before half-time, things didn't look too clever. They had scored three tries in the first twenty-five minutes, I had missed two or three kicks from long-distance. The message came down from the stands that 'ROG', as Ronan is widely known, was to take over the goalkicking.

He nodded as the decision was relayed to him, then turned to me and said, 'Daws, no way mate. You carry on.' That is another gesture I will never forget. Telling the world how much the Lions means to you and saying sorry a million times is all well and good, but being able to prove it by landing a winning conversion from the touchline with the last kick of the game says rather more. And that's what happened after we rallied in the second half and Austin scored his second try of the night after the hooter had sounded to signal time up. As the ball split the uprights I started to cry.

They were my first tears since I lost the final of a Minis tournament playing for Marlow Under-9s. I felt so emotionally charged I could easily have left the tour there and then and come home. My phone rang in my kitbag. It was Clive Woodward. I stared at his number and thought 'for God's sake will this ever end?'

'Oh you're jumping on the bandwagon to give me a bollocking as well are you?' I snapped.

'Actually, no I'm not,' said Clive, who had already called Graham Henry to offer his support in his position as one of the four home union head coaches, and was now phoning me as a friend. 'Of course I will support you, but you're going to have to get your head right. You just can't go doing that sort of thing.'

I needed to clear my head so Austin, Jason Leonard and Lawrence Dallaglio arranged for us to play a round of golf with a few other lads at Royal Melbourne on our arrival in the city the following day. Now this is a serious golf course, and not all the Lions were serious golfers. I discovered this as I approached the 18th green and heard a commotion on the tee behind. I later discovered Jason had topped his drive and because his ball did not make it past the ladies' tee, and naturally he felt obliged to unzip his flies and play 'elephant' golf to prove which sex he was.

Most people in that situation, particularly on such a classy course, might just pop the little fella out for one shot but Jason had it dangling from tee to green. Not that anyone noticed, as he strolled onto the green, slap bang in front of the clubhouse and tapped in his putt before, with a completely straight face, shaking hands with each of his playing partners. It was a gorgeous after-noon and standing beside the green waiting for them to finish I thought I'd take a photo to give the lads a memory shot to take home with them.

The shutter clicked, I stuffed the camera back in my pocket and thought nothing more of it. It was not until we were having a beer in the bar and the subject of Jason's tee shot came up that I was alerted to what had gone on. Jason was claiming he played the entire hole in a state of disrepair and nobody was having any of it. I switched on the camera and studied the photo. After zooming in a couple of times the evidence emerged. Sure enough, there was Jason's little pecker poking out of his trousers.

It was good to laugh again. For a moment at least I was able to forget the mess I'd got myself in. I was transported back to past rugby tours where fun had not been restricted to a day's play on a golf course. One in particular stood out from the others, the so-called Tour of Hell, England's 1998 tour to Australia, New Zealand and South Africa, where we were thrashed pretty much everywhere we went yet still found time for a good laugh.

There is the night in Dunedin where one of our number makes a female acquaintance, who returns with him to his room, along the corridor, as it happens, from where I am chatting to a few of the lads. Ten minutes later we hear screaming. We pile out of the room and there, hopping up and down and yelling, is our Romeo. 'My banjo! I've snapped my banjo!' I won't say exactly what happened but the words 'foreskin' and 'torn' appeared in the same sentence.

At least he lasted ten minutes. Another such liaison was over even more quickly and earned the player in question the nickname 'Countdown'. Although this chap shut his room door, he didn't think to draw his curtains. Half a dozen off us decided to go balcony hopping and peered into his room. As well as the curtains, the window was open and we could clearly hear the unmistakable sound of . . . Barrie White. As *Can't Get Enough Of Your Love, Babe* played in the background, this love machine went for it – and lasted less than a minute! As he rolled over, Barrie's dulcit tones were drowned out by the *Countdown* theme as six near-hysterical England players gave it 'di-du, di-du, di-du-di-du' at the top of our voices.

I had not laughed as much since an incident that took place on my first England B tour, to New Zealand in 1992. One of our front-row forwards persuaded a young lady to accompany him into the physio's room where he proceeded to grab a pot of Vaseline, dip his wick in it, and then crack on. The next day the boys were in for training and one of the locks opened said tub. As he wiped grease all over his forehead, neck and ears, he asked why there appeared to be a worm hole in the contents.

'You. Have. Got. To. Be. Joking!' he yelled, completely losing the plot, hurling the plastic jar against the wall, reaching for a towel and frantically attempting to wipe his head clean.

In four Tests on that ill-fated 1998 trip the try tally was twenty-eight to four against, and by the final leg the humour had run dry. There were various niggles before tensions spilled over one night in Cape Town. Austin Healey had had enough of Pat Sanderson and vice versa. We were out in a bar drinking with the South Africans and Austin leant through to get a drink and happened to nudge Pat. I think it was genuinely an accident but Pat reacted, telling Austin to get lost, to which Mr Healey maturely responded, 'Make me.' Cue a coming together and before we know it Austin had headbutted Pat, splitting his eye open.

Fortunately, England doctor Terry Crystal was on hand to take Pat straight from the pub to hospital for stitches. An hour or so later, just when I thought the tour couldn't get any worse, Pat marched back into the pub, his eyebrow needlework prominent.

'Where's Healey?' he asked. Here we go again, I thought. 'I'm here Sanderson,' says Austin. Then an extraordinary thing happens. Both start laughing. All's well that ends well.

Back in Australia in 2001 and I'm hoping the same rule will apply. It is half-time in Melbourne and the Lions lead the Wallabies 11–6. That's all three halves we have dominated in this Test series. It was as impossible to see a record Lions loss coming as it was to anticipate the elbow from Nathan Grey which crashes into Richard Hill's face, puts him out of the tour and turns the match on its head. By the end we have lost 35–14 and have enough injuries to fill an A&E ward.

Try though we might to get everyone fit – and somehow Jonny Wilkinson is cleared to play, having had his leg in plaster for a couple of days – there is no way back for Hilly, Rob Howley or Austin, who had hurt his back. I come in for Rob but Austin's late withdrawal leaves us without scrum-half cover on the bench for the decider in Sydney.

The selection meeting goes something like this. Graham Henry: 'Austin is out, anyone got any ideas?' Silence.

Donal Lenihan: 'Er, well I did see Andy Nicol yesterday.'

So did I but he was half-cut. Andy was Scotland scrum-half at the time. The previous year he had captained the Scotland side that beat the England team I was skippering, denying us a Grand Slam. He was a fine player but he was in Sydney as leader of a Lions supporters' tour. His idea of training in the second week of July was to walk to the bar – then four hours later try to walk back!

Imagine then his shock to receive a call from Donal the day before the final Test, while he was attempting to climb up Sydney

Harbour Bridge, asking him if he would play. He had just come off a massive night out, was severely hungover and, by all accounts, was needing every ounce of concentration to avoid puking up from vertigo.

'I was convinced it was a wind-up by someone with a comedy Irish accent,' Andy said. 'Then I realised it was really Donal Lenihan and he was being deadly serious!'

Fair play to Andy, he joined up with the team just nine hours before kick-off, was given a load of kit that didn't fit and packed off to a training session that was no more than a 'walk through' of set-piece moves. He spent what was left of the day learning the lineout calls before turning up for the game with the play book under his arm.

I wasn't too aware of his predicament at the time because I was concentrating so hard on the game, my first Test start of the tour. But I saw the panic on the touchline when I was caught at the bottom of a ruck inside the first five minutes and given a good old-fashioned shoeing all down my hamstrings. I thought that was that, I would have to come off. I looked to the bench and saw arms waving and a couple of coaches locked in conversation. Meanwhile Andy had not moved a muscle, let alone taken his tracksuit off and started warming up. He was staring at me as if to say, 'Don't even think about it, Dawson.'

He later admitted, 'I wasn't in great shape to be honest. I was with a supporters' tour and as happens on those trips you drink, fall down and then drink some more. I think the adrenalin would have seen me through the first five to ten minutes but after that I might have struggled. Luckily, Matt Dawson's body held together.'

As Lions careers go there has probably never been one to compare with Andy's, who ended the game having not got on, but still being selected as the one Lion to have to undergo post-match drug testing. Still, he knew the score, being a Lions veteran as he was . . . 2001 was in fact Andy's second tour. Would it be indiscreet of me to mention he wasn't selected for the first one, either? In 1993 he was flown out to New Zealand as temporary cover after Robert Jones was taken ill. He was there for six days, sat on the bench against Taranaki, came on for the last six minutes, and flew home the following day.

'Six days and six minutes of rugby,' he said. 'And that was the longer of my two tours!'

The only other contender for the shortest Lions Test career title I can think of is Eric Miller, the Leicester and Ireland back row, with whom I toured South Africa in 1997. Eric was due to be named in the team for the first Test but at the start of the week became sick. He was told to spend a couple of days in bed and he would be fine for the weekend. Unfortunately, his dad came to visit him, and with a father's concern for his son's welfare administered poor Eric with a rejuvenating equivalent of a Lemsip. James Robson, the tour doctor, visits him some time afterwards and by chance sees the wrapper in the bin beside his bed.

James looks at him incredulously and tells him he is screwed. The remedy contains a banned substance. So Eric is pulled out of the game but named on the bench for the second Test and happily gets his chance when Tim Rodber goes down with four minutes to go. Excited Eric is so desperate to become involved he sprints onto the pitch . . . and tears his quad. That was the extent of his Lions career.

The final whistle in Sydney brought heartbreak. After seven weeks away from home the series had come down to the final lineout of the final game in pretty much the final minute. Australia steal the ball on our throw-in and we lose 29–23.

There was a lot of chat afterwards that the Wallabies had cracked our lineout code, and two years later I had that confirmed. Speaking to Nathan Sharpe in the Cargo Bar in Sydney the night after the 2003 World Cup final, he told me they had known our lineout moves better than we had, and used to rehearse them in training.

It only added to my frustration about the whole tour as during an open training session before the final Test, Austin and I had spotted two Aussie fellas under an umbrella – one holding the brolly, the other with one hand tucked in his jeans and the other seemingly snug in his jacket pocket. Only it wasn't. In a crude attempt to disguise the fact he was holding a video camera, which we could see poking out, the bloke had stuffed his empty jacket sleeve into a pocket. James Bond need not have worried about competition.

'Donal, can we deal with these guys please,' I said to our team manager. 'They're videoing our lineout moves.' Donal went up to them, had a conversation, then came back and assured us they were just supporters.

It's fair to say we didn't give enough thought to protecting our secrets. Before the first Test we needed to rehearse our lineout calls but instead of finding a pitch we ended up at a shopping concourse. In the middle of it was some grass and on it, in front of thousands of 'shoppers', we did all our pre-match spotters. We went through our entire repertoire – every call, every combination – in the middle of town.

The series lost, we headed into town in our Lions blazers looking to drown our sorrows. We were told a bar in central Sydney called

The Establishment was the place to go and Austin and I hatched a plan to finance the evening. He would arm-wrestle, which believe it or not is his speciality, and I would find him opponents and take bets. It was a licence to print money. 'My scrawny little pal can beat you in an arm wrestle. You don't think so? Shall we say twenty dollars? Fifty?'

Very soon there was a queue of Aussie males lining up to take him on. Without exception they assumed it would be like taking sweets from a baby. Without exception he saw them off, as we both got battered on free drinks. Austin had not even taken off his blazer at this point. When he tried to, he ended up pulling through one of his sleeves to reveal a blue and white stripe lining.

'Hey Oz that looks quite cool,' I said. 'I'll have some of that.'

A couple of minutes later the two of us were wearing our blazers inside out, looking a proper pair of idiots, but as we were hammered and Austin was beating everyone left, right and centre we only saw the funny side of it. One of his beaten opponents did not, however, and reached over and ripped one of the arms off Austin's blazer.

Before Austin could react I had leant in and ripped the other one off. He stood there wearing what looked like half a tank top. We were a complete drunken mess and when he staggered outside to take a phone call we ended up losing each other.

After twenty minutes searching in vain for Muscle Mary I decided to get a cab back to Manly. The driver was a Welshman and almost immediately he started talking about the rugby and asked whether I had seen the game. I told him I'd come over to watch the Lions but before I could say anything else he interrupted me.

'By the way don't you hate that Matt Dawson? What a jerk. I can't believe he was playing today!'

I looked at his face reflected in the front mirror and his eyes were on the road. I was too drunk to argue so said, 'Yeah, yeah, that was a strange selection. Mind you, Rob Howley was injured.'

'He would have been better than Dawson even injured,' came the reply.

'Give him a break, Drives. With all the injuries the Lions had, Dawson was the best option. He has got some strengths you know.'

'No he hasn't. He's useless. He can't tackle, he can't pass.'

There I was, sitting in a taxi on the other side of the world, my Lions jacket inside out, being abused to my face by some bloke who didn't know it was me. As the cab pulled up outside my hotel I introduced myself and watched his face drop a mile. It gave me a measure of satisfaction but not much. I let myself into my room and looked in the mirror on the wall next to the bathroom door. I was a mess. 'Jesus, Daws, what are you doing? What have you become? Seriously.' There and then I made a pledge to myself. When next I returned to Australia, things would be different. Very different.

CHAPTER 5

A QUESTION OF TIMING

It's spring 2004 and my phone is ringing in the kitchen. It is the BBC. They want to know if I would consider making a guest appearance as captain on *A Question of Sport*. Frankie Dettori and Ally McCoist are team captains but Frankie is unavailable for three shows due to racing commitments. Would I fill in?

What, on my favourite show? The one Dad and I watched together throughout my childhood, first with my scrum-half rugby hero Gareth Edwards and Emlyn Hughes as team captains, then Billy Beaumont going up against first Willie Carson, then Ian 'Beefy' Botham. I knew everything there was to know about the show. Ally had moved into the hot seat in 1996, alongside world snooker champion John Parrott, before Frankie joined the show in 2002.

'Of course I'll consider it,' I say, trying not to sound too keen. Count to three, Daws, one . . . two . . .

'. . . The answer is yes! Thank you very much.'

I put the phone down and dance around the room. I am super

excited, like a child on Christmas Eve. I am a World Cup winner, England's most-capped scrum-half with sixty-five caps, and a two-tour Lion. But now, my life is complete. I pitch up at BBC Television Centre and am shown straight to the dressing room. Waiting to brief me are some of the production team, who advise that I should be myself, try to get some banter going with Coisty and encourage some of the guests around me. Sounds straightforward enough.

As I'm ushered into make-up, one of the guys, with a clipboard in his hand and headphones hooked round his neck, leans across. 'You may be interested to know, Matt,' he says. 'Frankie is unlikely to do the show next year.'

I had recently moved clubs, leaving Northampton and signing for Wasps. The decision behind the change was in part to explore career opportunities beyond rugby. I had no aspirations to stay in the game as a coach. I fancied getting involved in the media. Here is my chance. I am not about to waste it.

Confirmation comes in September. Frankie decides he needs to recommit himself to his day job, horse racing. He had almost been killed in a helicopter crash in 2000 and for four years after enjoyed what he referred to as 'nice safe work on the telly'. But now, he says, the hunger is back. He wants to be in the stalls again at Newmarket, Epsom, Longchamp and Dubai. Not in a television studio.

Horse racing allows the best to compete into their forties or, in Lester Piggott's case, into his fifties. Rugby is different. I am thirty-one and my playing career is approaching an end. Sooner or later I will be put out to pasture. I need to take control of my destiny. When the captain's armband is offered to me, I don't need to be asked twice.

A QUESTION OF TIMING

Quickly my life feels different. Although I am still a rugby player for Wasps and for England, and very proud of that, I have taken a step outside of the sport where I am known. People now look at me as someone other than a rugby player. After years of talking rugby with everyone I meet, I am all of a sudden seen in a different, broader light. The rugby chat continues, of course, but now conversations take in the world of television and light entertainment. I like it, but I realise I am unlikely to be able to straddle the two worlds for long.

So I meet with Andy Robinson one day in October. Andy has succeeded Sir Clive Woodward as England head coach and he invites me to his office as a senior player to talk through his plans going forward and what my involvement in his squad will be. I head to Twickenham knowing, in the back of my mind, that I have to bring to his attention that there is a *QOS* recording date coming up that clashes with England training.

He speaks first, announcing to me that he is going to make Jonny Wilkinson his England captain.

'Really?'

'Yes, really. He's a natural choice.'

'Okay, I'm not sure he's the natural choice. You've got to have him in your team but does he need to have that added pressure on him? I think there are some younger players who have the presence and skills set to be captain.' Robbo gives me that 'Growler' stare of his, then the muscles in his face relax, hinting at a smile, as if to say, 'Okay Daws, you're just airing your view, that's what senior players do now and again. I can accept that.' I sense an opening, an opportunity to strike.

'Oh, and Robbo listen, I need to talk to you about one of the training dates. Unfortunately, there's a clash with *A Question of*

Sport and I'm just wondering if I can have that Tuesday off.'

He goes quiet for a moment as he computes what I have just said and then speaks. 'Er, no. That will not be possible Matt.'

There's that smile again. Now what do I do? I am in a corner. I can't take 'No' for an answer. No equals 'Major Problem'. 'No' is not an option.

'Robbo, I've got to do this. I'm almost thirty-two, I've only got a few years left in my rugby career, I've got to plan for beyond that. This is about the rest of my life. I love playing for England, I want to play for England for as long as I can, but I need you to understand my position. This is an unbelievable opportunity for me.'

'I do understand that, Matt, but I need you to understand this. This is my first training session as head coach in charge of England and there is no way I can be seen to be having favourites. I'm going to have to say no.'

Nine months on I'm on an airplane coming in to land at Heathrow, returning with the British and Irish Lions from my third tour of duty. We have been to New Zealand and we have been smashed, losing the series three–nil. Worse still, I have come to the realisation that I am not capable of playing to the highest level any more, with the intensity, strength, power and athleticism required. I still have the rugby brain and the skills but that is no longer enough; not when those around me are quicker and more powerful.

As the wheels touch down on the tarmac I make a decision. Enough is enough. It is time to hang up the old boots. I will retire at the end of the 2005/06 season. I think back to that autumn morning in the office of the England head coach at Twickenham and the game of hardball I played with Andy Robinson. Thank God I held my nerve.

A QUESTION OF TIMING

'I have a long-standing commitment that I simply can't reverse,' is what I told the media in response to the Rugby Football Union press release announcing I had stepped down from the Elite Player Squad rather than risk losing my job on *A Question of Sport* before it had even begun. I'm telling the truth. The training session in question had not been arranged when I confirmed my availability to the BBC.

'Obviously I am disappointed to be out of the EPS squad, but I understand and respect Andy's decision,' I add diplomatically. I go on to say that being asked to become the fourth rugby player to be a captain on *QOS*, after Cliff Morgan, Gareth and Bill, is 'a milestone in my career' to set alongside winning the World Cup. I mean it too, but inside I'm not completely happy. I always thought I'd retire on my own terms, when I felt the time was right, not when somebody else decided for me. I make another decision. My rugby journey can't end like this.

MY *A QUESTION OF SPORT* XV

15) *George Foreman*
14) *Adam Jones*
13) *Michael Johnson*
12) *Paul Gascoigne*
11) *Laura Davies*
10) *Sam Torrance*
9) *Gareth Edwards (captain)*
1) *Gary Speed*
2) *Sue Barker*
3) *Ally McCoist*
4) *John Parrot*

5) Martin Johnson
6) Tim Henman
7) Will Greenwood
8) Paul Sackey/David Strettle

15) George Foreman

The first international star guest I have on my team, George doesn't do any of the meeting and greeting beforehand, he goes straight from his limo into the studio, escorted by his five sons – enormous fellas, all called George! They walk in through an audience of grannies and he sits himself down to my left. I say 'hello' and shake his giant hand. No problem so far. We don't ever give the guests advance notice of their questions so we all had fingers crossed he'd pick the right number and get a boxing question. He does. The sigh of relief from the production gallery is audible. The picture flashes up and the former two-time world heavyweight champion shakes his head.

'No idea, dunno.'

'C'mon, George,' I say. 'Look at the belt he's wearing, you recognise that, no?'

'No.'

I lean over and sort of tap him on the leg. 'C'mon, we can get this George.' He turns his head to me and fixes me with a glare.

'Don't you ever touch me again.'

I go scarlet. Rather than sensing my discomfort and the delicacy of the moment, Coisty then calls out, 'Ask him if he's got a grill in his boot!'

The show is spiralling out of control. I have Jason McAteer on my right, who is a funny guy, but even he is anxious.

Each of us gets a pad on which to make notes if we want to.

George isn't interacting at all. I'm trying to make small talk and he is just doodling on his pad. At the end of the show he rips all the pages off and puts them in his pocket, as if to say 'no one's having those', like they are pieces of art that are going to be worth millions. He gets up, walks out of the studio into his limo and I never see him again.

14) Adam Jones

The greatest of the great. Adam holds every record on *A Question of Sport*. Our series producer is a massive Welsh rugby fan called, would you believe, Gareth Edwards. He loves to get the Wales rugby lads on. In November 2009 Lions' prop Adam was on Phil Tufnell's team along with Phillips Idowu. On my team was AP McCoy and David Haye. Secretly, Adam must always have wanted to come on the show. When I saw his name, I was thinking, 'This could be hard work. I've never heard him say anything to be honest.' Hard work? He was on fire! He started off just answering his questions, then chipped in with all the rest.

The first round was an Opening Rally. Adam and his team had to name five sides playing in the Championship that season that had previously played in the Premier League.

'Newcastle United, Sheffield Wednesday, Middlesbrough, QPR and Barnsley.'

'Correct!' said Sue Barker. 'Right Adam, look at this action. 'Who is kicking this drop goal and who is the goalkeeper scoring from his own half?'

'François Steyn and Paul Robinson.'

'Correct!'

And so it went on. Who scored a try to help his club to Heineken Cup success before starting all three Tests in South Africa for the

2009 Lions? Who is the mystery cocktail maker in this clip?

'Jamie Heaslip and Nathan Hines.'

'Correct again!'

The Speed Pictureboard proved also to be a piece of cake, with Adam identifying Mike Phillips (rugby union), Laura Davies (golf), Stephen Lee (snooker), Iestyn Harris (rugby league), Gabby Agbonlahor (football) and Bernard Hopkins (boxing).

The show ended with a 'buzzer' round where you had to identify a shared name on three pairings. Adam correctly answered Jlloyd SAMUEL Peter, Bob and Mike BRYAN Habana and, to win the game with just two seconds left, Dilhara FERNANDO Alonso. Genius.

13) Michael Johnson

One of my sporting icons. Often when you meet these people you get slightly disappointed. Not with Michael. I was in awe of this guy. He was able to laugh at himself one minute, then get wound up in frustration the next as he was unable to suppress that competitive streak that made him such a great champion. In my pathetic, immature way I will laugh to myself when alone that I've been in japes and photos with one of the greatest athletes ever. Forget what they say about avoid ever meeting your heroes because you'll only be disappointed. In his case that could not be further from the truth.

12) Paul Gascoigne

Gazza only agreed to come on the show because Ally McCoist is one of his great friends and something of a mentor to him. He had a bag of wine gums in his pocket, which he was constantly dipping into. He was frail but switched on to the game very well, growing comfortable sitting around mates and trading a few stories. It was a Great North Run-themed show with Brendan Foster, Steve Cram and, I think, Peter Beardsley. There was a picture board and Gazza got a split picture of the racehorse Sunny Bay and a black footballer by the name of Jeff Whitley. He had to come up with a name, which of course was Whitley Bay. Only it wasn't immediately obvious to Gazza.

'Oh I know this, I know this . . . it's amazing . . . it's the name of the pub just down the road from me,' he finally said, excitedly. 'It's . . . it's . . . the Black Horse.'

There was this sudden moment of shocked silence, followed by nervous laughter. Our show is not *Have I Got News For You*, it's *QOS*. We're absolutely not here to upset anyone. Gazza sensed right away he had said something wrong and attempted to apologise. 'No, no, no, I'm sorry,' he said. 'I didn't realise the guy on the left is black.'

11) Laura Davies
One of the greatest golfers Britain has produced and an all-round lovely person. I once went to her house for a charity golf event. In her garden, amid trees and bushes, was a tennis court and a nine-hole pitch-and-putt with tee boxes all of which hailed from tournaments she'd won around the world. After finishing our game we all retired to her sports games room, which comprised six La-Z-Boy sofas and an enormous bank of TV screens showing every different sports channel. There was one fridge full of beers and another packed with soft drinks. It was heaven on earth.

10) Sam Torrance
Sharp as a tack is Sam. Comb your hair the wrong way (chance would be a fine thing!), wear a dodgy shirt, or take too long to hit

a golf shot and he's all over you. I love it when sporting greats come on and act like they do among their close pals at home. It's an endearing quality of the show that everyone is put so at ease. Sam was knowledgeable, quick-witted and unbelievably competitive. He also told a lovely story about Augusta, the US Masters and the American golfer Fuzzy Zoeller.

It's the mid-seventies and the pros are all given local caddies. Fuzzy issues an instruction to his. 'Whatever you do, don't talk to me during the tournament. Give me the yardage and if I ask for a club, you pass it to me. Is that perfectly clear?'

The tournament begins and Fuzzy is playing hole 13, Azalea, a 510-yard par 5. He tries to cut the corner off the tee and his ball flies past the brook and into the trees. Fuzzy gets to the ball from where the obvious shot is to chip out onto the fairway. But Fuzzy fancies a slinging, drawing miracle shot onto the green. He turns to the caddie to find him holding out the pitching wedge.

'Don't give me that,' snaps Fuzzy, 'give me the 2 iron.'

He then proceeds to smash this ball, with an unbelievably high draw, up out of trouble and down onto the top tier of the green. The ball lands, pauses, then spins back to within a few feet of the pin, from where he taps in for an eagle. The place goes bonkers and Fuzzy turns round to his caddie and says, 'What do you think about that then, eh?'

The caddie says nothing.

'No, no, you can speak now, what do you think of that? Tell me how good that was?'

Nothing. Fuzzy is now getting annoyed.

'Oi, don't be so rude. You didn't think I was capable of that did you? Did you?'

The caddie looks at him, finally opens his mouth and says, 'It wasn't your ball.'

9) Gareth Edwards (Captain)

Before anyone accuses me of brown-nosing my rugby hero, this is series producer Gareth Edwards. He was named after the Welsh legend, indeed he is himself Welsh, but much to his parents' dismay, he wasn't much of a rugby player. Instead he turned his concentration to sports trivia and television, and all of us on the show should give thanks for that. His one claim to fame is, allegedly, bowling Andrew Flintoff in the nets. Freddie must have been twelve at the time.

1) Gary Speed

An absolute *QOS* star and a huge loss to the world. Gary was a perfect gentleman in the Green Room before filming and always brought his family along to soak up the atmosphere. I have never known a footballer with a better knowledge of sporting trivia. For someone who spent so much time training, playing, coaching and keeping fit, I don't know how he found time to swat up. He loved being on the show and there is no better example of what *QOS* means to sportsmen and women, young and old.

2) Sue Barker

3) Ally McCoist

4) John Parrott

These three instigated the transformation of the show in the mid-nineties. The beauty of *A Question of Sport* is its ability to maintain all the tradition and history establish and by Messrs David Vine and David Coleman, while being bang up to date with its production, humour and imaginative programming. With their scathing banter, Sue, Ally and John reignited the nation's love for the show to the extent that it now works wherever it sits on the schedule.

One exchange I will always remember involved a series of clips followed by Sue asking the following question: 'What colour is the speed skater's helmet?' I look at her, then at Coisty, then back at her. Simultaneously we all begin to corpse. Coisty stands up and says, 'That's absolutely disgraceful to ask such a personal question.' Things are getting out of control. I try to steady the ship. 'He had a yellow helmet, Sue.' What was I thinking? McCoist explodes with laughter, before adding, 'You can get penicillin for that.' Thank God the show wasn't going out live.

A special word for Coisty, who was a huge influence and inspiration to me in how you should present yourself as a former sportsman. He never gave it the big 'I am', he was always very grounded. Of course it helped that he has the same childish sense of humour as I do.

5) Martin Johnson

'Statto', as he's affectionately known. In truth, his home questions should really be on American Football but name any sport and he seems to have an encyclopedic knowledge of it. My favourite Johnno moment on the show went as follows:

Sue: 'Home or away, Martin?'

MJ: 'Home please.'

Sue: 'Which Irishman holds the record . . .'

MJ: 'Willie John McBride.'

Sue: 'Er, yes that's right. Do you not want the question?'

MJ: 'I know it. Who holds the record for the most Lions appearances?'

Sue: 'Correct.'

6) Tim Henman

Pushes Adam Jones and Martin Johnson hard for the title of 'most knowledgeable'. Tim has never been on my team and I've never beaten him. No-one can ask him a question about tennis that he doesn't know the answer to but he's passionate about other sports, too, and one of the funniest guys you could wish to spend an afternoon with. That may surprise some, who know Tim just on and around the tennis court, but it's true. He is engaging and charming and his banter is so good he could easily have been a rugby player. He is Mr One-Liner. Whether its golf, tiddly-winks, or sports trivia he has to win . . . and not necessarily by fair means. Sledging is his speciality, particularly on your back swing.

7) Will Greenwood

Will and I obviously had the same sort of sports upbringing because our knowledge is remarkably similar. The fact we roomed a lot together with England certainly influenced that. My theory behind his wide-ranging sporting recall? He's a Manchester City fan, so unlike me (Everton), until recently he had no reason to follow football.

8) Paul Sackey/David Strettle

From one end of the spectrum to the other. These two England rugby wingers appeared one after another on successive weeks and didn't know a thing. Absolutely nothing. Not even about rugby. And people say it is the backs who have all the brains (and good looks, obviously)! This might come as a surprise but in my experience the consistently brightest rugby players are props – Dan Cole, Graham Rowntree, Phil Vickery, Jason Leonard, the list goes on. You might not be setting them a chemistry exam, but for common sense, general humour and dry wit, these boys take all the beating.

FIGHTING BACK

It's January 2005 and I have spent the winter playing club rugby for Wasps, while appearing weekly on BBC One. In my absence, England have had a mixed autumn at Twickenham. A 70–0 win over Canada was followed by a 32–16 victory over South Africa, in which Andy Gomarsall wore the No. 9 shirt and young Leicester scrum-half Harry Ellis came off the bench to make his debut. The following week England lost 21–19 to Australia in a match that earned the management a whole heap of flak for team tactics that backfire.

Given the last thing Andy Robinson said to me was that the door would remain open to me for an England return 'should my priorities change', I am surprised to get his telephone call inviting me to rejoin the squad. My priorities have not changed. What has changed is that England are under a bit of pressure and I'd got the better of Gomars in a recent club game. I am surprised also that Robbo claims to have 'always said' that 'I would consider bringing Matt back if I felt he was playing well'. I don't remember him ever saying that. Anyway, I am back and now I have the chance to sign off on my own terms.

The next phone call I receive from a rugby head coach excites me even more. Sir Clive Woodward is on the other end of the line talking about the upcoming British and Irish Lions tour to New

Zealand. He wants to know if I'd be interested and what my thoughts are on which other scrum-halves he should take.

This is not a call I anticipated. My last Lions experience did not end well and yet here I am not only being asked to come on the next tour but to advise the head coach in the selection process – to be a sounding board for him. It feels good, at least until we get to New Zealand.

2005 BRITISH AND IRISH LIONS TOUR (P12, W7, D1, L4)

1) ARGENTINA, drew 25–25 (Cardiff, 23 May)
2) Bay of Plenty, won 34–20 (Rotorua, 4 June)
3) Taranaki, won 36–14 (New Plymouth, 8 June)
4) NZ Maori, lost 13–19 (Hamilton, 11 June)
5) Wellington, won 23–6 (Wellington, 15 June)
6) Otago, won 30–19 (Dunedin, 18 June)
7) Southland, won 26–16 (Invercargill, 21 June)
8) 1st Test, NEW ZEALAND, lost 3–21 (Christchurch, 25 June)
9) Manawatu, won 109–6 (Palmerston North, 28 June)
10) 2nd Test, NEW ZEALAND, lost 18–48 (Wellington, 2 July)
11) Auckland, won 17–13 (Auckland, 5 July)
12) 3rd Test, NEW ZEALAND, lost 19–38 (Auckland, 9 July)

The writing is on the wall before we even leave home. Clive had put together a no-expense-spared extravaganza of a trip. There were more coaches and support staff than I'd ever seen in my life, and so many players that by the end of the trip I still had not properly got to know half of them. Yet for all the expense and all the detail, our opening match, a fixture against a depleted Argentina side at the

Millennium Stadium in Cardiff, did not go well. In fact, we only avoided becoming the first Lions team to lose a Test on home soil when Jonny Wilkinson tied the game with a penalty kick nine minutes into injury time.

At the time we don't see the signs. We are all caught up in Clive's grand vision. 'I make no apologies for believing this is the best prepared tour in the history of Lions rugby,' he said when we joined up. Given what has greeted us, it is hard to argue.

He seems to have every base covered. We are sent a package in which enclosed is a zipped red Lions folder containing a 'Power of Four' wristband (designed to create unity), the iPod, on which my favourite tunes are already downloaded, and a postcard on which is written on one side: 'What The F*** Is Going On?' and on the other: 'If you feel like this in any meeting, hold the card up or come and see me or call me on this number . . .' We are also presented with diaries in which there is a box for us to detail our sleeping patterns. We are required to rate our quality of sleep, with a mark between one and ten, and keep a note of our hours of slumber and consequent energy levels. Sweat analysis also takes place, though probably the less said about that the better.

There are seemingly no boundaries to Clive's pursuit of excellence. He even convinces himself that hiring Alastair Campbell, advisor to Prime Minister Tony Blair, as head of communications for a rugby team is a good idea. Last but not least, he tells us we will have our own anthem.

'Sorry. What did you just say?'

That's right. New Zealand have theirs so why shouldn't we, explains Clive. It's called *The Power Of Four*:

We're actually supposed to sing that? When you go on a Lions tour as an Englishman, you want to be a part of Ireland, Scotland

and Wales. You want to play with the best players. You don't need to be motivated to unite as the 'power of four'. That's what the Lions are about. That's what they stand for. I know the Lions are now the basis of a very successful commercial business, but it's not a corporation.

'I hope players and fans will welcome the fact we have our own song that can stir the passions,' Clive tells the media. 'It can help build the phenomenal camaraderie that is developing between the players of the four countries, who have come together as one.'

He also says the players will be expected to know the words by the time we play the first matches in New Zealand. I'm sure you can guess this for yourself but the first time we are put to the test it sounds like a load of wedding guests being asked to sing a hymn they don't know. Unbelievably painful.

So the Argentina game is not one to remember fondly, other than Welsh singer Katherine Jenkins giving *The Power of Four* its first official airing, God bless her. What none of us could have expected is that the 25–25 draw ends up being easily our best Test result of the tour. But hope springs eternal on Lions tours. It's the only way to approach them.

My frame of mind is clear. This is my shot at redemption with the Lions, an opportunity to put behind me once and for all the controversy of the 2001 tour. I'll keep my head down, work hard and complain about nothing. If they want me for the Test team, I'll be there, with bells on. If they want me to lug tackle bags, hold defence shields and turn out for the midweek boys, before cheerleading on the weekend, fine.

Of course, I am a more complex character than that. I don't see it at the time but there is still a lot of anger in me. I think I've changed and moved on with my life since 2001, that winning the World Cup and starting a TV career has ironed out all the creases. Not *Strictly* true. I head to New Zealand in a strange place mentally, verging on depression. I'm actually not very well. My diary constantly refers to 'fatigue', 'tiredness' and 'having the flu'. And that is before the really hard work begins. I spend a couple of days in bed. I wonder at one point why I have accepted the invitation to come on this tour. Don't get me wrong, I still enjoy the ethos of the Lions, but I am totally shot, rugby-ed out. It's an effort to get up in the morning, I limp around and really struggle to train twice a day. I don't think I'm alone, mind. After another long, long season a lot of the boys are just too tired to take part in all the activities.

In my case a lot of it is psychological. I sense early on, correctly as it turns out, that my role on the trip is going to be non-stop rugby. Dwayne Peel, my Welsh rival for the No. 9 shirt, is tearing it up. He is coming off a Grand Slam campaign and it is apparent to me that I am heading for a place on the bench. It is made equally plain that they want me to be playing in midweek, too. I'm in both squads and required to train every single day.

By the end of the trip I will have started two games – the fourth, which we lose, against the New Zealand Maori, and the eleventh (of twelve) which we win, against Auckland. I will also have been on the bench for another five, coming on in the warm-up games against Bay of Plenty and Otago, then in the first and third Tests. It becomes one long slog but I have pledged to take it all on the chin, and I stay true to that.

There are lighter moments along the way, such as the day Alastair Campbell has his trousers yanked down from behind by Donncha O'Callaghan. In his moment of embarrassment, as he reaches down to cover up his Burnley FC boxer shorts, he does not notice his mobile phone drop out of his pocket. Steve Thompson, the England hooker and my old Northampton team mate, does, and later we attempt to send love messages to Tony Blair. We scroll down his list of stored names but none is listed as Tony Blair or PM, Boss or even Gaffer. So we give it the carpet-bombing treatment. His entire address book gets an 'I love you' message. I know it is infantile but how often do you get a chance like that?

Then there is the night, also in Wellington, when we head into town for our team meal and some of us decide to go on to a late-night bar. I walk in with Dwayne and we see a load of Lions supporters. Dwayne stops dead in his tracks, like he's just seen a ghost. It turns out his dad is being chatted up by some scantily clad woman who has just taken part in a bout of jelly wrestling. I knew he was a quick mover – Dwayne I mean – but the speed with which he turns on his heels and escapes surprises even me!

My laughter is in stark contrast to the mood of the squad in the first week in New Zealand, where the Lions last won a series thirty-four years earlier, when John Dawes' wonderfully talented 1971 squad won two and drew one in the four-match series. Lawrence Dallaglio's tour-ending ankle injury in the first match is a blow to the entire tour party.

Spirits had been so high as well, after a journey over in which one of the backroom staff, Gavin Scott, forgot to eat before taking his sleeping tablet and passed out during supper. He had to be woken up with half a bread roll in his mouth. We then arrive in the Land of the Long White Cloud and Lawrence gets heavily fined for carrying an apple through immigration. Did we laugh? Did we ever.

But not now. We have just played Bay of Plenty in Rotorua and an opening Lions victory has been marred by Lol's horrific injury.

It is impossible to overstate what a blow this is. Obviously the English boys know that immediately, being well-versed in what he brings to any team, but Paul Wallace summed up what he meant to the other nationalities a week later after Lawrence hobbled into the changing room in Hamilton, before our game with the New Zealand Maori, presented us with our jerseys and delivered his emotional pre-match speech.

'He was the perfect person to do it,' said Wally. 'I'd played against Lawrence many times but having him on the same side makes you realise what an inspirational figure he is.' To a squad not given any chance of beating the All Blacks, Lol was completely invaluable, not only because of his influence within the team and in dealing with the referee, but because the opposition knew if they gave him an opportunity to steal ball, he would take it and if they didn't get the contact right, they would pay for it. He was so street-wise, his game management exceptional. When you hear people say, 'These guys will come back from this Lions tour as better players,' it's because of the likes of Lawrence. You couldn't help but learn from how he worked and played, but most of all from his attitude. When Lawrence played for England or the Lions, nothing else in the world mattered.

Despite his loss, and our defeat by the Maori, we arrive at the Test series without further incident. There is a lot of comment about the size of our squad and, consequently, the lack of opportunity for players to stake a claim for Test selection. There is also a widespread view that this is not an evolving Test XV, rather one that Clive pre-selected before leaving home, featuring the spine of his World Cup-winning England team two years earlier rather than the Wales side that won the Grand Slam just a couple of months ago.

A QUESTION OF TIMING

A week later, before the series opener in Christchurch, captain Brian O'Driscoll addresses the state of the Power of Four nation. 'We are building nicely to where we want to be,' he says. 'There's no need for any panic stations. This Lions squad has never lost a Test series in New Zealand, we've got to be fresh-minded and optimistic. We are a better team than four years ago. We have some real rugby greats in this team. The pressure is on the All Blacks.' Hmm, but what else was he going to say? A captain is never going to come out publicly and say there are things wrong on the trip. He is always going to put on a brave face. There is a huge amount of pressure on him as skipper. We all know we are about to take on the best of the best. Having to get your own preparation and performance right is enough of an ask, challenging the management and their processes along the way is a distraction you can do without. For the record, Brian was a very good captain under enormous pressure. I don't think he was in on team selection or even wanted to get involved in the dynamics of the process moving towards the first Test.

He has no say, either, in that decision to perform a response to the haka.

I try to imagine Martin Johnson agreeing to this. I can't. Not in a million years. I should say something, because experience has taught me you don't change your routine and do something out of the ordinary before the biggest games. But I don't. I think back to my pre-tour pledge. 'Keep your head down, wind your neck in and just concentrate on your rugby.' I remember why I took that oath – because I was on an exceptionally thin layer of ice with the Lions after what happened in 2001. Although I kept a private diary and would vent my frustrations there, this time it most definitely would not be for public consumption.

My only concession to public comment is a column I have

agreed to write for the *New Zealand Herald*, which I took on specifically as a vehicle for saying only positive things and because not only do I want to show my critics – of which there were many – that I can write a column without being negative, I am also determined to prove to the Lions' hierarchy that I am now grown up enough to be trusted again.

First Test: New Zealand 21, British and Irish Lions 3
Christchurch, 25 June 2005

Three hundred and fifty thousand Lions jerseys have been sold ahead of the series, a number bettered in the global replica shirts market only by Real Madrid and Manchester United. Anticipation is huge, fuelled by Clive urging Lions fans to rush out to New Zealand because something special is about to happen.

Not for us it's not. We line up for the haka, Brian does his bit, and the All Blacks look at us with an expression that does not suggest gratitude at the respect we believe we have just paid to their heritage. The game kicks off and within forty seconds play is stopped. As Brian O'Driscoll goes to drive through a ruck he is driven back, first by hooker Keven Mealamu and then, almost immediately, by Tana Umaga. Each lifts one of Brian's legs aloft and he comes down head first, avoiding actually landing on his head only by putting out an arm at the last second. His shoulder immediately dislocates. His tour is over.

'I had never been upended like that before in a rugby match,' Brian would later write in his book. 'Was I speared? I think so. Slam-dunked is probably the expression which sums it up the best. Not that it makes much difference – even if they just dropped me they were reckless as to whether I broke my neck or not.'

A QUESTION OF TIMING

The following morning his emotions would be red raw and who can blame him. 'There is a huge feeling of frustration and anger about the way it happened. I have absolutely no doubt that some sort of spear tackle ended my tour. It was completely unnecessary and certainly beyond the laws of the game. I have no way of knowing if the tackles were premeditated, but after only a few seconds (of the match) you can't help feeling more aggrieved.'

As Brian is carted away on the back of a golf buggy, Justin Marshall, All Black scrum-half and an all-round good guy, comes over and wishes him well. He is the only player on his team to do so. 'That should have been a common courtesy from one captain to another,' Drico would later say. 'So maybe there was an element of malice in it.' The game continues and Paul O'Connell is sent to the sin-bin, then Richard Hill wrecks the anterior cruciate ligament in his knee and his tour is also at an end. By the time the final whistle goes we have been beaten out of sight, and we are angry – an emotion that only grows when citing officer William Venter decides against referring the matter to the judicial panel, but he does cite Danny Grewcock for allegedly biting Mealamu. Dan strenuously denies it but is still kicked off the tour.

From this point until the end of the trip there is no other topic of conversation than how Brian was treated and how those responsible got away with it. Every day we are briefed on what we should and should not say. It becomes all-encompassing and a distraction. Danny's two-month ban only heightens our sense of injustice. The All Blacks are unrepentant, but fair play to the *New Zealand Herald* for penning the following words in an editorial:

It was, at the very least, a reckless and dangerous act. As such it was unbecoming of a man (Tana Umaga) who won plaudits for stopping play to tend to the unconscious Colin Charvis during a Test in Hamilton. It may even have been malicious. O'Driscoll's anger seemed directed as much at the All Blacks' reaction as the tackle itself. Quite reasonably he suggested it should have been a matter of 'common courtesy' for Umaga to check the condition of the opposing captain before he was taken by stretcher from the field. It is indeed unfathomable that a player of the All Blacks' captain's reputation did not extend that courtesy.

The recriminations following that first Test are not directed solely at the home camp. The Lions get it in the neck too, from one of their own, Welsh full-back legend JPR Williams. 'This tour has cost about ten million pounds and what have they got to show for it? All that money for nothing,' he is quoted as saying in a newspaper. Of more immediate concern to me is our lineout. The eighty minutes in Christchurch are calamitous for the Lions in that department. We lose eleven on our own throw.

The reason is that we went into the game with the most complex set of calls I have ever known – so complex that the players didn't understand them. They involved not only numbers and places but clubs of the players involved. Yet still that didn't necessarily mean the throw would go to that particular player. For example, if the throw was meant for Munster's Paul O'Connell, we might say Neath and a number. You're thinking a Welsh target but it was the 'N' of Munster to which the call referred. And if there was a number before or after the word, it would denote if he was going forward, straight up or back. It was phenomenally difficult but given that the Australians had cracked our code before the third

A QUESTION OF TIMING

Test in 2001, with decisive consequences, that was fair enough. We'd rehearsed them for weeks and just about understood them. The problem came on the Wednesday before the first Test when it was decided New Zealand knew our moves and we should change everything.

I remember being on a pitch at a college in Christchurch on the Thursday with Paul O'Connell referring to a piece of paper on which the codes were written. Our hooker Shane Byrne had the same. Two days before the first Test on supposedly the best organised of all Lions tours, no one knew where the ball was going.

As we move on to Wellington for the second Test and try to pick up the pieces, nobody hides from the touchline shambles. 'Our decision to change our lineout calls came back to haunt us,' admits Brian O'Driscoll. 'In hindsight that was suicide,' adds prop Graham Rowntree.

Forwards coach Andy Robinson says, 'We got our lineout communication wrong. We failed to get players in the air. It looked as though they could read our moves before we threw and we could not read their calls.' I'd say that pretty much sums it up! Professional rugby players will never admit defeat, no matter the circumstances, but I can't help feeling we are now chasing a lost cause.

We try to put the Test behind us and move on but it is difficult when our lineout has embarrassed us, one of our mates has been banned for a biting offence he insists he didn't commit, our captain has been forced out of the tour and another has career-threatening knee-ligament damage.

A clearly crestfallen Clive concedes, 'We let a lot of people down including ourselves. Test losses usually come down to a couple of things: the lineout or the scrum. In our case it was the lineout.

We made a strong lineout selection but this area was the disappointment.'

Were we right to be so paranoid about our code falling into enemy hands? Possibly, but not to the extent we took it. We were all aware New Zealand were doing whatever they possibly could to get some kind of intel on us ahead of the series. The country is rugby bonkers and I really wouldn't be surprised had they gone to the extremes of bugging certain places. That must have been a concern to the management, too, because they had rooms checked and double checked before we used them. I suppose that created a paranoia.

So here we are in Wellington in need of a pick-me-up. It comes with the appointment of Gareth Thomas as captain, in place of poor old Brian. Alfie, as he is known to one and all, immediately lifts the camp with his unique brand of humour and left-field take on life. He arrived late on tour, missing the first four matches to complete the French club championship season with Toulouse, but quickly became the life and soul. He is very different from Brian, not quite as eloquent or specific, but he perfectly captures the rawness of what we are about to do. We're a team of lads who don't really know each other too well and we are heading into the All Blacks' lair. Alfie tells the coaches to back off a little, arguing that we need to do less training and keep our powder dry. He calls us into a lot of huddles, pulls us tight, and time and again speaks from the heart. You can see in his eyes how much it means to him and you want to follow him. The tone of his message is not dissimilar to many of Martin Johnson's. 'F*** whatever else is going on in your life away from this field, what is important right now is that these twenty-one boys next to you are going to throw body and soul into

this game. Are you going to let them down? Of course you're not.'
Come Saturday, who scores the first try of the match? You've
guessed it. Alfie.

For all his inspirational effort, our morale is fragile. In identifying
reasons for this, one episode stands tall in my mind. It involves our
spin doctor Alastair Campbell and a talk he gives the squad a
couple of days prior to the second Test.

For reasons known only to Alastair, he thinks it a good idea to
compare our tour of duty with that of soldiers in Iraq. His theme is
that we players might think we are on a battlefield but we're not.
The guys in Iraq are on a battlefield and when soldiers lose, they
die. He suggests we lack desire and tries to use the example of a
theatre of war to put our situation into perspective. For him to
pretend that (a) he knows what we are going through, and (b) he
knows what those brave soldiers are going through is, to my mind,
both distasteful and inappropriate.

We don't heckle him. Rugby players tend to be a respectful
bunch and if you are asked to address the group, we will give you
the courtesy of being heard out. Unless, of course, you personally
insult someone. But as he talks I look around the room and
everyone's expression is one of disbelief. I am getting angry inside.
There are people who come in and deliver motivational messages
by talking about themselves in a way that resonates with you
as a sportsman, enabling you to pick out bits that lift you mentally
and make you a better competitor, at least for the next twenty-four
to forty-eight hours. This does none of the above and at the end we
are bristling.

My considered observation? What the f*** has that got to do
with us playing at the weekend?

Why has he chosen this moment to say that? We're 1–0 down in a series and we know deep down that, however tight-knit we are as a group, our chances of winning are slim unless we can find from somewhere another 5 to 10 per cent. So why, given that, would you put Alastair Campbell in front of the boys with a message like that? Does it give us the added motivation we require? Do I really need to answer that question?

Until that moment I actually didn't mind him. He got a lot of flak from the media but that was pretty much irrelevant to me. Clive wanted the best people around him, be they players, management or PR. He'd seen what Campbell did for Tony Blair and he must have thought to himself, 'If he can do that for the Prime Minister, he is going to do an amazing job for us.' It's not for me to say whether it was a vanity call or not. Clive had not got too much wrong in the time I had known him. If he wanted Alastair, why not? Without giving away any state secrets, he was quite candid about the political world in which he worked and initially I found him fascinating to listen to. Until, that is, The Speech.

It would be overdoing it to claim that as the turning point in the tour but, my goodness, it didn't help. I still can't believe he had the gall to say it, and that he was given permission by the management to address us in the first place. It left me asking, 'Where am I? What am I doing?'

If that was not surreal enough, I spend the following afternoon in a local coffee shop with Prince William and his entourage. The Prince is in town for the second Test and I've got to know him and his brother Harry over the years while playing for England. We drink lattes and eat cake and generally chill out. Can't imagine him being able to do that in many places in the world. We chat about how the tour is going and about life in general. He is relaxed and very at ease in the environment, just like a regular twenty-three-year-old. I remind him of the time Prince Harry came to Twickenham to watch England play Scotland six years before, and how, because I gave him my shirt after the game and showed him around the home changing room with my then girlfriend Natalie, he sent me this lovely letter.

'Thank you both so much for a lovely day, I really enjoyed it,' wrote Harry, who was fourteen at the time. 'The food was delicious and it was really nice to meet everybody. By far the best thing was the shirt. It was so nice of you to give it to me, especially with Twickenham dirt and your sweat. I haven't washed it yet and Nick Scott, who came with me, is my proof. I worship it every night! I am very happy to be playing No. 9 as you are. I hope to be getting tickets for the 20th against France, with help from Jayne (Woodward). I am definitely really looking forward to seeing you again and I really really hope that you kick France's butts. Thank you very much again and thanks for looking after us and introducing us to everyone. Lots of love from Harry.'

Coffee finished, William and his group depart, wishing me and the boys good luck for the second Test. We might just need it. Although the midweek team have stuck 109 points on Manawatu, with Shane Williams helping himself to five tries to book his Test jersey, I don't need to be told that Saturday's game is unlikely to have too much in common.

Very seldom have I ever watched the opposition, or any player on the other team, with such admiration as I do Dan Carter in the second Test. His is one of the great international performances by a fly-half. He helps himself to thirty-three points in the 'Cake Tin' stadium as New Zealand win 48–18 to clinch the series. I can't remember him ever playing that well before or after. This is the day the mantle of world's best No. 10 is passed from Jonny Wilkinson, who has held it for five years, to the All Blacks fly-half, or five-eighth. And if I'm honest, Carter takes it to a new level, scoring two tries and kicking nine goals as New Zealand recover from going an early try down to lead 21–13 at half-time, before pulling away to post a record score against the Lions.

Carter's attacking game as well as his strategic kicking and defence is without flaw. It is often an exaggeration to say an individual runs the show in an international rugby match. The truth is usually less simplistic. Not on this day. He is that good. As much as we play with great endeavour, the only player we have capable of reaching the heights he does in this game is Brian O'Driscoll, who was in the stands with his arm in a sling. And doesn't the world know about it, after a week-long PR counter-offensive.

The upshot of this is that rather than Tana Umaga feeling slightly intimidated by events in Christchurch, the stick aimed at him has the effect of empowering him and his team mates. They are galvanised by the media attack and it is their captain who scores their go-ahead try. His players mob him. Quite simply, we do not have enough fuel in the tank to repel what the All Blacks bombard us with. I later conclude that although we had some really good players in our squad, there were not enough great ones at the top of their form to live with New Zealand. In the third Test the following week, Umaga will bag two more tries. The 'O'Driscoll Affair' is clearly a PR own goal. That said, how the hell did Umaga and Mealamu not get banned?

The series lost, the only crumb of comfort is provided by the midweek team, for whom I finally start against Auckland. Ian McGeechan is the midweek coach and, needless to say, does a top job. We call ourselves the 'Midweek Massive' and before the game Geech gives us all T-shirts with the name written across the front.

A QUESTION OF TIMING

There is a feeling of unity and togetherness in our group, which is reflected in the results. The MM win five out of five.

Super Gav

The morning after the Auckland game I have to be up early because I am on the bench for the weekend and there is a training session for the Test twenty-two. I jump in the lift and there is Gavin Henson with a friend.

'How did it go last night?' asks Gav.

'What do you mean?'

'What was the score. Did we win?'

'You what?'

'Oh I didn't bother going to the game. I just went out with some of my mates.'

I had shared a room with him at the Vale of Glamorgan hotel before we flew out and thought he was a top man. Except for one thing. There was never a clean towel for me to use. Every day he would get up two hours early to prepare himself. For most rugby players this involves a quick shower half an hour before being due on parade. Not Gav. He would go into the bathroom and every single morning shave his legs and apply fake tan. He would then start on his hair. I kid you not, the whole room was full of cosmetics. Finally, he would come out, say good morning, and head out. I would then get up, go to the bathroom and find all the towels had been used and were completely orange. The place was an absolute bomb site.

Still, that was Gav and I could cope with that. But not turning up for a Lions match was poor form.

'We won by the way.'

'Oh great,' he replies, as the lift door opens. 'Catch you later.'

* * *

Like me, Gav succumbed to the temptation to compete in *Strictly Come Dancing*. Unlike me, he seemed to have a ball, reaching the semi-finals in 2010. Four years earlier I had hated the early stages of the competition and longed either to be eliminated or just to walk out. Although there was no repeat of my eve-of-competition panic attack, I did not enjoy being what I'm clearly not until I sat down to talk about it with former Manchester United goalkeeper Peter Schmeichel, who was also uncomfortable with the experience. We laughed at how we coped fine with Rugby World Cup finals and Champions League finals but could not handle a bit of Saturday night pantomime, and decided it was ridiculous to get so stressed out by what amounted really to nothing more than a bit of fun. 'Why don't we just throw ourselves into this? We've got nothing to lose,' said Peter. 'Why don't we ham it up and see where it takes us?'

From that moment on we both started to enjoy the show for what it is. I came to work with a smile on my face rather than a frown. Whereas before I would picture how I wanted the dance to look and, as far as I was concerned, fail utterly to replicate it, I stopped worrying about that. I still worked all hours with my dance partner Lilia, but with a more relaxed attitude I started to see the routine in my mind and remember the steps. We reached the final and finished runner-up to England and Surrey cricketer Mark Ramprakash.

MY *STRICTLY COME DANCING* XV

15) Bruce Forsyth (captain)
14) Anton Du Beke

13) Anne Widdecombe

12) Team Logan (Gabby and Kenny)

11) Peter Schmeichel

10) Lilia Kopylova

9)   Ian Waite

1)   James Jordan

2)   Brendan Cole

3)   Emma Bunton

4)   Gavin Henson

5)   Gary Rhodes

6)   Phil Tufnell

7)   Elaine Paige

8)   Austin Healey

15) Bruce Forsyth (captain)

The *Strictly* 'Godfather'. An absolute showman in front of the camera and my idea of a perfect granddad behind it. I loved the fact he always kept a throat lozenge in a little box in his jacket and before going on stage he would take a few licks of the sweet to loosen his vocal chords. He'd then prance on stage like a teenager with co-host Tess Daly. Admittedly, his auto cue was twice the font size Tess required, but age showed no signs of wearying him. He is a consummate professional and his ability to laugh at himself, after all he has achieved in life, was a lesson to us all.

14) Anton Du Beke

You have to admire Anton's stamina. Ten series of *Strictly Come Dancing* and all he has to show for it is one bronze medal! No one works harder with such tricky celebrities. My highlight will always be his time with Ann Widdecombe, when he responded to the challenge with humour and great showmanship to make an awkward, uncoordinated women move like Ginger Rogers. Saturday night television has to be entertaining and Anton embraces that challenge every year.

13) Ann Widdecombe

At the time Ann was flying high on *Strictly Come Dancing*, Sue Barker, Phil Tufnell and I were on the *A Question of Sport* tour. Sue is a huge *Strictly* fan and Phil and I also love to watch it behind closed doors. Each Saturday night the audience to our show were left wondering why our warm-up act, Andy Collins, put in a longer shift. It was because we refused to leave the Green Room until Ann and Anton had been on. The night she flew into the studio like a budgie on a perch I thought I'd die laughing.

12) Team Logan (Gabby and Kenny)

The rugby theme continued the series after mine, with ex-Scotland star Kenny Logan and his lovely and hugely talented wife Gabby going head-to-head. All eyes were on Gabby, who looked fabulous and danced amazingly well, but the British viewing public, being the mischievous souls they are, decided to keep Kenny instead. I can only imagine what Saturday nights were like in the Logan household after Kenny had been voted through to another week courtesy of some sort of Highland jig. Gabby's expression was a picture!

11) Peter Schmeichel

The man who helped me through those initial doubts and worries. Peter survived through to the weekend of his fortieth birthday, which he intended to celebrate by performing his favourite ballroom routine. Unfortunately, he got the Cuban heel the day before and had to make do with a birthday cake from me.

10) Lilia Kopylova

Lilia should be higher on the list because I'm not sure anybody else could have put up with me six hours a day for four months. My relaxed manner drove my Russian partner bonkers. Many people state how erotic some of the Latin dances look and believe me it can be a bit hot under the collar in training. While practising a certain samba move involving me being behind Lilia and being 'connected' in the hip area, we had to bend over and gyrate. Now I'm only human and therefore made plenty of mistakes with my footwork in order to repeat the move over and over. Twice I had to take a drink break when I wasn't thirsty. On the second of those she asked why I was facing the wall while sipping my water!

9) Ian Waite

The man who helped me find my camp side on *Strictly*. Yes, that was part of my *SCD* education as I needed to embrace the tight pink lycra and sequins in order to progress. My only gripe with him was that he claimed to have tablets that helped regenerate hair growth on one's barnet, and wouldn't share them. 'Daws,' said Ian sensitively. 'I'm afraid it's too late for you.'

1) James Jordan

Nice lad is James. We took a while to find common ground but a bit of a dust-up did the job. Brendan Cole was the show's resident bad boy but James fancied the title and went about his teaching in a military fashion. Poor Georgina Bouzova had a tough enough day job, saving lives and nursing children back to health in the TV show *Casualty* – she didn't need a dance partner giving her grief to make her foxtrot more foxy. I joked in an interview that Georgina wasn't allowed any sweets and produced a bag of chocolate for her to scoff. It was a bit of fun but did not go down well with the pro, who said as much afterwards in the foyer of TV Centre. I squared up to him, told him to get a grip and said if he really wanted to show how much of a man he was, to pick on me. It was a touch embarrassing but no handbags were thrown and it cleared the air.

2) Brendan Cole

The appeal of *Strictly* is so much more than a dancing competition. It's the comedy, the embarrassment, the surprise, the journey, and above all the gossip – and Brendan always tended to be at the centre of that Romances with contestants, arguments with judges, getting his own steps wrong are all on his CV, but my favourite Brendan memory came when I was backstage watching him and actress Claire King perform the samba. There he was, lost in the moment, performing this Latin American routine with eyes only for his gorgeous partner. Er, no actually that's not true. He was glancing over her shoulder to a group of girls in the audience and winking provocatively. Later that evening I saw him exchanging numbers with them in the bar. He had pulled while dancing the samba with somebody else, live on the BBC in front of ten million viewers. Stand up and take a bow my friend.

3) Emma Bunton

Ah the lovely Emma. When I was swinging my pants to *Wannabe* in Northampton's Cinderellas nightclub back in the nineties, little did I know I'd one day befriend Baby Spice; nor that I'd be in one of her music videos posing with a gorgeous dancer, looking all 007.

A QUESTION OF TIMING

Every Saturday morning we would meet for a run-through in Studio One at the Beeb and, as I was always positioned next to her, Emma and I would share a bacon roll and catch up on our routines. She naturally took pity on me as I was hopeless, but to my eternal gratitude she never let on.

4) Gavin Henson

The third British and Irish Lion to succumb to the bright lights and shiny floor. Gav definitely looked the part and was actually required to wear some of his fake tan in order to fit in! Like a few before him (Austin Healey, Mark Foster, Mark Ramprakash, Ricky Whittle) he liked to show off his upper torso but, fair play to the guy, he had a vision. By taking part in the most popular programme on British TV, minus his shirt, he then found himself starring in a dating show where he was the only man dating twenty plus women in Monaco. You have to admire that level of fitness and dedication to your job. I know it would be beyond me, even in my prime. If I ever had one.

5) Gary Rhodes

Sometimes *Strictly* just gives you special moments, which for the right or wrong reasons stick in your memory for ever. One of Britain's most-loved chefs pretending to play either piano or guitar – I'm still not sure which – on Karen Hardy's back was one of those. Even thinking about it now makes my toes curl. It wasn't the choreography but Gary's total lack of coordination. Yet in his mind he was absolutely nailing it. I'm going to YouTube it right now to check I'm not being harsh . . . no, I'm not!

6) Phil Tufnell

Maybe there needs to be a specific category for Tuffers, *'Strictly's* Toughest Celebrities'. The Cat actually had major surgery on a Tuesday before dancing. All those years of diving around in the outfield, taking amazing catches and stopping boundaries, finally caught up with my feline friend. The combination of seven-hours-a-day training and the rigours of professional dance moves gave the man no choice but to nip in to the local hospital for a knee op. A quick tidy-up of the cartilage and old snake hips was back swinging his bits around the floor. God help us.

7) Elaine Paige

Without fail the most popular question asked of me by women is 'Do you still dance?' My stock response is only at weddings and barmitzvahs but even then it would have to involve a bottle of Chardonnay and a partner who knew what she was doing. Unfortunately, that's exactly what Elaine Paige was hoping for when she was paired with me for *Sport Relief does Strictly Come Dancing*. From the moment we met in a studio in Fulham, we giggled our way through a tango routine. The problem was that the tango is fierce, mean and moody, so Elaine's high-pitched laughs and my Cheshire cat grin, to say the least, lacked conviction. It was then I realised how much I had relied on Lilia to drag me around the floor when we were competing in *Strictly*. Trying to lead someone is bloody difficult, particularly when that person is four foot eleven and you haven't got a clue what your next step is.

8) Austin Healey

Last but not least my old mucker Austin. Knowing no rugby player had lifted the Glitter Ball, he went the extra mile to become the first. When he phoned me in the summer of 2008 to ask for a little advice, I encouraged him to don the spats and swing the hips. Knowing him as I do, I thought it best also to mark his card that as the competition is about impressing the voting public rather than his fellow contestants, he should play the modest, unassuming card rather than the chirpy know-it-all Merseysider. He thanked me for the advice, and promptly ignored it. By week two he was oiled up and bronzed like Atlas, wearing the tightest see-through top possible. The first shot was of him standing behind Tess Daly tensing his biceps, which he'd named 'Con' and 'Crete'. I shook my head as I imagined a nation of elderly women deleting his voting number from their speed dial.

The midweek programme complete, some of the lads head to Queenstown, New Zealand's adventure capital, for a couple of days rest and recuperation. It's a well-deserved opportunity to kick back after an arduous six weeks – a spell in which I can count the really good times on one hand. I went on a helicopter tour of Wellington. On my own. I went on a hot-air balloon flight over Christchurch, again on my own, and first thing in the morning in order to get back in time for afternoon training. Scotland hooker Gordon Bulloch, who led the team to victory over Auckland and had a decent game, returns to the team hotel the night before the third Test feeling knackered and a little hungover. The following morning he gets a tap on the shoulder.

'You're on the bench, Gordie. Steve Thompson has pulled out.'

This was another Lions tour in which the injury count was ridiculous. We seemed to haemorrhage players. By the end I made the total number of lads selected by the 2005 Lions fifty-one. Alfie Thomas and Josh Lewsey were the only backs to start all three

Tests; Gethin Jenkins, Julian White and Paul O'Connell the three forwards. Josh played on the left wing in the third Test, the third different number he wore in the series. We lost the game 38–19, conceding five tries to one, and Dan Carter wasn't playing.

It was time to face the music. A BBC online poll at the end of the series wanted to know the main reason for the Lions' whitewash? Nearly 100,000 people responded. The results, in reverse order, were as follows:

6% – Lions squad too big
6% – Injuries to key players
30% – Clive Woodward's selections
58% – All Blacks just too good

New Zealand were not about to disagree, telling the Lions we were playing a brand of rugby that was basically past its sell-by date. 'The game has moved on,' was how forwards coach Steve Hansen put it. 'You now need a multi-dimensional game. I don't think you can pick a great big forward pack and a kicking nine and ten and win rugby games unless you play in a blizzard.'

There is an element of truth to that, but I don't think the Lions were alone. Defences had become too good, everyone was super fit and strong and the All Blacks were first to recognise that the time had come to start playing some rugby. The days of purely out-muscling a team for eighty minutes were gone. We learned that lesson the hard way.

When I think of the 2005 tour, what springs to mind? Probably that I don't think we ever stood a chance. We were up against a world-beating opponent and we had a lot of players, including myself, at the end of our careers. Some of us had been on a couple of Lions tours before, and maybe no longer quite had the mental capacity to win down in New Zealand. The scorelines in the Test series reflect that: 3–21, 18–48, 19–38.

From an England perspective, there were a lot of things we'd seen from Clive before. He thought he could drop back a couple of steps, introduce the Celtic nations into our way of thinking and bring them up to speed in time for the series. It turned out to be wishful thinking. His way of operating took a good four years to be fully taken on board by the England players, before we ended up using it to win a World Cup. The Lions had a week together in Wales, then five weeks on the road in New Zealand. With so little time we needed to depend more on instinct, as would be the case in 2009.

Maybe I should have said more. I was one of the senior players and, remember, Clive had picked my brains on scrum-half selection right at the start. But it's always difficult working out how brutally honest you can, and should, be with the man in charge. As I have learned the hard way, there is a very fine line between being constructive and being considered treacherous. The other point I would make is that with Clive, I was so used to him getting things right. In the seven years I played under him with England pretty much everything was spot on. Clive's style is not to skimp. Clive does all-singing, all-dancing productions, where money is no issue. A World Cup and a knighthood tells you he knows what he's doing.

I expected consultants to be brought in. I expected someone like Alastair Campbell to be the media liaison manager rather than any old PR guy. I expected to have loads of coaches and fitness people, masseurs, kit men, bus driver, chef, the whole shooting match. So there's no way I can now say I knew before the trip that 2005 was going to be a failure. We had been flogged to death on the training ground in 2001. The England players, in particular, didn't care for Graham Henry's methods because they were so different from what we knew under Clive, and I'm sure that reluctance to get our hands dirty and just get on with it like we did in 1997 was down to that cultural difference. So Clive would have recognised that trying to bring everyone into his, and England's, world was the way forward. He had the very best of intentions but, ultimately, was undone by lack of time.

That, and the fact the New Zealand team we faced was an all-time great one, even if it would be another six years before they won the World Cup. Richie McCaw, Dan Carter, Sitiveni Sivivatu, Doug Howlett, Aaron Mauger, Conrad Smith, Justin Marshall, Byron Kelleher . . . the list goes on and on. I never played against a stronger All Blacks team. There was no need to feel embarrassed. It never reached a point that I thought, 'People are going to remember us getting stuffed by the All Blacks for ever.' The players gave it their absolute all, but if you're going to win in New Zealand everything has to be 100 per cent right. Everything. If you are even a half percentage off, you're dead.

MY BEST LIONS' OPPOSITION XV

15) *Matt Burke*
14) *Joe Roff*
13) *Tana Umaga*
12) *Aaron Mauger*
11) *Sitiveni Sivivatu*
10) *Dan Carter*
9) *Joost van der Westhuizen*
1) *Os du Randt*

2) *Keven Mealamu*

3) *Carl Hayman*

4) *John Eales*

5) *Mark Andrews*

6) *Richie McCaw*

7) *George Smith*

8) *Gary Teichmann*

15) **Matt Burke** (2001 Wallabies)

I came across Matt on my first appearance at Twickenham for England in 1991. I was playing for England 18-age group and he was playing for the Grand Slam-bound Australian Schools team. I was running around like a headless chicken, so excited to be making my debut at Headquarters, whereas Matt was calm and composed, one of two superstar backs in the Aussie side, along with Peter Jorgensen, who would later go to rugby league.

Jorgensen had scored in each of the previous Home Nations matches and did so again against us, showcasing the strength and speed that would woo NRL coaches back home. He ran rings around us if I'm honest, but as much as he was the executioner, the brains of the operation came from the tall Burke, comfortable with ball in hand, strong in contact and possessing a boot Gavin Hastings would have been proud to call his own. I couldn't have imagined I would play against this guy for the next fifteen years of my life. Just as well, mind. The thought would have depressed me. On the Lions tour in 2001 the Wallabies were under all sorts of pressure after losing the first Test in Brisbane. Matt was given the unenviable task of shutting down the rampant Lions' back line. Sure enough the home defence was rock solid and he also dealt comfortably with the aerial bombardment. Without wishing to massage his ego too much, Matt was as close to a backs version of our immortal flanker Richard Hill as you could get.

14) Joe Roff (2001 Wallabies)

So relaxed he was horizontal. Not only in his languid running style but generally in the way he played his rugby. Think golfer Freddie Couples and you'll get the idea. The defining moment in the 2001 Lions series was his interception in the second half to bring the Australians back into the game, turning the whole momentum of the series. Joe would glide around the field picking wonderful lines off the midfield and would never go to ground, preferring to offload and continue the passage of play. He had a cultured left foot and when he was in the mood everything he touched turned to the colour of his national jersey.

13) Tana Umaga (2005 All Blacks)

'The Predator'. Unmistakeable in his appearance and just as noticeable with a rugby ball in hand playing for his beloved All Blacks. He will have to live with being remembered by many for his role in the 2005 Brian O'Driscoll incident but that should not erase an otherwise stunning career. He was the centrepiece in a back line that ripped the Lions apart on that tour.

12) Aaron Mauger (2005 All Blacks)

I sometimes think national teams in the northern hemisphere miss a trick when it comes to understanding the importance of a true footballer in the centres. Even though we have one of the greatest rugby players of all time in Brian O'Driscoll, the vast majority of teams up here steer towards the smash and bash approach. But look at Lions selections as far back as 1989 and the picture is different. It's all about balance. To enable players such as Manu Tuilagi, Scott Gibbs, Rob Henderson and Jamie Roberts to be effective, there has to be the brains and guile of a Jerry Guscott, Will Greenwood or O'Driscoll to complement it.

We get it at the very top level but the Kiwis see it as standard. They realise that the fly-half, or five-eighth, is under so much pressure from back rows that you need a playmaking inside-centre to share the load – to be his second pair of eyes and ears – which brings me to one of my favourite all-time players. Aaron Mauger was a joy to watch. Not so much fun to play against, but fabulous to admire from the stands. Yes he played with a formidable fly-half in Dan Carter but like our very own Jonny Wilkinson, who had Will Greenwood pulling the strings alongside him, Carter benefited hugely from Mauger's influence.

His delivery and communication was world class, he was almost a commentator as the match developed in order that his team mates knew exactly where to be and what to do. I bet All Blacks' coaches Wayne Smith and Graham Henry were gutted when he signed for Leicester; the Tigers, on the other hand, should be congratulated on one of the shrewdest overseas signings of them all.

11) Sitiveni Sivivatu (2005 All Blacks)

This guy plays a completely different sport from me. I never got close enough even to appreciate his electric speed and dazzling step. My memory of playing against him is running a covering line as any good sweeper should but, in this case, knowing I had absolutely no chance of altering the inevitable outcome. At best I could keep him from running under the posts so that the kicker would have a tougher conversion. But as the kicker was Dan Carter that, too, amounted to a waste of effort.

Still, every time I hear his name it makes me smile because I am reminded of my seasoned BBC colleague and rugby correspondent Ian Robertson who, for some unexplained reason, always uses his full name in commentary. I can hear it now ... 'Carter, miss pass to Nonu, who barges his way through the line and pops it to Sitiveni Sivivatu. Only one man to beat. Sitiveni Sivivatu going for the corner. Sitiveni Sivivatu will score. Nobody can stop Sitiveni Sivivatu.' Takes one to know one. When Robbo gets going no one can stop him either.

10) Dan Carter (2005 All Blacks)

Without a doubt one of the greatest fly-halves ever to play the game. Some national treasures and greats may be viewed with a slight bias, but no one in the world can argue that this fella is not a magician with the oval ball. I played against him in Dunedin on England's first tour as world champions in 2004. We had a decent side still and as World Cup holders and the No.1 ranked nation, we were considered a prized scalp. We looked at their line-up – the back line read Muliaina, Howlett, Umaga, Carter, Rokokoku, Spencer and Marshall – and we identified one weakness. You've guessed it, the young buck in midfield. Carter was inexperienced, a bit lightweight, a No. 10 playing out of position. You can also probably guess what happened next. We lost 36–3 and DC was sensational. He ghosted around, off-loading effortlessly to the big runners, then he would change gear and run some beautiful angles and arcs of which Philippe Sella would be proud. At the end his shirt was neither sweaty nor muddy. In fact I reckon the only dirt on him was the mark on his knee cap where he knelt down to fix the ball on the kicking tee before slotting three conversions from three, and five penalties from all angles. Each one was followed by that slow, lolloping jog back to his half, which became so familiar to us over his next 1,400 Test points.

For 2004 was just the start. I'm still to see a more complete performance from a fly-half against the Lions than his in the second Test in Wellington the following year. Remember the audacious run down the wing and chip and chase to beat his old foe Wilkinson to the touchdown, the shake-and-bake he showed Gavin Henson to set up the first try for his skipper Tana Umaga? What about his kicking display that night in the Cake Tin stadium, a notoriously difficult place for goalkickers due to the way the wind swirls around inside it.

When Dan was a child, his father bought him a set of black and white goal posts for his eighth birthday. The family lived in a small town called Southbridge on the South Island, and they had a long, narrow forty-metre strip of garden down the side of the house. It was there he spent his childhood, perfecting his kicking, and as the birthdays rolled by he took the tee back further and further. Accuracy was not an issue so he moved on to distance. Metre by metre he kept moving the tee back until he ran out of grass. Did he stop? No, he simply left his garden, went across the road and set up on the other side. The posts are still in the garden, by the way, so expect his son Marco to be teeing the ball up some time soon.

9) Joost van der Westhuizen (1997 Springboks)

When I came across Joost for the first time in 1997, he was a World Cup winner and the poster boy of South African rugby. His speed and strength were way beyond that of anybody I had ever played against, his ability to find holes around the fringes world class. He caused havoc in the first Lions' Test and we spent hours in meeting rooms and on the training field trying to work out a way to do something about it. We drilled ourselves not to buy any of his dummies or 'show-and-go's and in Durban the following week I watched him like a hawk, analysing his body language, monitoring his eye movements. I spent the game screaming, 'No dummies, no dummies!' to keep our forwards on high alert around the fringes of rucks. He still scored their first try, but that's what you do when you have the speed of a cheetah off the mark and an ability to duck through tackles as though you are coated in Vaseline.

He was the ultimate battler on the field and as I write he is showing the same qualities in his fight against motor neurone disease. I met Joost at a fundraising dinner in early 2013 and although physically he was unrecognisable, his smile and piercing blue eyes were as sharp and cheeky as ever. He mentioned in a TV interview that he has never forgiven me for throwing the dummy on him and his mates in the first Test of the Lions series in 1997. I take that as a big compliment from a man who ran riot for more than ten years and is now showing even more strength than that displayed by his 1995 World Cup-winning team. A true inspiration.

1) Os du Randt (1997 Springboks)

The rock on which South Africa's scrum was built in the 1997 Lions series. We all remember Scott Gibbs' unbelievable hit on him, but part of the reason that was so special was because he was such a key player for them, and symbolically it had great meaning. We gave Os a huge amount of attention in the build-up to the '97 series. I can't remember another time that I played against a team and paid so much attention to one of its props. Half-backs or open-side, maybe, but not a prop. In many respects, Os was the key to the series. If he was stable, the consensus was the rest of the South

African scrummage would monster us, which is why Paul Wallace had such a specific role to nullify him and, to be fair to Wally, by the end of the second Test we actually got the nudge on a little bit. That was some achievement as at the start we were shaken to the core by the rampaging home forwards flying into rucks. It was brutal that game and I was close to being scared of what was going to happen. We held on by our fingernails for much of the game, unable to get out of our own half. How I managed to survive eighty minutes I have no idea.

2) **Keven Mealamu** (2005 All Blacks)

People use the analogy in sport that running into a solid defender is like running into a brick wall. In Keven Mealamu's case it certainly was. Normally when you run into another human, there is a certain amount of give. You can work your way out of positions and bounce off them. Not Mealamu. He was like granite, a boulder, nothing soft on him at all. I knew if he got a forearm on me, I was going to go down. A couple of times he caught me in the bottom of a ruck. On one of those occasions he got me round the neck and put the squeeze on to the point I think I was turning blue! He was someone I would go out of my way to avoid. Even if there was half a gap I wouldn't really fancy taking it on.

3) **Carl Hayman** (2005 All Blacks)

Another All Black hard as concrete is Carl Hayman. The great props don't tend to resort to violence. They don't need to cross that line to intimidate. They just frighten you to death by playing hard and fair at the coal face. Another truism about props is that away from rugby they are among the most honourable men you could hope to meet – guys such as Jason Leonard, Phil Vickery, Os du

Randt and Carl. Nastiness in the front row, in my opinion, tends to come from the hooker. You might believe I'm thinking of Brian Moore when I say that. I couldn't possibly comment!

4) John Eales (2001 Wallabies)

He went by the nickname of 'Nobody', because nobody's perfect. It is hard to argue with that. John was a superb second-row forward who won two World Cups with Australia, in 1991 (on only his tenth appearance) and 1999 as captain, and also kicked goals prolifically at international level. John won eighty-six caps, and started every one of them, and could boast a 78 per cent win rate – though he was far too humble to boast about anything. That's only half the man. Away from the field he is charm personified. Whenever I see him he without fail asks after my family and shows an interest in what I am doing. The guy has no ego, yet he achieved more than almost anyone else has in the sport. It is no coincidence that no one ever messed around with him on the field; everybody had too much respect.

5) Mark Andrews (1997 Springboks)

Like Martin Johnson or Brad Thorn, Mark was a no-nonsense lock forward with real presence and no airs and graces. He just got on with it and I'd guess Johnno had plenty of respect for him. He was physical, confrontational, sometimes headless in the way he ran into brick walls without care for his own safety. There was no interacting with him on the pitch, not even a look. The 1997 Boks had plenty of hard men but at the bottom of a ruck you'd give most of them a bit of a wink and some banter. Not Andrews. He was one of those players whose eye you didn't want to catch.

6) Richie McCaw (2005 All Blacks)

If Eales was perfect, this guy was not and remains none too shabby. Richie captained New Zealand to the 2011 World Cup and is an all-time great open-side. What I admire most about him is the way he communicates with the referee. He has this knack of keeping the referee onside even when he himself is not. He does it by always keeping his cool and being very accepting of the few decisions that go against him. His spiel goes something like this: 'Okay, fair enough, Sir. So you're telling me I came in from the side there. So if I do it this way, does that mean it's okay?' To get rid of him the referee replies by saying, 'Yeah Richie, that'll be fine.' Richie remembers this and does it exactly as he's outlined to the referee, who now has nowhere to go. Referee management is a massive part of international captaincy and Richie's style of being positive and seemingly looking merely to clarify matters is very clever.

7) George Smith (2001 and 2013 Wallabies)

Very similar to McCaw in his ability to manage the referee, but sometimes the disruptive lines George runs in defence were, and still are, even better than those of his All Black rival. His timing at the breakdown is particularly impressive. It's not about him actually making a tackle, often it's the others doing that, but he is always on hand to pounce on the loose ball and he has this sixth sense of when not to compete for it. When I played against him for England, we had a rule that if you saw George near the ball, you had to get hold of him. Even if he was not in the ruck, make sure he became involved in it. Pin him down so he couldn't get to the next two or three rucks. He was – and remains – that influential.

8) Gary Teichmann (1997 Springboks)

You had to be a good player to keep Bobby Skinstad out of the South Africa team in the late nineties and Gary was that player. Quick, strong and tactically astute – as well as having great humility and a sense of fair play – he was a popular and successful No. 8 and captain, leading the Springboks to a record seventeen-Test winning streak in 1997–98. I'm delighted to say England brought it to an end at Twickenham and I kicked the decisive penalty. Have I mentioned that already?

Rocky.

CHAPTER 6

TAKING THE MIC

Johannesburg
1 June 2009

It is good to be back in South Africa. We are twelve years on from
the 1997 Lions series and I am no longer playing rugby, but returning to the land of the Springbok brings the memories flooding back.
My try in Cape Town, Jerry Guscott's dropped goal in Durban,
Barry Williams being taped naked to a lamppost in Johannesburg
not a million miles from the hotel in Sandton I'm just about to leave.

Outside is a car in which my two BBC Radio 5 Live colleagues
are waiting for me. Ian Robertson, the BBC's rugby correspondent,
and Ed Marriage, his trusty and dependable producer. Also with
them is Bex, daughter of commentator and former Wales captain
Eddie Butler. It's Monday in the second week of the 2009 Lions'
tour and we have the day off.

'We should go and take a look at Gold Reef City,' Ed had said over breakfast. 'It's a huge amusement park, with rides all based on the old gold rush. It will be a laugh.' Throughout the 2001 and 2005 Lions tours I dreamt of a day like this. 'Count me in buddy.'

'Can't we play golf?' protested Robbo.

We head south-east on Sandton Drive, take the first left into Grayston and then right onto the De Villiers Graaff Motorway in the direction of Jo'burg. As so often on the highveld in winter time, there is a clear blue sky. I sit in the back seat and feel pleased with myself. Pleased that I retired when I did, with my body still in one piece and having achieved more than I could have dreamt of in rugby. Pleased, too, that when the opportunity came along to add radio broadcasting to my BBC television work, I had the sense to jump at it.

Gold Reef City is on Data Crescent and as we turn left into it off Northern Park Way it's obvious it is closed. The car parks are empty, there's just a couple of lads at the traffic lights selling the *Johannesburg Star* newspaper, bottles of water and a selection of slightly manky-looking oranges.

'Any more bright ideas, Ed?' I say from the back. 'We should have played golf,' a Scottish voice pipes up. 'Robbo, is that all you ever think about?' asks Bex rhetorically.

I reach for the Johannesburg tourist guidebook on the back shelf and thumb through the pages. Funny that it doesn't mention the crime figures. I remember reading a piece on a website, which compared the number of murders and manslaughters in the UK and South Africa in the past year. One was in the hundreds, the other in the many thousands.

'What about we take a look at Market Square?' suggests Bex. 'Grab a coffee and maybe do a bit of shopping?'

'We'll have a coffee anyway,' all three blokes say in unison. We get there, park up, order a round of lattes, mess about for a while, then decide to head back to Sandton. I notice a police helicopter circling overhead but don't think any more of it. For once Ed doesn't check the map and sets off in the direction the car is facing. Quickly the arcade of shops disappears and we find ourselves in a pretty run-down part of town. But we know we are going in the vague direction of the motorway so we start talking rugby and dissecting the patchy performance of the Lions in their opener against the Royal XV up in Rustenburg.

We pull up at an intersection in the middle of downtown Jo'burg and as we stop we notice a lot of people milling around. Before we know what's happening a policeman spreadeagles himself over the bonnet of our car with his handgun drawn.

'I think we ought to get out of here fairly smartish,' suggests Robbo, a little more urgency in his voice than usual. 'We can't,' replied Ed. 'He's on the bonnet and there's another car right up our backside.' We hear a gunshot from across the road and as the copper jumps off the front of our hire car and takes cover, Ed hits the accelerator. There is another set of lights on red a couple of hundred yards down the road. Ed slams on the brakes and seeing another copper with gun drawn, winds down his window and calls out, 'Excuse me. What's the best way to the motorway.'

'Do yourself a favour,' comes the reply. 'Just get the f**ck out of here.'

The following day I come down to breakfast in the safety of our hotel and Ed and Robbo are already at the table, poring over the lead story in the *Star* with a colleague from the South African Broadcasting Corporation. 'Taxi War Shoot-out – Four Dead' screams the headline.

'We were there, we saw it happen,' says Robbo proudly. The guy from SABC looks at him wide-eyed. 'Ian, what the hell were you doing in that part of town? You do not go there.'

2009 BRITISH AND IRISH LIONS TOUR
(P10, W7, D1, L2)

1) *Royal XV, won 37–25 (Rustenburg, 30 May)*

2) *Golden Lions, won 74–10 (Johannesburg, 3 June)*

3) *Cheetahs, won 26–24 (Bloemfontein, 6 June)*

4) *Sharks, won 39–3 (Durban, 10 June)*

5) *Western Province, won 26–23 (Cape Town, 13 June)*

6) *Southern Kings, won 20–8 (Port Elizabeth, 16 June)*

7) *1st Test, SOUTH AFRICA, lost 21–26 (Durban, 20 June)*

8) *Emerging Springboks, drew 13–13 (Cape Town, 23 June)*

9) *2nd Test, SOUTH AFRICA, lost 25–28 (Pretoria, 27 June)*

10) *3rd Test, SOUTH AFRICA, won 28–9 (Johannesburg, 4 July)*

I am still in the honeymoon period between being a player and becoming a full-fledged media pundit, and, as I have played with many of the 2009 Lions, I spend much of the tour meeting up with them for coffees and a catch-up, getting the inside track on what is going on with head coach Ian McGeechan and forwards coach Warren Gatland, my last director of rugby at Wasps.

Their tour philosophy is based solidly around the need to restore respect for the Lions following the whitewash in New Zealand four years before. Nobody needs telling that the Lions have now not won a series in twelve years, but from Geech's point of view it is not just about the end result. It's about restoring the values and traditions for which Lions rugby is known: the 'missionary' work in communities where the tour stops off, coaching clinics in local clubs and schools, hospital visits. There was so little time for any of that in Australia and New Zealand on the previous two trips. They had become rushed, largely joyless affairs.

It is quickly apparent to me that this trip is different. There is a more relaxed feel to everything, or is it just because my circumstances have completely changed? I'm not permanently exhausted, living under the pressure of trying to win a Lions Test jersey. I am taking in the sights and sounds of the tour and, if I'm honest, enjoying being outside of the intense bubble in which players exist.

I try to get across to the management and to the players that when I am interviewing them for 5 Live, they are still talking to me, so they don't need to have their guard up in the same way they might when talking to journalists with whom they are not familiar. I mean it, too. I have no desire whatsoever to cause any controversy. I'm still all too aware that my credibility in Lions terms remains tarnished by my 2001 *Telegraph* diary. Eight years on I am still trying to rebuild bridges.

That should probably go for me and BBC 5 Live, too, after an incident that took place here in South Africa in May 2007 on my first England tour as part of their team. Thinking back on it now I laugh out loud, but there was a moment when it was not quite so funny. That was when I nearly killed Ian Robertson.

It was a couple of days before the first Test in Bloemfontein and we were in a restaurant down by a lake in the centre of town. We'd flown in a couple of days before and were in high spirits, Robbo, Ed, Eddie and the great Alastair Hignell. One bottle of red became two and for whatever reason we started looking through the contents of our wallets. There was the usual collection of rand notes, each with an animal on it. The 10 rand note had a rhinoceros, the 20 an elephant, the 50 a Lion and the 100 a Cape buffalo. Robbo claimed the 200 was illustrated with a leopard, but as no one else had seen one of them we told him to pipe down.

Robbo suddenly got up from the table, asked the waitress to point him in the direction of the toilets and excused himself – just as I opened my wallet and out dropped half a Viagra tablet. Don't ask me what it was doing there. I can only think some joker had planted it to try to set me up. Anyway, it gave me an idea. Robbo was always telling us stories about how he took Viagra. We didn't believe a word of it, of course, but . . .

I crushed it up and tipped the powder into his half-full wine glass. He returned to the table and knocked it back without even thinking. We didn't know where to look. We had all heard of Viagra and its supposedly magical qualities but none of us had seen it in action – until about thirty minutes later when Robbo moved to a neighbouring table and invited a women of mature age to sit on his knee.

She politely declined and soon after he returned to our table, sat down and spluttered, 'I don't know what it is but I'm feeling really horny.' He looked ready to go and hump the nearest lamppost. We roared with laughter. Imagine my shock then to come into breakfast the next morning and be told that Robbo had been taken to hospital with what he thought was some sort of heart problem but which turned out to be a quicker pulse due to the Viagra! He turned out to be fine, but I went as white as a sheet.

The Lions arrive at the Test series in good shape. They have played six games and won them all. Having struggled to get going against the Royal XV, in front of a tiny crowd in Rustenburg, they get the show on the road with a ten-try, 74–10 battering of the Golden

Lions, formerly Transvaal. It's the biggest score they've recorded in South Africa for thirty-five years. Being at the game reminds me of the same fixture in 1997 when John Bentley scored a miracle try, from inside his own 22, to put our tour back on track four days after losing to Northern Transvaal.

It is an emotional night for Brian O'Driscoll, who captains the side on his first return to a Lions side since his tour was so brutally ended in New Zealand four years before. He's not looking back of course, that's never been his style. But those of us who shared that experience with him in Christchurch are delighted for him. There is a popular phrase in Irish rugby: 'In BOD we trust'. It is an indicator of the God-like status accorded to Brian and the admiration in which he is held. His divine qualities do not extend beyond the rugby field however. At a function a day or two later Brian falls into a swimming pool and is fined £25 by the players' court. 'Brian is a great player,' said tour judge Alun-Wyn Jones. 'But I can confirm that he cannot walk on water!'

The tour continues to gather momentum, though there is a slight blip in Bloemfontein where in the second Saturday match of the tour the Lions give up a 20–0 lead and only nick a 26–24 win when the Cheetahs miss a last-minute kick at the sticks. Worse follows with confirmation that Stephen Ferris, who was shaping up to be the Test blind-side, and Leigh Halfpenny, who arrived late on tour due to a thigh problem, have sustained tour-ending injuries.

Still, victories follow against the Sharks and Western Province before the final game at sea level ahead of the opening Test in Durban cuts up rough. In fact the approach of the Southern Kings in Port Elizabeth reminds me of the game against South Africa in 2002 that almost ended my career and could well have left me paralysed.

It's clear to me that the Kings go out to soften up the Lions and attempt to dent their momentum with the Test series only days away. 'There were more cheap shots in that game than the rest of the tour put together,' Ronan O'Gara says afterwards, and he gets no argument from Gordon D'Arcy. 'We knew there was going to be some rough stuff on this tour and it arrived here,' he says. 'There was some stuff you would not be too happy with. Late hits, high hits, stuff like that. They talked in the papers about how they were going to rough us up ahead of the first Test and they did that.'

That view is supported by former Springboks star Bobby Skinstad, working for TV, who, live on air, asks captain Marco Wentzel whether the Kings were on a bonus for the number of Lions they could take out. 'The Lions come here and expect teams to be physical and we wanted to show them that,' is Wentzel's reply. 'The Lions are hardly angels themselves,' adds head coach Alan Solomons. 'I don't think anything untoward went on.'

It was a similar head-in-the-sand reaction to that of Springboks coach Rudi Straeuli after his South Africa side came to Twickenham in 2002 and wreaked havoc with one dangerous hit after another. It takes two to tango was essentially what he said afterwards. It was a ludicrous and irresponsible stance, given our post-match casualty list. Neil Back suffered a fractured cheekbone, Lewis Moody had a shoulder injury that required surgery, Jason Robinson was left with a perforated eardrum, Jonny Wilkinson sustained shoulder damage that would put him out until the following year, and I was experiencing alarming neck pains.

Whenever I turned my head I would feel pins and needles all the way down into my hand, and my index finger was numb. The specialist looked at my scan results and said, 'You may never play again.' Sky Sports pieced together footage of the incidents, which showed Corne Krige, South Africa's captain, launching himself at my head with a flying butt and later catching me in the face with a blatant forearm smash. Fortunately I got lucky. The swelling went down around my spinal cord and a couple of months later I was able to return to playing. I dodged a bullet that day.

With the start of the 2009 Test series a couple of days away, 5 Live ask me to host a live broadcast from our hotel on the Durban seafront. It is a beautiful spot, with the waves rolling onto the white sandy beach, and the sun has just dipped below the horizon when Ed Marriage gives me the nod that we're live on air. The gameplan is to interview Scott Gibbs and John Bentley, my 1997 team mates, and for them to tell good, clean stories to illustrate what a great time we had on that tour. For a bit of background atmosphere we have persuaded a few Lions supporters to leave the bar and join us, with the idea that from time to time I will ask for a fans' perspective.

All is going according to plan. Scotty and Bentos are in fine form and the supporters are laughing along with them and their tales. I then turn to these three Welsh girls, over from Swansea. 'You having a good night so far?'

'Oh yeah, wicked,' replies one. I start to ask her about their trip when she interrupts me and says, 'First of all can I say it's not the first time I've met you, Gibbsy.' I'm stopped in my tracks, Scotty freezes on the spot. He is live on air and he has no idea what she is about to say. Listeners obviously can't see it, but the colour has drained from his face and I'm now caught between wetting myself laughing and blind panic over what might be coming next. Scotty's look says 1. 'I really can't remember anything happening with you love'; and 2. if anything did happen, in the dim and distant past, please don't say it live on air.

'Yeah, yeah, I was in a bar in Swansea,' she continues, as the good people of England, Scotland, Ireland and Wales doubtless pause what they are doing and move closer to their radios. 'I got my tits out for you. Don't you remember? You signed them for me.'

Her words take a moment to register. Ed looks at me, I look at him, we both look at Scott. Do we pull out a plug, slap on a jingle, break off for a travel bulletin from back home. No need. 'Oh yeah, I remember,' says Scotty, clearly not, but rescuing the situation expertly, 'they were a fine pair.'

The Lions run out onto Kings Park for the opening Test and the thousands of red-shirted fans roar their approval. The hairs stand up on the back of my neck, goosebumps spring up on my arms. This is what the Lions do to you. For my money, there really is no other sporting show on earth like it. And for the first time since the 1993 tour to New Zealand I am not a part of it. Today I am in the stands with headphones and a BBC radio microphone, a mere observer of the sport that gave me everything.

My rugby after-life began with *A Question of Sport* in 2004 and I was having a ball doing that when my agent called to say I'd been offered *Celebrity MasterChef* – the first so-called celebrity version of the show – and did I fancy it? I talked it through with my mum. She laughed.

'What's so funny? Okay, it could have done with a bit more seasoning, but you ate my pasta bake the other night. Didn't you?'

In truth my nerves were less about appearing on television, because I had grown accustomed to that through QOS, than cooking on the telly. In fact it was not just a fear of cooking, but of the unknown. I'd watched the show but wasn't aware how it was put together, I didn't know how much it was edited to look like it was all very serious and competitive, or indeed how much help the contestants received and how much insight they were given into cooking certain types of food.

'Oh go on, I'll give it a go.'

It was my enormous good fortune to have met and made a friend of Mark Edwards shortly after our World Cup win in 2003. Mark is executive chef at the Michelin-starred Nobu restaurant in London and I just 'happened' to mention *MasterChef* to him one night when we were out for a beer and he said he'd love to help me out if he could. I jumped on his invitation to, as I put it, hone my skills.

Actually, I just wanted to ensure I didn't embarrass myself, which, as a professional sportsman, is always the concern. Before I knew it I was in Nobu every lunchtime and evening, being taken through various methods of cooking, practising my knife skills, seasoning, presentation, understanding my palate and taking tasting tests. Cooking is no different from sport in that if you do the basics well, you can look quite impressive. But a professional kitchen is a serious workplace. Chefs don't mess about and they don't tolerate fools. I was tucked well away.

The celebrities on my series included Tony Hadley, the lead singer of Spandau Ballet, fellow eighties pop stars Paul Young and Toyah Wilcox, and Olympic 400m silver medallist Roger Black – all big names from my childhood. *Gold* was the first single I ever bought so you can imagine how I felt to be in a cooking competition with Tony. Whenever I saw him I would start singing.

Well you have to, don't you? Tony is a top man and I will always remember the bruschetta he prepared for in the invention test. He presented the plate to the judges and Gregg Wallace, who co-hosts the show with John Torode, said, 'Now what have we got here?' Tony replied, 'It's bruschetta.' He then proceeded to list all the ingredients he had used . . . none of which are actually in the recipe. It was something on toast but bruschetta it was not.

The show was a hoot from start to finish. I don't remember any hissy fits. What I recall was how much everybody was into their food – even if some people's interpretation of being 'into' their food was slightly different from others.

I reached the final along with Roger and Hardeep Singh Kohli, the writer and radio and television presenter. I did so despite making a major cock-up of my orange and lemon tart. To be fair to me, it wasn't actually my fault. All the ingredients and pastry were top notch. The problem was the bloody oven with those push controls that you need a degree in mechanical engineering to master. I set the temperature, then carried on cooking everything else. At some point in the next five to ten minutes I must have leant forward and knocked the button, unwittingly turning the oven off. I didn't notice until the alarm sounded half an hour later and I opened the oven door to discover my tarts were raw. I was absolutely spewing. Somehow I still made it to the final cook-off, after which the judges said the following:

John Torode: 'Every single process Matt does, actually he does with exact precision. I think he's awesome, I think he's controlled, I think he's learned, I think he's disciplined and I find that extremely impressive. And today he produced food that was really, really sensational.'

Gregg Wallace: 'He delivered some of the most beautiful plates of food I've seen from an amateur ever. And he has really pushed himself in this final, because my worry was he's all Japanese, he's all Asian. No, no. He's really pushed himself. He's desperate to prove that he can encompass all cooking. And for me today I think he's proved it.'

As we filed back into the kitchen for the final decision, Gregg said, 'This is almost too close to call.' He is a massive rugby fan but, contrary to what some might think, he didn't want me to win. He wanted Hardeep, whom he felt had been the more consistent throughout the six or seven weeks of competition. John, on the other hand, was backing me. 'Look where Matt's come from,' he said. 'From making a tart where the pastry's uncooked, to then in the final absolutely nailing the same dish. He's gone on a journey and developed as a cook.' How ironic that three years after beating Australia to capture the World Cup, it should be an Australian helping a Pommie rugby lad to his next big success.

MY *MASTERCHEF* XV

15) *Phil Vickery*
14) *Lisa Faulkner*
13) *Tony Hadley*
12) *Toyah Wilcox*
11) *Richard Arnold*
10) *Roger Black*
9) *Jamie Theakston*
1) *Shelina Permalloo*
2) *Thomasina Miers*
3) *Hardeep Singh Kohli*
4) *Mark Moraghan*
5) *Gregg Wallace*
6) *John Torode*
7) *Lloyd Grossman*
8) *India Fisher*

15) Phil Vickery (England and Lions rugby player)

The player, not the chef. You can't help but be biased when seeing one of your old team mates going through the same pressures you once did. The shaven-headed former Lions, England and Wasps prop was known as Raging Bull for the way he played, yet give him a handful of veg and a rack of lamb and he became an artist. His soft tones when answering questions from Gregg and John in the most intense situations, plus the daintiest of touches in serving up, gave me a warm glow. I think I've watched every *MasterChef* show there's been but never have I cheered like I did when watching Phil in the final.

14) Lisa Faulkner (model, actress, TV personality)

This has nothing to do with the fact Lisa was one of the first women I saw online back in 1999. I remember one of the lads logging on to *FHM* magazine front covers and being wowed by this hot actress. No, my admiration is much more mature! Honest. I saw her being enraptured by cooking in a way I had been four years previously – turning a hobby into a passion because of the intensity of the competition. Her desserts looked fabulous, too, and I'm a sucker for a cup cake.

13) Tony Hadley (lead singer of Spandau Ballet)

So I rock up in east London ready to film a show that already intimidated me. What I don't need is to be paired with a bloke from Spandau Ballet. I introduce myself and inside all I can hear are the words of his songs, dying to be set free. We bond quite well and end up having a giggle at one another's efforts. Following his unique take on bruschetta (who needs basil, garlic or focaccia?) in the second round he makes a cracking steak dish, slaving away over a hot stove to produce a mash and meaty jus to accompany the ribeye. At least I think it's ribeye. I lose my focus when I notice the blue sweat dribbling down the side of Tony's face from his hair dye! I know, it's envy.

12) Toyah Wilcox (eighties pop star turned actress)

The second round saw us battle it out over a mystery recipe: dressed crab and soda bread. I nipped to the toilet and Googled soda bread recipes but instead linked to a spelt bread recipe, which didn't help at all. That'll teach me. Attacking a crab for the first time under pressure is a real challenge but I was determined not to leave any of the shell behind and, in my attempt to be precise, cracked the shell in two. Even worse was to befall Toyah, who was exactly as I imagined, a bubbly personality and slightly whacky dresser. That was also reflected in her food – lots of flavour and a little unorthodox. Her mayonnaise was pretty garlicky but Gregg loved it, until he crunched down on a piece of crab shell and almost lost a tooth.

11) Richard Arnold (television presenter)

It's semi-final time and with only four contestants left it dawns on all of us we could realistically win the first-ever *Celebrity MasterChef*. Our task is to cook for sixteen children staying at Great Ormond Street Hospital. After a briefing at 7am we have five hours to prep, cook and serve suitable kids' food. I go for spaghetti bolognese, Hardeep chooses shepherd's pie and Roger sensibly cooks up some chicken skewers. At the last moment John and Gregg throw a curveball, telling us we all have to create a pre-lunch nibble and the one with the most popular dish will score heavily. Richard Arnold is showbiz reporter on GMTV, a lively, camp, hilariously funny man who does not take anything too seriously and has a natural talent for cooking. He is a genuine threat! That is, until he announces his menu for children aged between ten and sixteen. For his hors d'oeuvres he thinks that baby gem lettuce leaves filled with cream cheese and chives is a good idea. Really? But that's got nothing on his main course: paella, complete with mussels, prawns and spices. Only because he laughs at himself do we double over when not one child picks either dish. Then there were three . . .

10) Roger Black (Olympic 400m silver medallist)

Roger brought to the competition everything you would expect from a 1996 Olympic silver medalist: determination, drive, passion – and sweat. He came up on the rails late in the series after being sent to a hotel restaurant. Something finally clicked in him and his messy, chuck-it-all-over-the-place methods became organised and well practised. He returned with his game face on for the final round, which required us to cook our best three-course menu in two hours. There was a lot of work to be done in a short time and as the clock ticked Roger realised he had left it too late to get his Chantilly cream as he wanted it on his dessert. He began whisking frantically. His beautiful floppy hair flapped about as his right arm began to tire. He kept going but all that whipping was making him perspire and, to his horror, a couple of beads of sweat splashed from his brow into the bowl. Within seconds the cream was clotted then, moments later, it curdled. At the end we all had to sample it. The memory of that slight salty taste has stayed with me ever since.

9) Jamie Theakston (TV and radio broadcaster)

Jamie and I have crossed paths several times over the last ten years, from enjoying the spoils of singledom to being happily married with fantastic kids and living a stone's throw away from one another in west London. Until we appeared together on the show I had no idea he had such a natural talent with food. You are not supposed to be able just to chuck a load of flour and water in a bowl and make bread. But he did. I remember his embarrassed laugh when he revealed his invention-test masterpiece at the end of the hour. Expecting to be humiliated by the verdict, he was instead bowled over to hear John Torode say, 'Mmm that really is lovely, Jamie. How did you make that?' JT's reply, 'Erm, not sure really.' Classic.

1) Shelina Permalloo (cookery author and TV chef)

Turning now to the first of a couple of real cooks, and natural ones too. Shelina won the 2012 *MasterChef*, specialising in Mauritian cuisine from her heritage. Gregg Wallace called her food 'Sunshine on a Plate'. People often talk about mouthwatering dishes, but in the case of her creations there is no other phrase. Throughout the competition her sincerity and humility shone through. A passionate, talented chef – I look forward to eating in her restaurant.

2) Thomasina Miers (2005 *MasterChef* winner)

I have eaten at Thomasina's restaurant and I loved it. Tommi won *MasterChef* the year before I went on the show and watching her perspire, shake and curse her way to the title made for awesome television. You can't help but cringe at the way we were all put out of our comfort zones in that kitchen, whether it was me with the Dorset crab or Thomasina in the fine-dining restaurant. Making a terrine looks pretty simple and slicing it with a professional knife even easier, but try it when the ingredients inside equate to £50 a slice. When the chef flippantly binned the first few slices and reminded Tommi of the cost of truffles and foie gras, I thought she was going to crack. I was wrong. She now owns a chain of Mexican restaurants called Wahaca.

3) Hardeep Singh Kohli (writer and TV presenter)

A Glaswegian comic of Indian parents, whose knife skills in the kitchen were as sharp as his wit. Our battle went all the way to the final, me preparing sushi (which drove him bonkers as he didn't see it as cooking) and then serving up spaghetti bolognese (which I don't think he thought was much better). The final was quite a head-to-head: my sporting determination against his twenty-five years' experience of family kitchens and experiment-ation. Fortunately, sportsmen tend to stick together and Olympic athlete Roger Black was the third finalist. In the heat of the contest Roger casually wandered over to the fridge to set his pud. Seeing an empty tray on the top shelf he took it out to make room and threw it into the washing-up. Twenty minutes later Hardeep went to the same fridge to check the champagne ice he was pre-paring for an overly pompous dessert. Only kidding, Deep! 'Where's my champagne? Who's moved my champagne,' There it lay, covered in soapy bubbles. Was it the difference between first and second? Maybe. But I did offer him a glass of my winners' bubbly afterwards. #awkward

4) Mark Moraghan (actor and singer)

A sort of *MasterChef* hero for me. Us 'celebs' were put through the mill a little as the production was always leaning towards jeopardy and that one moment when a slightly burnt corner of a mille-feuille could be catapulted into a headline on the 10 o'clock news. The pressure was intense but most contestants adapted and responded to it. Not Mark. During a tricky service at the Knightsbridge restaurant Marcus Wareing at the Berkeley, he lost the plot. The soap star represented all those reality contestants who have thought, 'What am I doing? I don't need this, I don't want it, I'm out of here.' And off he went. Out of the shot, out onto the street, into a cab. I applaud you, Mr Moraghan.

5) Gregg Wallace (*MasterChef* judge/presenter)
Where would we be without the rugby-mad veg seller and teller of constant gags of varying humour? I think Gregg was slightly put out when I attempted to replicate the infamous hot white chocolate and frozen berries that The Ivy restaurant has served for years. I placed my own spin on it – vanilla in the white chocolate – but tradition lies deep with Wallace. It was as if I'd betrayed the chef code.

6) John Torode (*MasterChef* judge/presenter)
You know which one he is. The one who always clatters the spoon full of dessert into his teeth when he's tasting. John and Gregg really are a cracking couple of lads, who love their job, are passionate about food and represent the *MasterChef* brand fantastically. A typical Aussie with great banter and an ability to take it in return, he was an inspiration and mentor to me on the show and I'll forever be grateful.

7) Lloyd Grossman (TV presenter and gastronome)
We shouldn't forget *MasterChef* has been going since 1990 when a well-spoken, if at times slightly patronising, Lloyd Grossman presented a series of regional heats to find the cream of the crop. That original format was what got me hooked on the show. Lloyd's

brutal honesty was television gold. Not for him the manufacturing of drama, he was merciless. If you were good, he told you; if you were not, watch out.

8) India Fisher

Go on then . . . Have a guess who India is? There have been many great moments on the show, tasty food, awful food, even some raw, inedible food. There have been tears, cheers, laughter and downright embarrassment. One person has captured it all. India is the voice of the show, literally setting the tone and drawing us back to our TV sets week after week. Silky smooth, like my mum's gravy, India makes a plate of scallops on cauliflower purée sound as saucy as a Jackie Collins novel. Sorry. Lost myself there for a moment.

First Test: South Africa 26, British and Irish Lions 21
Durban, 20 June 2009

A case of what might have been. The Lions know they need a big start yet they are left in the blocks as the Boks blast away. The tourists' set-piece is bullied and obliterated and South Africa lead 26–7 after fifty minutes. Then comes the reaction. Realising this is the only Test of the series at sea level before they head to altitude, where their hosts have an inbuilt advantage, the Lions launch a counter-offensive. Tom Croft, who was not in the initial tour party, has scored one try already, and dots down another. Mike Phillips crosses, too. All of a sudden the Lions are up 3–2 on the try count and down by just five on the scoreboard. Yet South Africa dig in. The Lions make five line-breaks without reply but the home side, with three times as many tackles as their resurgent opponents, hold firm. The Lions are heroic in defeat, but the harsh reality of

Test match rugby, particularly in Lions' series, is that that counts for nothing.

The second Test in Pretoria is now win or bust and although the second half revival at Kings Park has given the Lions some momentum, a midweek draw against the Emerging Springboks does for that. A try and a touchline conversion in the last play of the game in wet and windy Cape Town is a body blow to morale and a crucial moment. That said, it's nothing to the pain they experience at Loftus Versfeld four days later.

Second Test: South Africa 28, British and Irish Lions 25
Pretoria, 27 June 2009

A Test match that has everything but the one thing the Lions need – a victory. There is bitter controversy when Schalk Burger gouges Lions wing Luke Fitzgerald in the first minute and somehow escapes with a yellow card. There is a quite extraordinary performance from Simon Shaw, winning his first Test cap twelve years after his first Lions appearance. And there is unbearable anguish for the Lions right at the death when my old mate Ronan O'Gara misses a tackle on Jaque Fourie to let South Africa in for a late try. Then, with four minutes of injury time played, the scores tied and the series poised to go to a decider in Johannesburg the following Saturday, RoG is adjudged to have taken out Fourie in the air. Up steps replacement fly-half Morne Steyn and, from his own half, plunges a dagger into the heart of the Lions.

If O'Gara is in pieces emotionally afterwards, a number of his team mates are the same in a physical sense. Five Lions end up in hospital. Gethin Jenkins has a broken cheekbone, which requires surgery, fellow prop Adam Jones has had his shoulder dislocated by Bakkies Botha (later banned for two weeks), Brian O'Driscoll has concussion and midfield partner Jamie Roberts has a badly sprained wrist.

I pop round to the Lions' hotel later that evening and there are haunted expressions everywhere, and disbelief that in the space of eight days their dreams have been shattered. This is what the Lions can do to you. As I found with the third Test in 2001, defeat in that red shirt rips you apart. You feel responsible to the thousands of travelling fans, but above all you feel responsible to the badge.

The third Test is now a dead rubber but you would not know it, such is the anger swirling around the squad over Burger's act and total absence of contrition, and Boks' coach Peter de Villiers' subsequent remarks on the subject.

'If you know Schalk's nature and character – if you know the man as I know him – he would never do this,' claims de Villiers in his press conference. 'We have brilliant players in this country, most of them world class. We do not prepare them to do little small things that belong out in the bush veld. If you want to gouge a lion, that is where you go. But we must understand here very very clearly that rugby is a contact sport – and so is dancing. If we are going to win games in board rooms and in front of television cameras and in shops, we must say to ourselves, 'Do we really respect this game that we really honour so much?' If it's the case that we are, why don't we all go to the nearest ballet shop, get some nice tutus and get some great dancing going on? No eye gouging, no tackling, no nothing. Then enjoy. There are no collisions in ballet, but in this game there will be collisions. If people want to make it soft because we won a series, I cannot do anything about it.'

It is a preposterous outburst and one that antagonises everyone concerned with the Lions, for whom the 2005 All Blacks' spear tackle on Brian O'Driscoll – and, again, absence of apology – is still all too fresh in the memory.

Brian takes it upon himself to react on behalf of the tour party. 'When I heard those comments, I wondered how someone could get away with something like that. I find it an absolute disgrace that a coach of a national team can make comments about gouging being part of the game. I can't be more adamant about that. I think it needs to be voiced. I think a senior player needs to say it. If there are kids or parents watching an interview like that, questioning whether they should have their kid play rugby or soccer, that's their decision made right there. To hear a national coach saying that, in any shape or form, gouging is acceptable in the modern-day game is despicable. I find it mind-boggling. Essentially, it brought the game into disrepute.'

Though Burger is banned for eight weeks, the judicial officer clears him of an intentional act. He said it was 'clearly reckless but I am unable to conclude that there was eye-gouging in the sense of a ripping or aggressive intrusion in the eye area.' Had he been asked to give the Lions team talk he could not have done a better job.

Third Test: South Africa 9, British and Irish Lions 28
Johannesburg, 4 July 2009

What a performance! South Africa go looking for a first clean sweep over the Lions and get a hiding instead. Despite making ten changes, they don't see it coming. The Springboks had lost just once in twelve years at Ellis Park. Make that twice. Two tries for Shane Williams and one for Ugo Monye give the Lions a win that equals the Invincibles' record victory over South Africa in the second Test in 1974. I later hear that Warren Gatland had walked into the changing room before the match, held a Lions jersey aloft, told the older players it was the last time they would wear it and asked, 'How do you want to be remembered?'

So why is it that the 2009 Lions tour is remembered so fondly by all who were on it, players, coaches, support staff, media and supporters alike? And why is it considered a success despite the series result going the same way as 2005 and 2001? Quite simply, the man they appointed to lead it. Not for nothing is Sir Ian McGeechan known as the 'Lion King' and the Lions committee deserve a huge amount of credit for that decision. It would have been very easy to go with Warren Gatland as head coach, or any of the other obvious contenders for the top job who were knocking around. But after speaking to former players and management, they realised the previous two tours had moved away from what the Lions are supposed to represent and that one man above all others had the expertise to get it back on track.

Sir Ian held the whole thing together in 2009. Gats, Shaun Edwards, Graham Rowntree and Rob Howley obviously did a lot of the coaching, but Geech's imprint was on everything. I was there only as an observer, but I could tell it was completely different, from the moment the squad arrived. There was a more relaxed feel to it, a different camaraderie. There were smiles on faces, everyone knew everyone else. There was certainly nobody vowing never to go on a Lions tour again, as Ben Cohen did in 2001 when he was so shabbily treated, given one opportunity to shine then dropped like a hot coal. It took me back to 1997 – because it was in South Africa and because, as was the case back then, the coaches knew they were working with the best British and Irish players, and their clear focus was to do everything to enable them to shine.

Each tour has its own identity, based on the people involved in it – 1997 was absolutely nothing like 1989, the previous winning Lions tour captained by Finlay Calder, and '89 was nothing like the Syd Millar–Willie John McBride-led triumph of 1974. Each tour needs to capture the unique character of its group of players. For some that might mean a boozy night to get things started, then doing hardly any training and using the early tour games as their physical preparation to hit the Test series at full pelt. Others might be better suited to hitting the ground running with training from the start, then tapering down as the Tests approach. You have to sense what is right for your group of individuals.

That's what Geech did in 2009. He and his coaching team absorbed the lessons of the previous tour and took the view that the simpler they made it for the players the greater the likelihood they would excel. They gave everybody a chance, they also socialised well together and along the way had a lot of fun, which bonded the group tight. Lions tours should be enjoyable. They should be special. Geech got it spot on. They came up just short on the scoreboard but they put the Lions back on the map and secured the future of the brand. Great to see.

CHAPTER 7

RETURN OF THE ROAR

Isleworth, south-west London
20 May 2013

We are heading for a pub, five British and Irish Lions and me. There's captain Sam Warburton, George North, Ben Youngs, Geoff Parling and Rob Kearney – all gathered to discuss the upcoming tour. After all I went through as a Lion, the good and the bad, there's one thing I want to know. Has the Lions concept lost any of its appeal for the modern-day professional player? Is being a Lion still as good as it gets?

The lads arrive and walk through the door into a bar absolutely rammed, to be greeted by a chorus of 'Lions . . . LIONS!!' Rob smiles. He was on the 2009 tour. He knew what was coming. The others almost take a step back. Not in shock as much as in wonderment. These guys have played for their countries in Six Nations and World Cups. They've been around the block. But this is something else. They have not encountered this sort of passion before.

George will go on to become a star of the 2013 tour to Australia, providing the iconic moments of the first two Tests with his sixty-metre try in Brisbane followed by his 'tackle' on Israel Folau in Melbourne. He is the ball carrier running into contact, yet he lifts six-foot-four Folau on to his shoulders like a bag of coal and continues upfield. Sitting in the pub before the tour has even started, he has the look of a kid on Christmas Eve.

I ask him about his first day as a British and Irish Lion, when the squad assembled for kitting out, team photos and a general get-to-know each other. 'I couldn't believe it,' says this Grand Slam winner and huge hero of Welsh rugby. 'I was sat next to Paul O'Connell in the dressing room, opposite Sam and Manu Tuilagi. I'm surrounded by three of the big names in world rugby, all getting changed into our Lions kit for the photo. Then Paul turns to me and says, "Well done, you've had a really good season." I couldn't believe he was saying that to me.'

There, it seems, is my answer. It doesn't matter who you are, whether you're a superstar winger like George or one of the greats of the game like Paul, you are genuinely excited by the chance to play with the best. George's boyish enthusiasm took me right back to early 1997 when I was injured and ruled out of the Five Nations Championship. I would sit on an exercise bike in the gym, pedalling away while watching old Lions games on the television up on the wall. When it started getting tough and my legs began to burn, I would imagine myself in a red shirt, digging in alongside Jeremy Guscott and Scott Gibbs. I remember it like it was yesterday. Back then every rugby player in Britain and Ireland had that aspiration, that dream, to play in a Lions team. It was that special, so clearly the pinnacle of rugby achievement. Eighteen years since the switch away from amateurism, with the World Cup now dominating the rugby landscape, I wondered if that had changed.

Listening to George's response cheers me. The Lions clearly are still relevant and, thanks in no small part to the restorative work of Sir Ian McGeechan and his management team in 2009, seem to matter as much as they ever have done. Success as a brand is one thing, however, success on the field another. The Lions' last series win was in 1997. We are now a generation into full-blown professionalism. With each passing year the odds are stacked higher against the great touring team. The host nation has significantly more time to prepare for the challenge of taking on the best of Britain and Ireland. This year, the first time the Lions meet as a complete squad will be to check-in at Heathrow. Even the week of bonding has been lost to the demands of the club season.

Still Gatland is bullish. He talks openly about winning, rather than of restoring respect, which he says was the objective in 2009 following the whitewash of 2005. I like his chat, always have. And evidently I am not alone. Unlike with fellow New Zealander Graham Henry in 2001, there is very little criticism this time about the Lions appointing an overseas head coach. Other than sharing Kiwi blood, the two of them arrived at the job along very different paths. Graham came to it cold whereas Gats was on the previous tour, learning the ways of the Lions, familiarising himself with the workings of the Lions camp. Sir Ian McGeechan might have headed up the management in South Africa, but Gats did a lot of the coaching.

His style of managing and coaching is not dissimilar to that of Geech. They share the hard-nosed touring mentality of training your socks off then going out and having a beer. Both know what it feels like to be around Lions fans on tour when they're going completely loopy, both understand the pressures the players are under day-in day-out. Gats has added credibility in taking charge of the best of the four home unions, having coached the national teams of Ireland and Wales and also enjoyed huge success in English club rugby.

No, he's not British, nor has he been a Lion himself. But he possesses a lot of the traits needed to be one: the passion he feels for the badge, a selfless work ethic and his natural ability to feed off the emotion and the tradition of sport in general. He felt the same about the All Blacks when he was a player and coach in New Zealand. He'd want to speak to the former players, he'd want to know why the All Blacks were so special. Ditto when he came to Wasps. He studied the club's history, quizzed the old guard. He wanted to know why they say, 'Once a Wasp, always a Wasp.' It isn't just a slogan, it's a way of thinking ingrained in those privileged to pull on the black and yellow. Gats took that on board. That curiosity, that hunger to immerse himself in the 'family' around him, means that, for my money, he is an ideal choice to lead the Lions, for whom tradition and history play so big. He gets it.

I'll give you one example of how Warren Gatland's man-management approach brings the best out of his players, how he puts himself onside with his men by going that extra yard for them, on condition he gets it back in return. It involved me in 2004 and came just after I had been dropped by England because I had a prior commitment with *A Question of Sport*, which clashed with the national team's rearranged training session. I had just joined Wasps, where Gats was in charge, and each Friday we would be given our training schedule for the next seven days. I knew I had a day of recording the following week, but usually *QOS* were flexible enough so that I could train and go into the studio afterwards. On this occasion, though, Gats decided at short notice to move a session to later in the day, which left me in the lurch.

I knocked on the door of his office. 'You got a moment Gats?'

'Sure, what is it?'

'I want to be open and honest with you here. I haven't caused any problems previously . . .'

'What is it Daws?'

'I'm down to film *A Question of Sport* on Tuesday and training has been rearranged and it's created a big problem for me. I don't know what to do.'

He looked at me and half-laughed, a bit like England head coach Andy Robinson had a few weeks before, prior to telling me he could not and would not help. I was pretty sure I knew what was coming.

'Hmm,' he said. 'What happens if I bring training forward by an hour and a half, would that give you enough time to make it to the studio?'

I stopped staring at my shoes. 'Bloody hell, yeah. That would really, really help. Top man.'

I turned around to leave and he laughed. 'Daws,' he said, stopping me in my tracks. 'F*** me, mate, you'd better play well at the weekend!'

That's the deal with Gats. He realises that to get the best out of a team you have to make the odd sacrifice yourself. If his staff or players waste those opportunities or take liberties, he knows where he stands with them. More likely than not they don't get a second chance. His philosophy is straightforward. You've got to give individuals the opportunity to succeed – or fail.

He loves a joke, and the occasional pint, and is game for a laugh but he is nobody's fool. He watches his players like a hawk, in training, in the dining room and in the team room – who's getting on with whom, who's winning the pool and the table-tennis leagues, how much banter's flying around, who's creating the stories and who's had a night out. He squirrels away all that knowledge then uses it to his advantage when he comes to build his team.

2013 BRITISH AND IRISH LIONS TOUR
(P10, W8, D0, L2)

1) *Barbarians, won 59–8 (Hong Kong, 1 June)*
2) *Western Force, won 69–17 (Perth, 5 June)*
3) *Queensland Reds, won 22–12 (Brisbane, 8 June)*
4) *Combined Country, won 64–0 (Newcastle, 11 June)*
5) *NSW Waratahs, won 47–17 (Sydney, 15 June)*
6) *ACT Brumbies, lost 12–14 (Canberra, 18 June)*
7) *1st Test, AUSTRALIA, won 23–21 (Brisbane, 22 June)*
8) *Melbourne Rebels, won 35–0 (Melbourne, 25 June)*
9) *2nd Test, AUSTRALIA, lost 15–16 (Melbourne, 29 June)*
10) *3rd Test, AUSTRALIA, won 41–16 (Sydney, 6 July)*

The 2013 Lions tour explodes into life before the players have even assembled as a squad. On the Saturday before their Monday flight the Aviva Premiership final takes place at Twickenham between Leicester and my old club Northampton. It is a feisty affair, which on the day results in Tigers winning a superb game of rugby but would later see two significant suspensions handed out. Richard Cockerill, Leicester's director of rugby, gets a nine-match touchline ban for using 'obscene' language towards the fourth official. Of greater concern to the Lions is the eleven-match suspension slapped on Saints' captain Dylan Hartley for verbally abusing referee Wayne Barnes. Dylan was seen by many as the Lions' starting Test hooker. Not any more he's not.

I applaud the decision. I always had plenty to say to referees, but I don't remember ever raising my voice in anger to one. I might have moaned to a captain or a coach and implored them to deal with some problem or other, but nothing more. Dylan's case – calling a referee a 'f***ing cheat' – is so black and white that I'm pleased Wayne took the action he did. It sends a great message to the whole sport. Referees up and down the country will feel a lot stronger for knowing that if they are sworn at by a player, they can send him off and say, 'You saw what happened in the Premiership final mate, that's what you get.'

It cost Dylan a Lions tour, which is a huge price to pay. I would not wish that on anyone. And I know from my Lions experience in 2001 that to be in the eye of a media storm is horrendous. You feel a raw, gut-wrenching churn in your stomach when you know you've done something wrong and you've been caught. There's nothing you can even try to do because anything you say only makes things worse. You come out in a cold sweat. You've got no excuses, nowhere to go. You just have to take it on the chin. As I did, I'm sure Dylan will learn from this.

Talking of sweats, the Lions tour opens up in Hong Kong to much debate. How on earth is a game against the Barbarians in 94 per cent humidity going to help them win a series in Australia in less than a month's time? At least that is the chat after a 59–8 win. In oppressive conditions, play was painfully slow and the only real fight shown by the BaaBaas was when Schalk Brits attempted to lamp his Saracens club mate Owen Farrell, who reacted by putting him on the deck.

I always thought it a great idea – the Hong Kong leg that is, not smacking Faz. Great for the brand and for the tour sponsors, and perfect for the players not to have to make a long-haul trip in one hit. Ironically, my one concern afterwards is not for the Lions but for the Barbarians. They are great for the sport and the ethos of the game, but they need to be competitive. England embarrassed them the previous week at Twickenham and the Lions dust them without getting out of first gear. I suspect the BaaBaas will continue but I'm less sure whether their future is playing top-drawer opposition.

As for the Brits–Farrell incident, I seriously don't understand it, particularly as Saracens pride themselves on being such a 'family'. They make so much of their in-season squad trips abroad to the Oktoberfest, to Verbier, to Cape Town. We're always told how they all love each other and get on so well, how they sing their team song after every game. And then, the first time two of them come up against each other, Brits lets fly. Not with a swat, a backhand, a swipe in frustration against some unknown opponent but a vicious punch, which, had it connected, would have knocked Owen clean out. I know Owen was tugging his shirt but come on! If you punched someone every time that happened, there would be no one left on the pitch.

As the tour leaves Hong Kong for Perth, Warren Gatland and the media are united in their concern over Owen's retaliation, the way the fly-half tripped Brits and put him on his backside. Rightly so. The Aussies will see that as a weakness they can exploit. You can never lose sight of the fact that on a Lions tour you are playing against not only a national team but an entire nation – the supporters, the ball boys, every single player, the officials in the changing rooms, the bus drivers. Everybody will do their utmost to make sure their country beats the Lions.

More of a concern for me is that Owen's competitive streak has a tendency to boil over and he runs the risk of losing focus. He's superfit, he makes some great tackles and he throws himself around. He's keen as mustard, and that is fine. But I don't want to see a fly-half going into rucks and trying to kick the ball out or steal it. That's not his job. If he's doing that, he's out of position and more likely to get injured.

Owen sits out the first game in Australia, at least for an hour, before coming on to score one of the Lions' nine tries in a 69–17 pasting of Western Force. That makes two easy hit-outs for the tourists – far from ideal given the speed with which they are hurtling towards the Test series. I agree with Sir Clive Woodward's view that the Force's decision to rest half their team in favour of a domestic match four days later shows disrespect for the Lions.

A Lions tour generates millions of dollars for the Australian Rugby Union and the host nation's economy. If you want the Lions to tour your country, go out and show it. Half-baked teams do nobody any good. My sympathy is as much with the Western Force players as anyone else. Those guys who were rested in order to play in a dead rubber against New South Wales will never have another chance to play against the Lions. It doesn't matter who you are, and what sport you're in, you want to test yourself against the best. For those boys not to be given that opportunity I think is irresponsible on the part of the Force management.

Queensland get it absolutely right in the third game. With soon-to-be Wallaby coach Ewen McKenzie in charge off the pitch and Quade Cooper their captain on it, here is a club fully determined to embrace the whole ethos of Lions tours, both in the strength of the team they put on the park and the way they play the match. The Lions do well to win 22–12. The Reds don't just give it a lash, you can see they've thought it through. How can we dent the chance of the Lions winning a Test series? Well, we can run them into the ground and knacker them out. It almost works. They lead after the first quarter and are within a score until Owen's late penalty kills them off – his sixth success from six attempts at goal.

Owen has landed twelve out of thirteen in two games, an impressive response to earlier criticism. It keeps him in step with Leigh Halfpenny, who nailed eleven out of eleven from all angles, most of them acute, against the Force and will add another maximum with eight goals and two tries in a brilliant thirty-point display against the New South Wales Waratahs. The tour is now properly up and running. Jonathan Davies is superb, scoring one try and making the other four in the 47–17 win. And the performance of the pack augurs well with the first Test now only a week away.

It is obvious Gats targeted the Waratahs game as the big warm-up match. There are Test match combinations all over the team sheet, in all three rows of the forward pack and in Jonny Sexton and Mike Phillips at half-back. The one point of confusion is that Brian O'Driscoll captained the midweek team in a 64–0 defeat of a Combined Country select XV four days earlier. I can't really understand that, if he's needed for the first Test, as he surely is. Unless Gats is thinking of pairing Davies and Jamie Roberts?

Ah, the best-laid plans. It wouldn't be a Lions tour without the scourge of injuries. Props Cian Healy and Gethin Jenkins barely make it to Australia before being shipped off home, Tommy Bowe breaks his hand against Queensland, George North tears a hamstring against Country and now, against the Waratahs, Jamie has done likewise. Undoubtedly, Tommy, George and Jamie were earmarked for the Test XV in Brisbane. Just as the Lions hit their stride, they pull up lame.

available on board. How close did he get? Er, to about Alice Springs before he passed out! No kerfuffle, no 'OMG I'm going to be sick', he just closed his eyes and started snoring. By my calculations he'd had twelve beers, which equates to twenty-four in Boon-speak. Not even halfway. It was a classic case of a bloke being egged on through the first three or four then, as the pace slows, people becoming distracted and going off to watch a film or pose for pictures with the trophy with fellow travellers. All of a sudden, from having a gallery of people giving him support, he's left on his own with another fifteen cans to go and no one watching. Even in his inebriated state Tins starts to wonder what on earth he's doing.

These are games very much in the image of the coach. Warren Gatland loves a laugh. He's demanding of his players but he knows how to keep them sweet. At training one day, for instance, he sees the boys are knackered. 'Right Faz,' he says, throwing a ball to Owen Farrell on the halfway line. 'Knock it over from there and we'll end training here and now.' The faces of the props, in particular, light up. Owen promptly does what he did all tour – and is buried underneath Adam Jones and the rest of a relieved front row.

Even the captain and head coach are not immune. Sam Warburton and Gats throw a five and on different days are left behind after training. A passing tailor takes pity on the skipper and drops him back to base. In return, Sam takes to Twitter to endorse the quality of the chap's suits. Another day another Warburton forfeit, this time for forgetting Christian Wade's name! Sam throws a four. Onto the phone he goes to tell Cardiff Blues' director of rugby Phil Davies that he is a ready-made club captain. 'Having led the Lions, I feel I'm now qualified to captain the Blues . . .' Safe to say Phil smells a rat.

Last but not least in the dice game is the number six, which means spending a night sleeping with the kit man. Hilariously, team manager Andy Irvine pulls that one. The card, I mean. What sort of warped mind came up with that, I wonder. Then I remember Paul Stridgeon is on the tour. For anyone unfamiliar with Paul, nicknamed Bobby after the Adam Sandler character in the nineties film *The Water Boy*, he is the Lions fitness coach and a former freestyle wrestler who competed for England at the 2002 Commonwealth Games. He's the guy on whom Gats and Shaun Edwards took bets during the 2009 Lions tour that no player could get the better of him in a wrestle. Bobby's only five foot eight and he can't weigh more than 12 stone stone soaking wet, but sure enough no player got the better of him.

Anyway, Bobby is the life and soul of any squad, particularly on long tours. Not only does he have this party trick of clambering up any pole or road sign and being able to suspend himself horizontally (except once on the 2009 tour when the lamppost snapped – I hardly laughed at all!) he has devised something called the Bobby Cup.

It began when I was at Wasps and Bobby was our fitness conditioner. Gats asked him to present the Bobby Cup to the man of the match but only when we won. Bobby thought he could have a bit of fun when presenting the award and persuaded one of the young analysts to set off with a camera randomly to video something funny. One day, for example, Bobby dressed in the all-in-one costume of the Wasps mascot and went and annoyed commuters on the London underground. Another time one of the fitness guys dressed up in a *Baywatch* outfit and was videoed running across Trafalgar Square complete with red float.

The idea was just to give everyone a laugh and it became a ritual.

When we won a game, we'd come in for analysis on a Tuesday and there would be a three or four-minute video of entertainment before the cup was handed out. Bobby is completely mad and the videos quickly became a highlight of our week.

When I joined Wasps in 2004 I sensed that everyone at the club had pre-conceived ideas about me. I had my *A Question of Sport* work to keep me busy, so I was very much head down and get on with it. One day Bobby asked if I could help him with the Bobby Cup by setting something up with *A Question of Sport*. I said it would be a pleasure and arranged for him to come into the studio one afternoon where we made a video to show to the squad the following Tuesday.

The day arrives, Bobby pushes the play button and the theme music and opening credits for *A Question of Sport* come up. All the lads, I sense, are thinking, 'What the hell? I don't want to watch this prick Dawson. He's only been here two minutes and already he's showing off.' As the credits finish Sue Barker welcomes every-one to the show and then says, 'Before introducing you to tonight's guests I'd like you to meet my co-presenter.' The camera pans to Bobby, who's sat next to Sue, and he introduces Will Greenwood and Graham Thorpe with the most inappropriate comments.

Bobby was always telling us how well endowed he is and, as a result, was nicknamed 'The Rope'. As he stops talking Sue says 'Right, thanks very much Bobby . . . Er, can you just please take your hand off my knee.'

Bobby replies, in his broad Wigan accent, 'That's not my hand, Sue. That's the Rope.'

Anyway, the Lions had the Bobby Cup on the 2009 South Africa tour and, in keeping with Wasps' tradition, these videos were a cross between being horrendous and sensationally funny. There's only one example of his work that I can get away with mentioning here. It was a 'Day in the Life of the Lions' mascot Lenny. The video began with Lenny waking in his own bed, showed him in the shower, then down in the gym where his paws were strapped to a barbell holding about 200k (which a couple of lads, either side and slightly off camera, lifted). The video went with Lenny drinking his protein shake, hanging out with the rest of the lads and having an afternoon snooze, before going out for dinner.

In the nightclub afterwards the storyline begins to deteriorate. Lenny goes off to the toilet and comes back with a white powdery substance on his nose, which he claims, unconvincingly, is talcum powder. He sits down in a private booth and two scantily dressed young ladies appear and begin kissing him and stroking his inner thighs. As his tail begins to stiffen, the camera pulls away.

Bobby is mates with the 2009 management and as all but Shaun Edwards are re-selected for 2013 – Andy Farrell going as defence coach in his place – nobody is safe. Early in the tour when Mako Vunipola, the young Saracens and England prop, is awarded man of the match, Bobby takes the opportunity to embarrass the coaches by interspersing shots of them blasting players for making mistakes with clips of them making exactly the same mistakes in their own playing days.

He shows Andy Farrell talking about self-discipline – then runs footage of Faz appearing to put the nut on an opponent in a rugby league match. Next up is Gats hammering home some point about defensive line speed – and then he flicks to a clip of Gats missing his man while playing for Waikato. The boys love it. And he is not finished. Rob Howley is shown throwing a pass over the head of his fly-half and Neil Jenkins is caught rifling a kick straight at the referee, knocking him out. Perhaps worst of all, Bobby finds an old tape of forwards coach Graham Rowntree talking about being a financial planner and insurance broker. Yaawn!

The lights come back on and the joker, aka Paul Stridgeon, clears his throat. 'And the Bobby Cup goes to this man for taking down the biggest whale in Brisbane.' Cue a clip of Mako, not making a try-saving tackle on a giant second-row, but appearing to chat up this rather big woman in a bar!

The Lions arrive at the Test series with some good and some bad news. The latter is that they have surrendered their unbeaten tour record to the ACT Brumbies, on the same pitch in Canberra where I kicked the conversion in 2001 to ensure we avoided the same fate. That game was a hugely emotional affair for me, coming immediately after my diary episode and apology in front of the whole squad. The 2013 version, however, is a limp affair, not helped by the Lions backline never having met let alone played together. England trio Billy Twelvetrees, Christian Wade and Brad Barritt have answered a Mayday and are newly arrived on tour to provide injury cover. Brad didn't even have any boots as he was on holiday at Disneyland in Los Angeles when his call came. Then there is Shane Williams. Remember him? With major injury concerns over wings Tommy Bowe and George North, Wales' all-time record try-scorer is flown in from Japan – and out of international retirement – on a one-match deal.

Against understrength sides, such as the Barbarians, Western Force or Combined Country, these changes wouldn't have mattered. Against Australia's top Super Rugby team, albeit one missing a stack of Wallabies, it does. Despite a second-half comeback, after the Lions clear their bench, the Brumbies deservedly win 14–12. I struggle to think of a worse Lions performance that I have seen.

The damage to morale and momentum is fortunately limited. And the reason for that is the good news to which I referred. George North, ruled out of the first Test by the medics a week earlier, amazes everyone by being passed fit to play in the opening Test at Suncorp Stadium. His Grade 1 hamstring tear is not completely mended but it is near enough for Warren Gatland to take the risk. Knowing Tommy Bowe will be available for the second Test, after recovering from a broken hand inside three weeks, gives Gats the confidence to take a calculated gamble on George. Even if he pulls up, runs the logic, Bowe will be fit to take over in Melbourne.

The boost to team spirit is evident in the body language of every Lion ahead of kick-off. Not only is their barnstorming winger back, their Saturday team is coming off the performance of the tour in Sydney against the Waratahs. There has been pressure on captain Sam Warburton to put in a big performance to justify his place in the team – he delivered in style. The bigger the game the better that guy plays. Alun-Wyn Jones, who has had a quiet tour to this point, also enjoys a massive night; one only surpassed, perhaps, by the virtuoso midfield display of Jonathan Davies, whose Test place alongside Brian O'Driscoll is guaranteed when fellow centre Jamie Roberts limps off with a hamstring tear. Jon is on fire, he makes so many things happen.

First Test: Australia 21, British and Irish Lions 23
Brisbane, 22 June 2013

How will history recall the opening Test? Well, for starters, there were four tries to take the breath away, one each for Lions' wings George North and Alex Cuthbert and a brace for Israel Folau, a former rugby league and Aussie Rules professional making his Test debut on the Wallaby wing.

North has an extraordinary match, particularly given the concerns over his fitness. He catches a stray kick and runs it back sixty metres, through at least six defenders, to score in the left corner. It is another Jason Robinson moment: Lions debutant, left wing, skinning the Wallabies to score. Two men, twelve years apart, united by moments of individual brilliance. Tom Croft says later that George's name will become synonymous with the Lions. He could well be right, but there are no guarantees in a sport as physically brutal as ours. What is beyond doubt is that we're going to see replays of this try for years to come. There are a dozen or so moments in Lions' history that stand out in the memory. This is one of them. His try is sensational.

The Lions lead and seem to have the game in the bag, but back come Australia only for Kurtley Beale to miss two late shots at goal, either of which would have won the game. The second of the two, after the final hooter, is a forty-six-metre effort in the muddiest part of the pitch. Why he plonks it there I can't think. His body language screams 'I don't fancy this one little bit'. Kurtley is wearing short moulded studs. As he plants his left standing foot it gives way and he slips as he strikes the ball. He still manages to make contact but the kick is short and wide. The Lions breathe a huge sigh of relief.

To think I tweeted 'Game over' after the first scrum, which the Lions blitzed. Premature? No way. You don't win Test matches by being undone like that in the scrum. All the Aussies had at the time was Will Genia's individual brilliance and Israel Folau finishing like a veteran in only his thirteenth game of rugby union. Fair play to them, however, for getting their act together after half-time and almost making me look very foolish.

* * *

The Lions know they have dodged a bullet, that Australia really should have won the match – and perhaps would have had Beale worn longer studs. Nonetheless, after sixteen years of misfortune, they are not about to apologise for getting lucky. There wasn't a lot of good fortune going the Lions' way in 2001 when Nathan Grey's elbow put Richard Hill out of the series in Melbourne, nor four years later when Brian O'Driscoll was speared and Lawrence Dallaglio and Hilly suffered tour-ending injuries. This time it is the Wallabies turn to curse Lady Luck. In addition to Beale's misses, they pick up a stack of injuries. Three backs are stretchered off, two more need help getting to the medical room.

It's a long time since I've seen a Lions side enjoying the rub of the green, be it the bounce of the ball, the opposition missing kicks or the opposition captain getting cited. For standing on Alun-Wyn Jones' face, Wallaby skipper James Horwill will surely have the book thrown at him. Add to all that we have key players coming back from injury. I can't ever remember that happening on a Lions tour.

Wait up, I've spoken too soon. Dr James Robson is in front of the cameras. He's delivering a devastating medical bulletin. Paul O'Connell, pick of the Lions' forwards so far, will play no further part in the series as he has an arm fracture. What's more he did it during the first Test and refused to come off. The guy is seriously hardcore. He battled on in the set-piece and in the mayhem of the breakdown, to bring home the win. Only when victory was guaranteed did he let on.

RETURN OF THE ROAR

MY TOP-TEN TOUGHEST LIONS

1) Andrew Sheridan
2) Will Greenwood
3) Paul O'Connell
4) Scott Gibbs
5) Mike Teague
6) Lewis Moody
7) Wade Dooley
8) Robert Jones
9) Darren Garforth
10) Jeremy Davidson

1) Andrew Sheridan

After an outstanding display for the 2009 Lions it was put to England prop Andrew Sheridan that his performances on the 2005 tour in New Zealand had not really done justice to his talent. Sheri looked his questioner in the eye and said, 'I played five games with a cracked fibula on that tour, so I feel I did do myself justice.' You what? 'I'm serious. I tore ankle ligaments two weeks before the trip but because my leg wasn't X-rayed higher up, we didn't know it was more than ligament damage. All I knew was that I was very sore. I was on a lot of painkillers throughout the tour. I only found out my leg was broken in the final week.'

2) Will Greenwood

If Sheri totally gets my admiration then so certainly does Will, my great pal and former England team mate. During a match in Bloemfontein on the 1997 Lions tour Will was knocked uncon-scious for seventeen minutes. Dr James Robson has seen most things in his long and incredibly distinguished Lions career but this was of a different order. There was real concern on his face that Will was going to die, and James certainly doesn't exaggerate things. I can think of plenty of examples of players getting knocked out cold and coming round and behaving strangely, none better than Paul Grayson getting back up on his feet with the game still in its first half and, thinking it was over and we had won, walking to the stand to applaud the crowd. In Will's case, he came round, sat bolt upright in the back of the ambulance and said to the medical team, 'Tell them it's my hamstring,' before lying back down again. Why did you say that, I asked him later. 'My dad,' Will said. 'He told me never to admit I had concussion.'

3) Paul O'Connell

Paul kept his right forearm fracture a secret until after the 2013 Lions had won the first Test. When the news came out, the Wallabies were stunned. 'Our physio came on the pitch and said, "He's just broken his arm",' said prop Ben Alexander. 'But he got up and packed those last few scrums. After the game we shook hands and I thought, "Ok, maybe he doesn't have a busted arm".' Only he did.

4) Scott Gibbs

Scotty was a tank, but when he injured his ankle early in the 1997 Lions tour, I thought that was that, even for him. I helped carry him off on the stretcher, and back then there were none of the automated ice machines there are today. He had to wake himself every two hours through the night to apply the ice. He did it for days and by the start of the series he was back firing on all cylinders.

5) Mike Teague

The year of the Teague was 1989. It started with him so pumped up before England's match against Wales that when his team kicked off he ran after the ball, crashed into someone, knocked himself out, and was stretchered off after just three seconds' action. He says that was the most embarrassing moment of his career. But his proudest followed soon after. In the Lions' triumph over Australia that summer Mike was voted Player of the Series, not bad for a guy almost forced home by a shoulder injury before the first Test. The Lions brought in a replacement while he recovered, and Mike had to sit in the stands in his tour blazer and hear his team mates subjected to fierce sledging from the locals. It wound him up so much that when he was passed fit to play he was unstoppable.

6) Lewis Moody

I look at the smiling, genial media persona of Lewis today and it's not the bloke I remember at all. All suited and booted and softly spoken, he looks suave, sophisticated even. Nothing like the Leicester, England and Lions' open-side who had this annoying habit of walking up to you, no matter the occasion, and flicking your bollocks. You could be at a buffet function with a plate of food in one hand and a glass of bubbly in the other and he would walk past and give you a flick. Unlike the rest of us, he never tired of this prank. Not for nothing was he known as 'Mad Dog'. He had absolutely no fear. He would run into rucks, run after kicks and just soar in the air. He wouldn't care where or how he landed. Playing for England against New Zealand once at Twickenham he went so high at the kick-off that he landed his wedding tackle on his opponent's shoulders and had to come off. A lot of his team mates didn't have too much sympathy. That kind of serves you right, we thought, for flicking us in the bollocks.

7) Wade Dooley

I can't remember big Wade ever actually enjoying playing rugby. The six-foot-eight lock's pleasure came purely from the physicality. 'I was never malicious but I used to stand up for myself,' is how Wade remembers it. When he scored a try, there was no celebration. He'd just get up and walk back. I remember Will Carling jumping on him after he scored a try against Wales and Wade giving it 'Don't touch me, just get on with the game'. One of my team mates at Northampton was Martin Bayfield and he played alongside Wade. Bayfs wanted to be skilful and fit and agile, but Dools would say, 'That's rubbish, you've just got to be big and strong.' He had a real old-school mentality, always in the thick of the action. He's now an RFU citing officer. You couldn't make it up.

8) Robert Jones

A cheeky little scrum-half who will always be remembered for starting the brawl during the Battle of Ballymore, the second Test on the 1989 Lions tour, with a lovely little stamp on the foot of Wallaby captain Nick Farr-Jones. Rather than blow his whistle, the referee jumps in to try and break them up. Then captain Finlay Calder gets involved before the big guns arrive. Wade Dooley lands a load of punches. Paul Ackford doesn't.

9) Darren Garforth

Strictly speaking he doesn't qualify as he wasn't a Lion but I wanted to get the story in about one of my favourite opponents at club level and a team mate with England. We called Garf 'The Samoan' because of his build and he was, and still is, a lovely, lovely guy. Even when you were playing against him and he was being very tough and physical, he'd always have a glint in his eye. We were on a coach heading back from an England A trip when the beers came out. Only one problem, we had no bottle opener. No problem, says Garf, who picks up a bottle and presses it against his eye socket before turning it 45 degrees. Off flew the lid. It was proper bonkers.

10) Jeremy Davidson

Dubbed 'Dangerous Brian' on the 1997 Lions tour because he seemed to injure one player after another. Jerry was a hard and sometimes uncoordinated second row. Whether playing touch or full-on, with him it was always full-on. I remember Tony Underwood stepping Jeremy and getting grabbed by the scruff of his neck. It was like a scene from Tom and Jerry. His legs just went away from him.

Second Test: Australia 16, British and Irish Lions 15
Melbourne, 29 June 2013

So the Lions draw first blood but at a massive cost. Paulie, as he is known to one and all, had inspired the entire squad early in the trip by telling them, 'This is your shot at forever – don't let the opportunity pass you by'. Now he must rely on those same team mates to realise his dream. Not that he is going anywhere. Paul agrees to stay on in a support role – a boost to the tourists when all the good news suddenly seems to be going Australia's way. Horwill, caught on camera bringing his foot down onto the face of Alun-Wyn Jones, is somehow cleared of foul play at a disciplinary hearing, not once but twice. So while the Lions have lost their most influential forward, the Wallabies have got theirs back. As the series moves to Melbourne it is the home camp that is suddenly buoyant.

'Losing O'Connell is a massive blow,' Aussie prop Alexander says. 'In this country he's got humongous respect. The Lions are going to miss his presence and that hardness the Europeans see week in, week out when he plays for Munster and Ireland. He's one of the greatest players I've ever played against and he's a big loss for the Lions.'

I sense Gats recognises this. He is agitated after the game; thrilled to have won of course but quick to recognise that all is not well. The first Test tends to be the Lions' best opportunity of a victory. The opposition are traditionally under-cooked. They've been in camp for weeks, whereas the Lions have been playing warm-up matches twice a week. As we know from this tour, not all of those matches provide a stern examination, or anything close, but nonetheless you get my point. And yet here in Brisbane the Lions could and probably should have lost. They know it and the Wallabies know it, too.

I love watching Gats in action at times like this. Some people think he is an off-the-cuff speaker, saying the first thing that comes into his head. Untrue. He moves quickly to put the pressure back on his squad, to give a clear impression that far from being thrilled by the result he regards it as a defeat. He knows the quicker he gets the players into that mindset the better chance they have of closing out the series in Melbourne in a week's time. He then has a personal dart at Kurtley Beale. Talk about kicking a man when he's down! Beale has only recently returned to the Aussie squad after treatment for alcohol-related issues and now he's missed two kicks, which has cost his country victory against the Lions. Gats goes for him, slamming him over his choice of footwear.

'Why has he come out on the field wearing that sort of footwear in those sort of conditions?' he asks. 'You have to turn up with the right tools. It's part of your job, making sure that you are prepared.' I'm sure he could imagine his own players thinking, 'Mate, is that really wise?' Perfect. That's the reaction he wants. That will put them on edge.

Gats allows his squad the evening to enjoy the victory, then turns up the heat again, warning the players that changes are almost inevitable, given how close they had come to defeat. He tells the midweek team, 'Your tour's not over. There are chances for people to be involved either this weekend or the following weekend.' It's a decent attempt to get them on edge, back to that emotional high they were at before the first Test. But it is devilishly difficult to manufacture desperation – particularly in a best-of-three series when your opponent must do or die.

I like the way the Lions don't overplay their irritation at Horwill being cleared, remembering how going overboard in our response towards the O'Driscoll spear tackle in 2005 probably worked against us come the second Test. I look at the five changes they make for Melbourne and think that is about right, too, particularly Ben Youngs for Mike Phillips at scrum-half. By his high standards, Mike had a poor game in Brisbane, while Ben has been flying.

One point I try to flag up is the importance of the half-time break in Test match rugby. The Lions' return to Melbourne takes me back twelve years to when we went into the interval bossing the game and within forty minutes of ultimate glory – and ended up losing the Test by a record margin and, the following week, the series. Aussie sportsmen, in my experience, are notoriously difficult to kill off because they don't get too wrapped up in the emotion of a game. They assess a situation dispassionately – even when their backs are to the wall – and they adapt. What we should have done in 2001 is to put ourselves in their shoes and thought how, at that moment, they would be changing up their game to combat us.

You spend your whole week preparing for the contest yet it is at half-time when you're at your most vulnerable because all the emotion, physicality and fatigue is swirling through your mind. Be assured that that is the time the Aussies will go to work. The Lions must be alive to it. If they are, the series will be theirs.

Twenty-four hours later they lead 12–9 at half-time and end up losing the game 16–15. A converted try by Wallaby centre Adam Ashley-Cooper, five minutes from time, puts Australia in front and with the last kick of the game Leigh Halfpenny is unable to land a fifty-five-metre penalty shot to reverse the result. It is torture to watch. A huge opportunity to close out the series goes begging.

Now there is no need to manufacture desperation. It's in all of us, even those just looking in from the outside. We all have that horrible sense of deja vu. Surely it can't be 2001 all over again, where we lost the series after winning the first Test. And what do the Lions do? They get on a plane to the Sunshine Coast for a couple of days off followed by selection and two more days of light training. This may well have been put in the itinerary with a view to the Lions already having the series wrapped up, with Noosa seen as a good place to let off steam away from the prying eyes of a big city.

Sir Clive Woodward is concerned that four nights in a resort before the Lions' biggest match in many a year does not sit comfortably, and he says so. But these boys have had a hell of a season – not just the tour. It's been an unbelievably long campaign, and knowing what a deciding Lions Test is like, the mental stress you are under, trust me you get close to meltdown with it all. Without some release it's not easy to deal with.

Thinking back to 2001, I'd love to have had two days away from it all to have a little bit of a giggle and a laugh; maybe play golf, go on a jet ski, have a quiet beer even. Just switch off ahead of the most stressful weekend imaginable. Not that the 2013 management will recall Noosa as a stress-free environment, the calm before the storm. For them, and Warren Gatland in particular, it proves to be a media tempest to overshadow even the storm to come. While the players surf, take to jet skis or sip cappuccinos along Hastings Street, the Lions' coaches go into conclave and reach a decision that sends shockwaves around the sporting world.

They decide that Brian O'Driscoll, the four-time Lion and senior figure on this tour, should not be involved in the final Lions Test of his career. While the four home unions await confirmation that Drico will captain the team in the absence of Sam Warburton, who had to be helped off the field of play with ten minutes to go in the second Test and was subsequently ruled out of the decider with a very nasty hamstring tear, Gats drops the bombshell.

'I have never done sentiment,' he tells the press lads. 'I have to put my hand on my heart and say it's the right rugby decision. Brian is obviously very, very disappointed. It's hard when you've been the number one in your position for fifteen years and first choice on every team you've been a part of. But I would hate to go home thinking we had made calls based on what was the right political decision.'

Gats says he expects it to become a 'major story and debate for forty-eight hours'. Even he cannot foresee the firestorm that blows his way as he names ten of his Wales side in a Lions XV dubbed the 'British Ieuans' while Drico is dispatched to coach kids at a local rugby club before going out to dinner with the other players not required at the weekend.

My old pal Keith Wood brands it a 'terrible mistake'. Willie John McBride says he is 'gutted because Brian O'Driscoll has been in my era and in my life, the greatest player we have ever produced in Ireland.' Lions team mate Ian Evans, sitting around the dinner table with Drico, attempts to lighten the mood. 'I know you're disappointed but try being me, the only Welsh bloke on tour not involved in any Test. How shit must I be?!' My take on Drico's omission appeared in the *Daily Mirror* the day before the game.

It's not about Brian O'Driscoll and his personal disappointment.

It doesn't matter how many Welshmen are starting the game, or that England, Ireland and Scotland contribute only half as many players between them.

The style of play Warren Gatland deploys to beat Australia won't bother too many people either if it gets the job done.

Tomorrow in Sydney is all about the Lions winning a game of rugby and achieving the one goal they set before they left home – regardless of who does what and how.

Of course players are desperately disappointed not to make the 23-man squad. Naturally Drico, denied a farewell Lions Test when he might have expected the captaincy, is one of them. But come lunchtime tomorrow the entire squad will celebrate if the Lions win. Because that is all that counts.

That is the reality of a Lions tour. These boys are team mates for a fleeting moment in time. The 2013 Lions came together at the end of May and they cease to be after this weekend. It's about getting the job done.

Sir Ian McGeechan says it takes an entire squad to win a Test series, because the reaction of those not selected sets the tone for the group. That is never truer than before a deciding Test.

Which is why Brian's reaction to being left out was so important. He voiced his disappointment then went straight to the training ground to fulfil a commitment to take a kids' coaching session.

Of course he feels hurt. I know from experience the horrible sick feeling you get in your stomach when the coach asks to meet you for a coffee. You know full well what the conversation will be. You don't need the coffee.

But Brian is an unbelievable pro. He realises his responsibility to the group, understands there is a bigger picture even if rejection is wounding and completely alien to him.

Whether it's the right call depends on the Lions continuing to play as they have been, without a set-piece platform and having to try and force some momentum into midfield.

Jamie Roberts is undoubtedly the man for that pattern, with his Wales midfield partner Jonathan Davies the perfect foil. That makes sense to me for where the Lions are at this moment.

They haven't yet nailed their strategy – no one really knows how they're trying to play. So naturally Gats has turned to the players he knows best and who best know his pattern. It's a strong team and it's a good team. In fact, had he picked it for the first Test I don't think he'd have had too many complaints.

Say what you will about Warren, he's a straight shooter. For good or for bad with him you always know where you stand.

The last time a Lions series went to a deciding Test I was in the team. There are obvious parallels between now and 2001 in that we won in Brisbane and Australia in Melbourne.

Yes we then lost in Sydney but the circumstances were very different. We had injuries all over the place, this is a strong Lions team. We were completely drained, these boys have just had two days of complete down time on a beach in Noosa.

Knowing what a deciding Lions Test is like, the mental stress you put yourself through, the ongoing 24/7 thinking about rugby, Noosa will have done them the world of good.

As the pressure spikes, you feel close to a mental meltdown. Everyone is talking Lions, the supporters are everywhere, the history of Lions rugby hangs over you.

Five minutes from glory, the Lions blew their opportunity last week. They know that. But they will be stronger mentally and emotionally for that.

These players will want this like they've never wanted anything before whereas I think the Wallabies could struggle to get back up to where they were in Melbourne.

My heart says Lions, my head doesn't know. I can't wait to find out.

Gats is stung by the criticism but he has strong support from defence coach Andy Farrell, who has greatly enhanced his coaching credentials on this trip, and forwards coach Graham 'Wig' Rowntree, whom I've long admired. Wig and I go back many years, to an Under-21 match between England and the French Armed

Forces, played at Twickenham before the 1992 Pilkington Cup Final between Harlequins and Bath.

I was picked in my then club position of centre and my opposite number was the best player in their team. In the changing room, or rather a Portakabin in the West Car Park, I was nervous as hell. But then Wig and his Leicester front-row mucker Richard Cockerill began their preparation for the physical battle ahead. Forwards usually have a huddle, shake one another about a bit, maybe even a few whacks on the chest but this was some weird East Midlands stuff. They started by gripping one another's shoulders and slamming together chest-to-chest to the point you could hear the wind being knocked out of them. Next was a WWE-type square-up. Nose to nose, forehead to forehead, chanting and screaming about how they were going to smash up their opposite numbers. A few slaps around the face followed and the attention of the room turned to these nutters. They were both sweating profusely and looked like their eyes were about to pop. But the best was yet to come. In a grand finale with the whole team watching and only moments to go before we walked onto the hallowed turf, the pair started to head-butt one another. And not just a little nudge or rub of the brow, this was full-on Kirby Kiss-style, like rutting stags.

I'm not sure it worked for everyone but my fear of the opposition suddenly disappeared. I thought, 'If these boys are on my team and can do this to themselves, what the bloody hell will they do to the enemy!' I'd have them on my team any day.

And now the same Graham Rowntree is in the Lions changing room, hours before kick-off in the same Olympic Stadium where Jason Robinson scored his try, where I made my break, where Jonny Wilkinson dropped that goal, where Martin Johnson lifted the Webb Ellis Cup aloft. That was as big as it got for England

and there can be no overstating the size of this occasion for the Lions. Lose and with New Zealand up next in 2017, it's reasonable to suggest it could be another eight years before they get their next shot at a series win. That would be 2021, twenty-four years after us old boys got the better of South Africa. That is too long between drinks.

Along the corridor in the home changing room the pressure is no less. The Lions are not due back in Australia until 2025. That is a long time to dwell on a series defeat. Robbie Deans, the Wallaby coach, probably won't survive another week if that happens. He knows that, the boys in green and gold know that.

Just as last week, Gats has decided to keep the build-up simple. Before the opening Test he had asked Sir Ian McGeechan to present the jerseys. In the Hilton Hotel in Brisbane, Geech got straight to the point. 'You cannot be frightened about what lies in front of you,' he said. 'You have to embrace it all and not be daunted by the prospect. You have to grow, not shrivel, get more out of yourself than you have ever done before, and get more out of those around you. You have to become bigger, stronger and better than you have been before. If you get it right, then the experience will stay with you for the rest of your life.' The Lions, of course, won that day but Geech's message was powerful enough to last the series. It did not need to be repeated every Friday evening.

In fact, his words from four years before were still echoing around the Lions' team room as game time approached. The 2009 Lions had gone into their final Test against South Africa under instruction to lay a foundation for 2013 and, ultimately, for this very day. 'The biggest thing you earn in this jersey is respect and reputation,' Geech, then head coach, had told the boys that day in Johannesburg. 'We can leave a legacy today for the players who pick up that jersey in four years' time. Please give them something to play for. Play for everything we want that jersey to be.' The Lions won by a distance.

Third Test: Australia 16, British and Irish Lions 41
Sydney, 6 July 2013

The 2013 Lions have something to play for all right but they badly need to get off to a flier. I make a mental note of three areas where the tourists must quickly gain ascendancy: at scrum-half, where Australia's Will Genia bossed the first two Tests; at scrum time where the Lions need to make a statement after coming up short for a variety of reasons in the first two Tests; and finally on the scoreboard.

The game starts, Genia drops Jonny Sexton's kick off, the Lions bulldoze the scrum and Alex Corbisiero scores under the posts. Seventy-eight seconds on the clock, all three boxes ticked. My BBC pal Jonathan Davies warned beforehand that for the Lions to win they must take no prisoners in the scrum, that two Tests worth of set-piece frustration must be vented on the Wallabies. His instructions are followed to the letter. The Lions' set-piece is so dominant that goalkicker Leigh Halfpenny helps himself to a Lions Test best of twenty-one points and has smashed the record for most points by a Lion in a series long before the game is over. He would end up with forty-nine points and being named Player of the Series. Not a bad response to missing that pressure-laden monster kick in Melbourne.

Australia make a game of it in as much as James O'Connor scores a try on the stroke of half-time to peg back a 19–3 deficit and reignite the contest. When Christian Leali'ifano adds a couple of penalty goals soon after the restart, the Lions' lead is down to three points. Alun-Wyn's men are rocked. It's then Warren Gatland's half-time words come into play.

'We spoke about being prepared to go to a place that not many players go, in terms of pushing your body to the limit,' Gatland would later reveal. The Lions do just that. Cue three tries in thirteen minutes, all for them. I'm sitting there pinching myself as Jonny Sexton, then George North, then Jamie Roberts all touch down.

By the end the Lions will have posted their highest-ever Test score and recorded their second-biggest Test-winning margin. Two snapshots of the evening stay with me, both involving the vast travelling support. First, the English, Irish and Scots joining with the Welsh to serenade the Lions with *Bread of Heaven*. Then the 30,000 visiting fans standing together and waving goodbye as Australia's supporters leave en masse following Jamie's try, eleven minutes from time.

The final whistle brings jubilant scenes that take me right back to England's 2003 World Cup final win on the same pitch. Sam Warburton joins Alun-Wyn in lifting the Tom Richards Cup, Brian O'Driscoll brings baby daughter Sadie onto the pitch. All around there are broad smiles. I think back to that November night in 2003, coming off the pitch to be greeted by a drug tester. He wanted me to give up the greatest moment of my career to follow him into another room to give a sample. I politely declined. 'Mate, I can't pee at this moment, and I'm not leaving the changing room right now. I've worked all my life for this. Please, you'll have to stay with me.' To be fair he agreed and stood watching me as I downed champagne with the boys and posed for photos. Then he watched me shower before peeing in his bottle. Ten years on and I'm watching from afar as into the Lions changing room goes James Bond star Daniel Craig. How fitting. The Lions really are in Double-O-Heaven. Sorry! I call a mate on the team. His phone is on voicemail. He gets back to me three days later.

'Sorry Daws, it's been absolute madness here,' he says, before detailing the two hours of celebration in the changing room, the official function at Sydney Opera House followed by an all-nighter in The Ivy nightclub, during which the Lions' media manager is thrown fully-clothed into a swimming pool by Ben Youngs and Tom Croft. From there a bus is laid on to take the entire Lions squad, minus Warren Gatland, to Bondi for an all-day beach party. Gats has flown home to New Zealand.

He was in no mood to celebrate, publicly at least, after what he described as 'vitriolic' abuse aimed at him over his decision to axe Drico. Ironically, that call and the result that followed has raised his stock to an all-time high. His is a special talent born of tremendous skill and enormous courage. I can't think of another coach in world rugby who'd have had the balls to do what he did. He did not allow his heart to rule his head. He stayed true to himself. Even as the storm raged around him his primary focus remained on what needed to be done to win. It was a remarkable performance really.

As he says his goodbyes he has one message for his history-making players. 'Go let your hair down boys, you deserve it. Just promise me one thing. Don't do anything too ridiculous that lets down what you've achieved.' Not even the sight of Scotland full-back Stuart Hogg parading around town dressed only in Speedo swimming pants, can do that.

EPILOGUE

Bondi Beach, Sydney
7 July 2013

They are on a beach drinking beer, just like we were. The clock is running. Time is against them. In forty-eight hours the 2013 Lions will cease to be. They look around at team mates to whom they are forever bonded by one six-week 'moment' in time and think: 'The next time I see you I'll be trying to knock seven bells out of you.'

It happened to me sixteen years ago. Scott Gibbs and I sat with a case of beers on Durban's North Beach, watching the sun come up over the Indian Ocean, hungover from a night on the sauce following what turned out to be the 1997 series decider, which the Lions won to take an unassailable 2–0 lead over South Africa.

We were brothers in arms, united forever by what we had achieved side by side at Newlands and at Kings Park. Yet a week later the '97 Lions were no more and within two years Scotty would be breaking my heart with that bloody late try for Wales against England at Wembley, which robbed us of the Five Nations title and a Grand Slam.

The realisation that the end is nigh makes this an incredibly special time and Warren Gatland's Lions are not about to waste it. They have written their names into history, done what no Lions squad has managed since 1971 in coming back from losing the second Test to take the series. And they have done it as one totally united squad.

After defeat by Australia in 2001 and the whitewash by New Zealand in 2005 I worried for the Lions, feared that the concept of four nations coming together once every four years to take on the best in the southern hemisphere was outdated and incompatible with the professional era.

I should have had more faith. Despite another loss, this time to South Africa, the 2009 Lions eased my concerns for the brand. Sir Ian McGeechan returned to restore the old-school Lions' values and prove they could work in the 21st century. In so doing he banished the angst of the previous two tours. But still the Lions needed a win for their credibility going forward. And with the world-champion All Blacks up next there were plenty who felt 2013 amounted to a now-or-never opportunity.

That sounds daft, now the Lions have put the Wallabies to the sword, doling out such a thrashing in the deciding Test that we have all come away from Australia daring to believe New Zealand can be toppled four years hence.

If anyone doubts the power of the British and Irish Lions, look at Brian O'Driscoll out there on Bondi Beach, necking a can of beer and sharing fully in the glory moment. A legend of the game, Drico was widely expected to captain the Lions the previous night yet was instead dropped from the squad. It was a hammer blow to the Irishman ahead of what would have been his final Test, but he sucked it up, took his seat in the stands and was on the pitch at the end in his suit to help lift the Tom Richards Cup.

Listen to the words of a player who in his *Daily Telegraph* column admitted to a 'massive mix of emotions' when the final whistle blew to bring to an end his twelve-year quest for a Lions series win.

'I do not want today to end because you are with guys you know you are not going to hang around with ever again,' he says. 'You look back on this moment together. I will never get it back. We will never be together again. It is bonkers that we will not be together for much longer but that is why you gotta love the Lions.'

All day long the Lions party swap memories and get increasingly pickled. Good on them. They've earned it ten times over. Jonny Sexton and Tom Croft are going home to get married, Geoff Parling to see a baby daughter born while he was away. Life will move on, but not quite yet.

At 7pm the Lions team bus arrives. It has been there for them through good times and bad. In Canberra and Melbourne where games did not go according to plan; in Brisbane, where Tommy Bowe broke his hand, Newcastle and Sydney, where George North and Jamie Roberts tore hamstrings and feared their tours were over. And now it is at Bondi preparing for one last journey.

The boys climb aboard, a couple of them still wearing the Wallaby jerseys of their opposite numbers. The bus pulls away and heads through Sydney's eastern suburbs towards their city-centre hotel.

'Wait up, driver!' yells a voice from somewhere near the back. 'There's two of the Aussie lads.'

The driver hits his brakes and the bus comes to an abrupt stop. To cheers from the entire squad up the steps bounds Adam Ashley-Cooper who, just a week before, had scored the match-winning try that forced the series into a deciding Test. At the time it was a dream-killer for the Lions. Now he is welcomed aboard like an old friend, accompanied by Wallaby legend Nathan Sharpe, who gets the full 'Sharpie! Sharpie!' chant treatment before both are made to sing for their lift.

This, ladies and gentlemen, is the British and Irish Lions, one of the finest concepts in all of sport. Now and forever. Let nobody tell you differently.